SPECIAL LIBRARIES

SPECIAL LIBRARIES

A Survival Guide

JAMES M. MATARAZZO AND TOBY PEARLSTEIN

WITH THE ASSISTANCE OF SYLVIA JAMES

INTRODUCTION BY BARBARA QUINT

 LIBRARIES UNLIMITED

AN IMPRINT OF ABC-CLIO, LLC
Santa Barbara, California • Denver, Colorado • Oxford, England

Library of Congress Cataloging-in-Publication Data

Matarazzo, James M., 1941–
    Special libraries : a survival guide / James M. Matarazzo and Toby Pearlstein with the assistance of Sylvia James ; introduction by Barbara Quint.
        pages cm.
    Includes bibliographical references and index.
    ISBN 978-1-61069-267-0 (hardcopy) — ISBN 978-1-61069-268-7 (ebook)
1. Special libraries—Administration.   2. Corporate libraries—Administration.
3. Special libraries—Case studies.   4. Corporate libraries—Case studies.
I. Pearlstein, Toby.   II. James, Sylvia R. M. . III. Title.
    Z675.A2M375 2013
    025.1'96—dc23   2013000610

ISBN: 978-1-61069-267-0
EISBN: 978-1-61069-268-7

17   16   15   14   13   1   2   3   4   5

This book is also available on the World Wide Web as an eBook.
Visit www.abc-clio.com for details.

Libraries Unlimited
An Imprint of ABC-CLIO, LLC

ABC-CLIO, LLC
130 Cremona Drive, P.O. Box 1911
Santa Barbara, California 93116-1911

This book is printed on acid-free paper ∞

Manufactured in the United States of America

For Paul, who always listened patiently and was
never bored

CONTENTS

FOREWORD

It was a great privilege and pleasure to be asked to assist with this book. I have spent many months reading and thinking about the contributions and the story they tell about corporate libraries. From the core articles written with some distinction by Jim Matarazzo and Toby Pearlstein that provided the idea for this book, to the most recent updates from a wide variety of writers, it is a fascinating account. Each chapter, update, and companion piece has its own distinct voice, which resonates with the main theme of the book on whether the corporate library and more importantly the role of the corporate librarian will survive as we know them today.

Living and working in Europe, the development, or perhaps should I say nondevelopment of corporate libraries has taken a very different path from those in North America that are described in the book. The lesson to be learned from the demise of corporate libraries in the United Kingdom is tantalizing and the fact that such corporate units were never very prevalent on continental Europe, even in the largest companies, tells a tale in itself. From my perspective, I have been fascinated to be an observer and participant in both models of corporate libraries on both continents. I have worked in both regions and in fact managed a large corporate library throughout the 1980s that worked closely with a sister company in the United States that had a similar sized unit. Even then, in what could now be regarded as the heyday of the corporate library, we never felt particularly secure in the corporate hierarchy. There were always issues to be defended about our viability to a series of constantly changing line managers. There were regular reviews of our size, the headcount needed, and most importantly, the amount of expensive prime real-estate square footage we occupied in offices in the center of London, which was then as now, one of the most expensive cities in the world in which to run an office. This factor seemed to exercise our senior management more than any other in considering our future. In those days our collections were mainly paper and microform based and required large immovable filing machines to hold them, so that we could cram as much as possible into the smallest possible space. My solution and survival guide at the time was to rapidly develop an expertise in managing filing systems and developing creative storage solutions for the vast sets of documents created every week. This was an essential way of proving our value to the management that made the crucial decisions on our destiny at that time. Interestingly, these same line managers were completely disinterested in the state-of-the-art corporate finance research service we also offered and which if asked, would have considered our greatest value to the firm.

How times have changed. No management would approve the existence or development of this type of corporate library today. The paper-based document storage and retrieval services of which we developed an expert knowledge are much less important in these days of digital documents. As a consultant, with a specialty in all kinds of use and applications of corporate research, I no longer regularly advise corporations on how to manage their corporate libraries and how to develop new services. When I first began to work independently in this field in the late 1980s, this work used to be the mainstay of my consultancy.

So the corporate library and librarians need to be quite a different model if they are to survive. They may now be completely outsourced and the same personnel might be employed and managed by a different company, while still working in the offices of the company they once were fully employed by. The service might be outsourced to another location altogether and operate entirely remotely, employing none of the former staff. The central department may have been completely dispersed and the former corporate librarians may be working within other departments, fully "embedded" with their former clients. All this change has required the corporate librarian to embrace the flexibility and readiness to adapt to new economic realities and conditions in order to survive. Many rose to the challenge and welcomed the changes and the opportunities they offered. Unfortunately, many more were never given the chance to work in any of these new incarnations of the corporate library and were made redundant. More often than not the whole corporation in that location was closed and the corporate library completely disappeared, never to reappear or be relocated anywhere else within the organization. All the expertise and knowledge died with the closure and became lost to the corporation. Who knows what might have been accomplished had the corporate librarians been better prepared, thought out a plan of campaign, and attempted to move their unit to another part of the corporation, finding a host department who might take it under their management.

All these models, possibilities, and survival tools are described in this significant book on corporate libraries and the consequences and possible closure avoidance actions are discussed.

I recommend that all corporate librarians read the book. It will also be an excellent primer for library students hoping to work in this field. Looking back, I wish I had a book like this to guide my faltering steps when I first landed a position to manage a corporate library, nearly 40 years ago. Most of all, it would have been so supportive to have so many good examples and case studies of state-of-the-art corporate libraries to study. Many of ideas and practices described throughout the chapters of this book would have been so useful to me in my day-to-day interaction with skeptical line managers, bent on trying to close the service down. As a corporate librarian, you are no longer alone in trying to work your way through the problems and challenges that came up, especially the ultimate survival test, keeping your corporate library alive!

Sylvia James
Sussex, England

INTRODUCTION

BARBARA QUINT

What is burning there is the memory of mankind.
Let it burn.

Bernard Shaw put that first line in the mouth of an Egyptian leader agonizing over the fire destroying the ancient library of Alexandria in his play, *Caesar and Cleopatra*. But Caesar's response, "Let it burn," may have a chilling resonance to embattled information professionals today. It's an end-user world and the success of the Internet and its Web has enriched every life. Nonetheless, the information professionals who run libraries fear the loss of quality content in the erosion and threatened collapse of traditional information infrastructures. The future may hold dire consequences for "the memory of mankind."

Historically, librarians and libraries have had two primary missions, archive and access. By the last half of the 20th century, the archiving of substantial content—science, technology, social science, arts, humanities, government actions and policies, news reports, and so forth—were set into established and relatively durable infrastructures. The work of scholars, researchers, scientists, business writers, journalists, bureaucrats, and other credentialed experts were published and recorded by numerous publishing outlets. Publishers ranged from commercial and trade publishers to scholarly societies and government agencies. Networks of libraries insured that the products of these infrastructures were archived and protected and, to some extent, made available to the public.

Computer technology played an important role in enhancing the functionality of these infrastructures, but its most vital and most revolutionary role has come in the provision of access. As the technical developments in computers and networks moved from niche markets, such as publishing, to the workplace and then the home, the mass market of computer users grew exponentially. In the course of creating and serving this market, of course, the price of hardware, software, and network support dropped like a stone. The traditional information industry had developed its products and services for niche workplace markets, often staffed with information professionals who could handle the complex data structures. Now the industry faced not only the re-tooling required to service end-user markets, but also having to convince those end-users to accept subscription prices that often exceeded the costs of the equipment the content ran on.

Disintermediation—the elimination of layers of enabling players, each getting their piece of the pie, lying between the originator of the content and its ultimate user—has pervaded this process. With the World Wide Web reaching into every office and home and now, through mobile technology, into practically every place, the tools needed to create and distribute content have become available globally to all. The universal availability of the ability to create content digitally has sped the erosion of established sources. How many breaking news stories now cite Twitter or Facebook items? An egalitarian digital democracy puts professional established sources cheek by jowl with individuals who may, or may not, have special knowledge or insightful opinions, but—good, bad, or indifferent—here it all comes.

Digital content is inherently fluid, expanding to fit the need, to reach anywhere and anyone. Libraries as institutions have clienteles limited by geography and/or jurisdiction. This has made them an excellent market for traditional information services, both print and digital. A publisher takes one piece of content from an author and prints multiple copies for sale to libraries around the world. But Web-based information sources don't follow that pattern. They don't make and sell multiple copies. They move multiple users to the single digital copy. The originator or the vendor can deal directly with the public without a third-party library. Librarians who used to carefully select their acquisitions find themselves just signing checks for "big deal" collections, "libraries in a box" supplied by publishers or database aggregators.

Librarians are all too often prisoners of their constituencies. Regardless of the sweep of online resources they can array, of the expertise they can bring to the search processes of users, of the experience they have accrued in solving particular kinds of problems, they can still only serve a ZIP code or a corporate logo. They cannot match their abilities and talents with the needs of a Web world of users. They cannot exploit the full power of digital content because of the strictures of pre-defined, Second Millennium constituencies.

Much of today's valuable content and much more of tomorrow's is born digital. Print is becoming a format output option rather than a standard form for delivering and storing information. E-books have passed the tipping point and are now assuming avalanche-like speeds, turning the image of libraries as buildings full of books into a negative. Publishers are scrambling to survive the changes.

As a profession, librarians were the first to adopt online and recognize and enable its revolutionary effect on humankind's future; but, now reference librarians, who had gone through a generation of empowerment as professional online searchers, gatekeepers to the wonders of online, find their former and future clients doing their own searching. They may well argue that end-user searching is not as good as it should be, but the argument may seem self-serving and moot.

In this process, all libraries face challenges, even public and academic libraries with their semi-obligatory status. ("Hey! This town doesn't even have a public library. How hick can you get?!" "The accreditation committee will look at your library next. WHAT??!!") However, the most challenged are special libraries, those libraries created by institutions; corporations, government agencies, hospitals, or law firms specifically to perform efficiently for the benefit of the institution and its employees. Special libraries must function well and prove their worth to clients and upper management every single day. In the past, it meant acquiring and managing print sources and distributing usage to whomever needed them. As online arrived, it meant having the right people to tap the complex, unforgiving data structures and keep the price-to-value ratio working in the institution's favor. But now, as end-user systems—often priced at free or not much more—improve and ease the search process for even expert sources, special libraries face the brunt of the threat to the future of libraries.

We must remember, however, that though special libraries may face the greatest challenges today, they are only the first in line. All libraries have tough times coming. The bad economy accelerates the threat.

So what are librarians to do to face these hard times? That's the focus of this book and the series of articles in *Searcher* Magazine on which it is based. The authors have grouped their thoughts into three parts: Part I: You Are What You Measure—The Importance of Data as a Survival Tool, Part II: Strategies and Tactics for Survival, and Part III: So What Does Your Manager Think? The practical focus emphasizes staying alive in today's realities but with a firm focus on the future. In the case of special libraries, that means understanding institutional goals and meeting and exceeding institutional expectations. The authors draw on the work and perspectives of senior colleagues in the field as well as their own lengthy and distinguished experience. Of particular interest, they chronicle actual cases of established libraries that went under or skated free by the skin of their teeth.

Initiating the series led me to the two authors. To tell the truth, when I first approached them, all I hoped for was the name of a potential author or authors for the series. When they volunteered to do it themselves, well, I can tell you (but never whisper a word of this to my other authors, wonderful people but sensitive), I was so proud that *Searcher* had qualified as an outlet for the two most prestigious writers in the field. They hold a unique status in writing on this subject over the years.

The authors have focused on the challenges to special libraries in particular, appropriately recognizing that the first wave of serious assaults on the profession is taking place in that arena. Most importantly, however, they have recognized future dangers as coming from the threat to the profession more than to libraries as traditional institutions. And the greatest danger to the public would lie in the elimination of information professionals working solely for their benefit. Information professionals working in the information industry do wonderful and often highly principled work, but they must serve the interests of their employers first. Information professionals working in libraries have always placed the clients' interests first. Frankly, if librarians hadn't placed those interests first and foremost, online services might have had a much more difficult time climbing up that hard, steep path to the tipping point. How many users today get their first training in serious, multisource searching (aka from Google to the stars) from librarians?

Back when I first started searching online (wearing a stunning, polyester, dinosaur-skin pant suit), I had an epiphany. I realized that I could do full-scale literature searches from a phone booth, as long as my Rolodex included a number for a document delivery service. And since that epiphany, I have always believed that people may not always need libraries, but they will always need librarians. We librarians must survive as a profession or future clients, the citizens of the world, will suffer. That may sound self-serving, but it is still true. In the eternal march of humanity from the vulnerability of ignorance to the safety of knowledge, humanity's chances of reaching that safety depend on guides and guardians working to clear the path, to fix the potholes, and to find or, if necessary, construct functional alternative routes.

What course can librarians follow to survive and in time, to prevail? Our professional ethics hold the beginning of the answer. We inform. We serve the information needs of our clients. That is what we do. We are not defined by buildings or piles of print. Like coral reefs, the leftover detritus of the tiny living coral, libraries are just what is left over when a librarian goes home. If the Internet and its Web have solved the problems of our clients, Hallelujah. One job done. Now what's next?

Close to 30 years ago, I made my first speech to information industry executives. I was working in a library for librarian wages at the time and felt at something of a disadvantage, but the feeling evaporated as the day proceeded. I recall the last thing I said to them to this very day. "I wear polyester. You wear natural fibers. I walk on linoleum and have to chin myself to see the sky. You walk on wall-to-wall carpeting and work in window offices. But we both feed off of human ignorance. We'll never starve."

Or will we? Time and the tide of history will tell. But if we librarians do fail, if our profession ceases to function, what happens to history? Will the "memory of mankind" burn? Could the problem by libraries in the Second Millennium—Archiving—recur in the Third Millennium? Here's a test. Try to picture this scenario. It's 2112. Google's founders are buried in a Silicon Valley version of the Arlington memorial cemetery. Amazon's Jeff Bezos has a virtual tombstone there with a streaming video of his actual grave in Washington State, along with a graphic of Amazon.com's recent stock prices and an ad with a discount offer. Libraries are gone. And where does that leave history? Where are the records of past lives, past business and government actions, past scholarly investigations, past scientific experiments? As the intellectual activity of humankind went all digital, of course, it was archived, but for how long? Under whose charge? Have all the individuals pouring their lives into the social networks paid the nets for permanent archives? How many relatives failed to renew those subscriptions after deaths in the family? Has Twitter kept all its postings relating to news stories that broke 40 or 50 years ago? Has the Open Archive kept up with the Open Access movement? Are Wikipedia and Project Gutenberg still fully staffed with second and third generations of volunteers? Are they still around at all? Speaking of around at all, writing corporate histories or even tapping the lessons of past businesses is a lost art. Remember that social network that was so popular long ago? Face-something, I think it was. It went public a century ago in 2012, but 50 years later it was just a penny stock and in 2073, it vanished. I wonder where all their corporate records went, much less their postings. Nowadays in 2112 rumors buzz that even mighty Google may have to reduce their petabyte storage towers again under pressure from the EPA over the climate-altering heat, a decades-old controversy. Of course, Google Books took the big hit back in 2085, eliminating the last usable source of pre-Third Millennium content. So sad.

Problems solved can re-emerge in new and more challenging forms, but so can opportunities. What matters is insuring the continuance of libraries and, more importantly, in my opinion, of librarians to solve problems come back from the grave bigger and grimmer than before, solve them with new ideas and new tools but old, established principles and goals. Taking opportunities to create new and better access is essential, not only to guarantee our relevance back in the good old teens of the 21st century, but also to insure that our clients will see our role in making them safe from humanity's ancient arch-enemy, Ignorance. These days the enemy can come hidden in a deluge of data, creating an overload that leaves people without the information they really need or want and discouraged by the sheer quantity of data into continuing the search. That's when our profession steps up. That's when we structure answers to suit the questioner. That's when we find and even create the new sources for future questions.

But to do all this, we must stay in play. We must work smart and plan carefully. We must respond to today's challenges, anticipate tomorrow's, tap collegial networks, and create strong alliances. We must protect our clients' interests and expand their view of what we can do for them and for others.

You start now with this book, but this is just the beginning. And this book will focus on the beginning of the trend to shut down libraries, at where it hits the hardest. The problems faced by special librarians are ultimately shared by all librarians—proving one's worth; one's value as information professionals in an end-user world where the people who assign one's budgets are themselves end-users. Whether a corporate executive, a government manager, or a university dean, to whomever we librarians report, we must prove our worth. We must endure first to prevail later. And we must prevail or our clients will suffer, if not today or tomorrow, still too soon.

PART I

YOU ARE WHAT YOU MEASURE: THE IMPORTANCE OF DATA AS A SURVIVAL TOOL

INTRODUCTION

JAMES M. MATARAZZO AND TOBY PEARLSTEIN

The first three chapters focus on the importance of data collection and pragmatic research to the sustainability of our profession and your employment. In the first chapter, "Corporate Score," Matarazzo and Pearlstein present a customizable framework for the collection and characterization of data in a way that will help you demonstrate the contribution of your information services in a mission-centric and customer-centric fashion. This approach is illustrated in the second chapter by a case study of the AT&T Bell Laboratories Network that reminds us that many of the alignment and measurement techniques we currently use are tried and true and that while technologies and labels have changed, the past is indeed prologue and we should also be looking backward to find lessons that can be applied anew for future success. To illustrate what we mean, we have taken the liberty of leaving in place Don Hawkins' original labels for the services and products the AT&T Bell Laboratories Network provided, and juxtaposing them with what the same services and products might be called in today's parlance.

In the third chapter, looking at research related to the management of corporate libraries, the case is made for the necessity for more of this kind of research both by practitioners and academics and the support and encouragement of this research by information professional associations such as the Special Libraries Association. As a profession, we simply do not do enough in the way of collecting data about special and corporate libraries—data that are so important to our understanding of where opportunities may lie. Too few practitioners currently take the time to codify their practices for sharing with colleagues, and this leaves a real gap in the ongoing education of corporate Information Services management. And too few faculties in library and information science (LIS) programs choose to seek out grants and publication opportunities in the area of special libraries, especially those in corporations. This chapter reviews the challenges of finding funding for this type of research and suggests several topical avenues and constituencies that are ripe for attention.

CORPORATE SCORE: MARRYING TWO EXPERT TOOLS WILL HELP YOU SUSTAIN YOUR CORPORATE LIBRARY

JAMES M. MATARAZZO AND TOBY PEARLSTEIN

The library manager of a large insurance company rearranges the library's print collection to resemble a large bookstore, set up mostly by subject with excellent signs above each section. In consultation with her corporate supervisor, she purposefully makes the library's onsite services 95 percent self-help. Now she focuses her team on the main goal: supporting the sales team in its efforts to sell insurance. In positioning the library to strengthen the firm's most important activity, the library manager reasons that if the company is successful and the library can point to its contributions to that success, it will be successful too.

A large professional services firm reshapes its organizational structure around industry-specific goals in order to remain competitive. The manager of the firm's research service knows it must adapt also or become marginalized. He assigns industry-specific researchers to provide more contextual products to the firm's teams. By demonstrating that the researchers are aware of the firm's strategies, and by aligning their services to these changes, the library becomes a full partner in supporting the organization's new reality. These two scenarios demonstrate a transition of library services from an older warehouse model to one focusing on client-centered uses. Corporate librarians hold the key to determining new ways to work within their environments. They must drive the process to change the view of the company library as a liability—as overhead, as a cost center, as part of the problem—to the library as a solution center, a necessary investment.

For the sixth consecutive year, we hear that corporate libraries are losing both space and staff, closed by management who believe that any needed information is freely available on the Web. While no official tally is kept, the magnitude of the problem can be estimated by reviewing Special Libraries Association (SLA) membership data and our own experience.

We calculate a more than 20 percent decline in SLA membership since 1997 (a figure SLA confirms), roughly when the Internet began having an impact on the lives of librarians and information science professionals and their clients. Even if only half the special librarians in the United States and Canada belong to SLA, and even if this represents only a portion of closures, reductions, or voluntary and involuntary early retirements, it is clear that to help themselves, company librarians must find a new path to success.

STRATEGIC THINKING IS KEY

With this in mind, we suggest two tactics to achieving full alignment with your parent organization. First, become a thought leader. Second, measure your contribution in language your boss understands. While this has been said before, it is crucial to use professional tools paired with management tools to prepare yourself, your team, and your library for success. These are, respectively, the SLA's *Competencies for Information Professionals* (SLA 2003) and the Balanced Scorecard construct, introduced by Robert S. Kaplan and David P. Norton in 1992 and continuously expanded into its current version (*Alignment: Using the Balanced Scorecard to Create Corporate Synergies*, 2006). These aids help connect the competencies to your strategy and create a balance between operational and financial measures so you can showcase your library's contributions.

In its *Competencies for Information Professionals*, most recently revised in 2003, SLA's focus is necessarily on core skills and services relevant to the parent organization. The whole process of ensuring both personal and professional competencies can help define the value of the librarian and library services to the business. Value becomes somewhat easier to demonstrate because the library's benefits are designed and implemented to enhance larger corporate objectives. While SLA's competencies can help a library manager manage

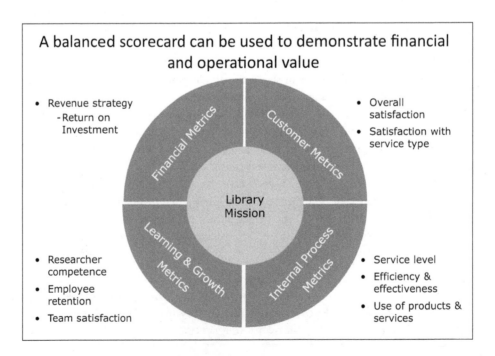

A balanced scorecard can be used to demonstrate financial and operational value

- Revenue strategy
  - Return on Investment

Financial Metrics

- Overall satisfaction
- Satisfaction with service type

Customer Metrics

Library Mission

- Researcher competence
- Employee retention
- Team satisfaction

Learning & Growth Metrics

- Service level
- Efficiency & effectiveness
- Use of products & services

Internal Process Metrics

"down," so to speak, the balanced scorecard is a tool for managing "up." It can bridge the library-oriented/phrased competencies that you and your team will have no trouble understanding and the business-centric assessment of the value of the library to your organization. The scorecard helps translate your strategy into measurable objectives and concrete actions.

If you already capture metrics about your offerings (reference requests, hits and click-throughs on your library's website, user stats on online products), you are ahead of the game. If you don't, the scorecard can be a good guide for thinking about what your organization will find important to track. It enables you to set goals and measures for both the financial and operational side of your services and can be an indicator of what really matters and consequently how to focus your discussions with decision-makers. When the boss asks you to explain why it's important to invest in realizing the competencies, the balanced scorecard can be your Rosetta Stone (or BabelFish if you prefer).

BECOME A THOUGHT LEADER

In order to implement the balanced scorecard and competencies fully, you'll need a plan for becoming a thought leader. We've developed five critical points.

Understand Your Customers

You and your team must understand what the organization does. Find out what your customers do in their daily work and where gaps exist. Focus groups, individual interviews, or surveys will help you learn what information and services are necessary for your customers to succeed.

Know How Management Defines Success

Show senior management how your services can contribute to their success. Start by answering these critical questions: What are the higher goals your company seeks to achieve? Which units are key to achieving these goals and what information services will enhance their productivity? Align your strategy with those goals.

Refine the Services Offered

Most company librarians provide services to anyone at the firm. It is a mistake to offer a little help to hundreds of employees in scores of departments. This only dilutes your support, and when cuts must be made, no one will stand up for the library because no one receives substantive assistance. Instead, prioritize your target audiences and create champions—thinking first of those on whom the success of the firm depends.

Be Client-Centered

Get inside the key units of the firm. The more time you spend "connected" to those you bolster (whether virtually or physically), the sooner you will be seen as a valued member of the team and your contribution to the team's success acknowledged.

Provide Leadership

The "library as place" in today's business environment must give way to the "library as provider of services" that permeates the organization and is integrated, as much as is practical, into its daily workflow. It is the manager's role to be a well-informed information professional who thinks strategically and is able to recognize and create opportunities to make an impact on the organization's business goals.

While there is no magic bullet to guarantee success (sometimes even the most cogent argument will not influence corporate decision-makers to see beyond short-term solutions), the general direction is clear: the greatest chance of success will come from affiliating the library with the unique goals of its parent organization and the needs of the people working to hit those targets. This goes beyond parroting a mission statement or tweaking position names and titles; it demands practitioners who are strategic thinkers. Librarians must become the catalysts for increasing the productivity and effectiveness of their customers, whether they be bench scientists or management consultants.

STABILIZING OUR FUTURE

Views vary widely about the causes of downsizing and closures of corporate libraries. Corporate libraries and librarians have been affected even in environments where a strong library foundation has been traditional. But as traditional library services are vanishing, so are its traditional practitioners.

What should alarm us is that more companies don't recognize the utility of their library during times of downturn. Rather, the library is often seen as a handicap. Whether as a result of consolidation, outsourcing, offshoring, or just plain naïveté about the Web's capabilities, there is no question that the closure of many corporate libraries and attendant job losses are having an effect on corporate librarians. Minds won't be changed without us. It's our job to show the companies we work for why our services are essential.

REFERENCES

Competencies for Information Professionals of the 21st Century. Rev. ed. Special Libraries Association, 2003. http://www.sla.org/content/learn/members/competencies/index.cfm (accessed February 1, 2013).

Kaplan, Robert S., and David P. Norton. *Alignment: Using the Balanced Scorecard to Create Corporate Synergies.* Boston: Harvard Business School, 2006.

2

CASE STUDY: THE AT&T BELL LABORATORIES LIBRARY NETWORK

DONALD T. HAWKINS

From its inception in 1973 until the historic dismembering of AT&T that began in 1984, the AT&T Bell Laboratories Library Network stood as a shining example of a highly successful organization serving the employees of AT&T-Bell Laboratories (AT&T-BL).

Originally, the corporate name of Bell Laboratories was "Bell Telephone Laboratories, Incorporated," but in the 1970s, AT&T changed the name to "AT&T Bell Laboratories."

Libraries were an important support to AT&T-BL's mission from its formation in 1925. In a seminal book chapter, Kennedy (Jackson et al. 1978, 165–76) described the AT&T-BL Library Network and its services and noted, "It is not surprising . . . that the numerous information sources and channels available to an R&D community are heavily used . . . The role of the technical libraries in Bell Labs is major. . . . " Jackson and Jackson, authors of the book in which Kennedy's chapter appears, concurred: "We consider this Network to be the most advanced, most centralized industrial information system operating today."

This case study reviews some of the history of libraries at AT&T-BL and the development of its Library Network, with an emphasis on the management philosophies, options, and services that permitted it not only to survive but to also become highly successful.

AT&T-BL CORPORATE STRUCTURE AND HISTORY

Gertner (2012) called AT&T-BL "the most innovative scientific organization in the world." Its mission was to support the R&D initiatives of its owners, AT&T and Western Electric (WE), its manufacturing unit. AT&T-BL became a highly desirable place to do research. Indeed, many employees (including those in the Library Network) considered it an honor and a privilege to work at AT&T-BL. One significant indication of the caliber of AT&T-BL's scientists is that several of them won the Nobel Prize.

Initially headquartered in New York, AT&T-BL moved to Murray Hill, New Jersey shortly after World War II and also established two other large locations nearby, at Whippany and Holmdel, New Jersey. As WE grew and expanded, small AT&T-BL branches were incorporated at many WE locations. The motivation for this was to foster close communication between the AT&T-BL scientists and engineers and the WE engineering and manufacturing personnel. At its peak, AT&T-BL was comprised of four main locations (three in New Jersey and another one in Illinois) and seven branches.

Each AT&T-BL location had a physical library that focused on the subject area relevant to the work done there. The main research library was located at the Murray Hill headquarters where much of the company's basic research was done. Initially, all of the libraries operated semiautonomously, but as networking and computer technology advanced, it became evident that operating as a network would lead to significant enhancements in the services rendered to users as well as cost savings resulting from elimination of duplication of efforts across the libraries. Thus, in 1973, the AT&T-BL Library Network was formed. (The library at the Western Electric Engineering Research Center was also included in the Library Network.)

LIBRARY NETWORK ORGANIZATION

The Network was organized in three major departments: Systems, Library Operations, and Administration. Its guiding philosophy was that the entire AT&T-BL library operation and its related functions should be managed as a single unit. Thus, the Library Network operated in a hybrid mode, with services applicable to the entire Network operated centrally, but still maintaining local libraries at the main and branch locations, where most of the interaction with users occurred. The libraries at the main AT&T-BL locations were each managed by a supervisor who reported directly to the head of the Library Operations Department. At the branch locations, the library supervisor reported to the local AT&T-BL Operations Manager, with a dotted-line relationship to the Library Operations Department. The Library Systems Department developed and managed the computer systems that operated the Network, and the Library Administration Department was responsible for budgeting, resource acquisition and management, and similar functions. The heads of the three departments each served as a direct liaison to one or more branch libraries.

The management of the Network held meetings three times a year, which were attended by all first-level and higher managers. These meetings were extremely valuable because they gave managers from remote locations a chance to interact face-to-face with people with whom they dealt by phone or interoffice mail. A unique policy was that newly hired information professionals in the Network who were below the manager level were invited to two management meetings early in their tenure so that they could see and understand how policies were formed. They were treated as full participants at the meetings, not simply observers, and were provided with all the background documentation, meeting minutes, and so forth. (On a personal note, I was at the meeting in 1973 where the concept of a library network was introduced, and it was extremely instructive.)

LIBRARY NETWORK SERVICES *[EFFICIENT AND EFFECTIVE SHARING OF SERVICES]*

Kennedy (Jackson et al. 1978) lists the following centralized services provided by the Network. He noted that it would have been inefficient, uneconomical, or impossible to provide many of them on a local level.

- Acquisitions and cataloging
- Current awareness services
- Specialized information directories
- Advanced information retrieval services
- Translations
- Computing information services
- Technical report services, such as acquisition, indexing, announcing, and so forth
- Management information reports
- Systems design and development

Several of these services will now be discussed in detail.

Internal Technical Information *[Library Services Moves toward Knowledge Management Services]*

A major operation, the processing and handling of internal proprietary information, became part of the Network's services shortly after it was founded. This service included the acquisition, indexing, and distribution of all Technical Memoranda produced by AT&T-BL staff and could be considered as a full-fledged information service in its own right. Not only were authors able to designate report recipients by name or department number, but readers (who well may have been unknown to the author) were also able to request copies of reports issued, either by author or department number. This and other Network services were designed to foster the widespread dissemination of information, getting it into the hands of the scientific and engineering staff for use in their research quickly and easily.

Acquisitions and Cataloging *[Acquisitions and Cataloging Create Opportunities for Alignment]*

Before the inception of the Network, each of the AT&T-BL libraries had a conventional card catalog. One of the earliest Network projects was the production of a printed union catalog in book format (following which the library staff at several locations had the enjoyable task of tipping thousands of catalog cards into a dumpster!). As Kennedy remarks, this was the first time that AT&T-BL staff at all locations were able to see all books held in all of the Network's libraries. Copies of the catalog could also be held locally by departments, thus providing convenient access to the libraries' collections. Of course, today a printed book catalog seems quaint and obsolete, and in time, it gave way to a modern online catalog incorporating all the functions library users have come to expect.

Book acquisitions did not occur in a vacuum. Spaulding and Stanton (1976, 269–80) describe the creation of "selection profiles" for each library in the Network. Researchers in the various subject areas of interest to AT&T-BL were recruited to serve on a selection committee that advised the librarians on their information needs. Before the formation of the Network, selections tended to be parochial in nature and were not coordinated with the other libraries, but with the development of computer systems, reports on departments' usage of resources could be used to guide selection policies (see "Management Reports" subsequently). The supervisors and reference librarians, who had responsibility for selecting new titles to be added to the holdings of the libraries in the Network, used the resulting selection profiles. Profiles were organized in three levels:

1. Representative collection
2. Research collection
3. Comprehensive collection

In the case of materials applicable to a number of locations, one library was designated to collect such materials and serve as Network source for them. The selection profiles thus helped to provide a sharper focus on the collections and reduce unnecessary duplication of purchases.

Current Awareness Services [Enhancing the Dissemination of Information to Users]

The Library Network had a significant current awareness effort that took the form of periodic abstract bulletins covering areas of interest to AT&T-BL. The bulletins were coupled with a request service, so that a user wishing a copy of an article needed only to write the item number on an order form printed on the bulletin cover and place it in their interoffice mail. The numbers were entered into a system that generated address labels, and a photocopying operation produced the copies. (The photocopying operation was supported by a "captive" collection of frequently requested journals.) Later, a special command library (Waldstein 1986), was written by the Systems Department and added to the company's UNIX® machines, so that users could simply enter their requests online and e-mail them directly to the Library Network for processing. This is another example of how the AT&T-BL Library Network enhanced the dissemination of information to users. After the current copyright law was enacted, a new system, BELLPAY, was created to generate reports so that appropriate royalty payments could be made to the Copyright Clearance Center (CCC) (Stanton 1978, 326–29). AT&T-BL was one of the earliest users of the CCC.

Because of the major subject interests of AT&T-BL, subscriptions to the INSPEC, SPIN, and NTIS database tapes were obtained and used to generate the major alerting bulletin, *Current Technical Papers* (CTP), which covered most areas of the physical sciences, engineering, and technology. Hawkins (1985b, 187–204) describes CTP and the bulletin production system (Bell Laboratories Library Publications and Retrieval, BELLPAR) in detail. The database tapes were processed in-house, and appropriate articles were selected and printed in the bulletin. It is important to note that no individual user interest profiles were stored for these current awareness services, thus eliminating staff time and the costs that would have been incurred in managing a large number of profiles. Instead, global company "profiles" were used to extract information from the databases.

CTP was issued twice a month in five subject sections and announced about 2,000 items in each issue. It was sent to about 5,500 subscribers. In addition to the bibliographic data for each item, after 1976 the CCC royalty fee was also shown. (Items for which copying permission had not been secured were not given an order number, but they were listed because it was found that users wished to be made aware of their existence.) An active publisher contact program attempted to secure copying permission for uncopyable journals.

In addition to CTP, current awareness bulletins on management, computing, and telecommunications were produced. These took the form of listings of the tables of contents of appropriate journals, which were manually keyboarded and assigned order numbers so that users could request them through the BELLPAR system. The basic philosophy of the

Network's current awareness services was ". . . projection rather than reaction, which implies going to the users; making it easy for them to learn about, request, and get information; marketing the library image . . . and developing information and alerting and access packages addressed both to known and forecasted needs" (Kennedy 1982, 128–47).

Information Retrieval Services *[Focusing on Client-Centric Needs: Connecting Competencies to Strategy]*

Although a major responsibility of the reference librarians in the local libraries was to find information for the technical staff, they frequently had neither the time nor the expertise to conduct lengthy or complex searches. To satisfy those needs, the requesters were referred to the Network's centralized Information Retrieval Service, which was staffed by subject experts with PhD degrees. The thinking behind the creation of the centralized service was that PhD-level staff could use their specialized knowledge to help them in satisfying their requesters' needs. This policy turned out to be highly successful: Not only were the information scientists able to interact with the researchers at an advanced level, but they also were available for special tasks; for example, indexing books written by AT&T-BL authors. One of the major services provided was the compilation of extensive bibliographies, each of which contained key word in context (KWIC) and author indexes that were produced by the Network's in-house BELDEX program (which had been one of the earliest applications of computers to information systems [Lowry 1972, 841–46]).

Before the advent of online information retrieval systems, searches were done manually; on occasion, searches were purchased from services such as the Illinois Institute of Technology's Computer Search Center (Schipma 1970, 105–8). However, when the commercial online services appeared around 1972, the information professionals in the AT&T-BL Library Network were enthusiastic early adopters and began to use them extensively. Hawkins has published a number of articles describing the implementation and use of online searching in the Network (Hawkins 1974, 105–8; Hawkins et al. 1976, 31–55; Hawkins 1976, 28-4; 1980, 97–126). In addition to traditional online searching, the online services were used for specialized information projects, such as bibliometric studies (Hawkins 1977, 13–18; 1980, 475–82), "printing" search results to magnetic tape for further processing (Hawkins 1981, 253–56), and experimenting with searching by end users (Vollaro and Hawkins 1986, 67–72; Hawkins and Levy 1986, 167–74).

Initially, only the centralized Information Retrieval Service used the commercial online services and the costs were absorbed by the Network. As usage increased, all the reference librarians obtained access, and the costs of expensive searches were charged back to the user. Awareness of the benefits and power of online searching grew with end users following a publicity campaign (Hawkins 1977, 48). Publicizing online services was not undertaken when they initially became available because of fears that the library services would be overwhelmed by requests, but when this did not occur, the initial limited publicity was expanded with favorable results.

Library Network Systems Development *[Technology Facilitates Workflow]*

Lowry (1972, 841–46) discussed the early development and use of computer systems in the Network and some of the information products produced. Online circulation control in the libraries had been a reality since 1968 when the Bell Laboratories Library Real-Time

Loan System (BELLREL) was launched (Jackson et al. 1978, 165–76). As the Network grew and demand increased, many other systems were developed to automate various Network functions.

Initially, the Library Network was just one of many users of the Murray Hill computer center. As its load grew, it became clear that development of new systems would be significantly enhanced and become more cost effective if the Network had its own computer. Negotiations with the computer center resulted in a machine named Diana (Diana was an appropriate name for a library's computer because Diana was the goddess of the hunt in Greek mythology) and running the UNIX® operating system being dedicated solely to the Network. Although the AT&T-BL computer center maintained the system, the Network's programmers controlled the process flow, thus spurring the development of systems and greatly enhancing the management of the Network. And, as usage by end users grew and increased the load on the machine, it allowed the development of a decentralized client–server architecture that avoided unacceptable response times (Brown-Woodson 1998, 178–79).

Management Reports *[Demonstrating Contribution]*

No organization can operate effectively without relevant and timely management reports generated from real-time measurements of various activities, and the Library Network was no exception. The power of the computer systems developed in the AT&T-BL Library Network was heavily exploited to develop innovative and useful reports that kept the Network running smoothly and also allowed it to react to the unusual circumstances that beset the telecommunications industry during the 1980s. Such information was critical in providing timely and relevant response to the information needs of the AT&T-BL technical staff, and that, in turn, contributed to the excellent reputation enjoyed by the AT&T-BL Library Network.

Because the Network had its own systems and computer access, the routine creation of such reports at regular intervals could be integrated into existing workflows, and when special circumstances arose, generation of customized reports was easily accommodated. Kennedy (Kennedy 1982, 128–47) described some of management functions that became possible in the Network as a result of the development of computer systems. The use of selection profiles to drive acquisitions has been discussed above; examples of some other reports produced include:

- *Titles in Demand* (TID). The TID list was produced by the BELLREL system and listed books for which five or more people were waiting. Not only was the TID list a guide to the books for which additional copies were needed, but it was also a measure of researchers' interest in a subject area. Using the TID list, the library supervisors held a weekly conference call to decide which titles would be purchased and by which library, thus enhancing service to users by shortening waiting times.

- *Zero Activity Report.* This report, at the other end of the spectrum from the TID, identified titles that had not circulated in a given period of time. Generally run annually, it was used in weeding the collection.

- *Reserve Queue Aging* (RQA). Run weekly, the RQA report listed unsatisfied requests for books and was used by managers to decide on purchases of additional copies of books. The related *Get Off the Shelf* list identified books that had been requested and should have been on the shelf but had not been checked out to the requester for one reason or another. It was used by the clerical staff in their efforts to locate such books and send them to the requesters.

- *Loan History Report.* This report listed books checked out by members of a given department and was used to establish a local collection of frequently used books when a department was moving to a new location.

- *Journal Usage.* The BELLPAY system produced a report of the number of photocopies made of articles from each journal title held by the Network, arranged by the time elapsed since the publication of the article. With the increase in journal prices (even in the 1980s!), this report provided input to decisions on which journals to cancel and which new ones to subscribe to.

- In the acquisitions area, financial data, vendor performance, and workflow through the processes of order receipt, cataloging, and distribution of ordered items to libraries was tracked by management reports.

Kennedy sounds a useful caution that remains important today. "The very ease with which elegant compilations of all kinds can be produced may encourage excesses in reporting. The results may be unhappy." However, he also goes on to note, "the value to information managers of a carefully defined, coherent management information program can hardly be overstated" (Kennedy 1982).

KEYS TO SUCCESS *[KEY TAKEAWAYS]*

Why did the AT&T-BL Library Network achieve such a good reputation and become so successful in the years leading up to the momentous events of 1983 and the following years? (The post-1983 period will be described briefly below.) There appear to be five major reasons:

- *Management support.* The Library Network enjoyed strong support from the upper management of AT&T-BL, and the managers of the Network made special efforts to remain in favor with the AT&T-BL management. A Library Committee composed of executives reviewed the operations of the Network and were kept apprised of new services and systems. Senior executives frequently used the resources of the Network to support their own activities, and their requests gave the Network staff an opportunity to showcase the various services available through the Network. The Network was well supported financially; in 1982, its book budget was about $587,000, and in 1988, the budget for the Library Network Support group, which included purchases of books for the 22 units of the Network and for individual employees, was $3.5 million (Talcott, personal communication). These are 1980s' dollars, which would equate to at least twice as much today.

- *Professional staff.* Virtually all of the Network's professional staff members had master of library science or other advanced degrees. Many of them were active in external professional societies, attended conferences, gave presentations, and published articles in leading journals. Such activities were encouraged and supported by the Network managers. The information professionals were thus able to command the respect of their colleagues and effectively help to satisfy their information needs.

- *Advanced services.* Many of the services offered by the Network went well beyond traditional library services, such as specialized information retrieval, a wide range of current awareness services, and attention to technological advances in the subjects of interest to AT&T-BL. These enhanced the Network's reputation within AT&T-BL.

- *User involvement.* The Network took a strong proactive approach to its users, consulting with them in the design of new services. This was formalized in the form of a Library

Users Committee at the major locations, which provided frequent feedback to supervisors. And of course, frequent informal communication from regular users was also solicited and valued.

- *Marketing* was not neglected. Feature articles appeared regularly in company house organs such as the *Bell Labs News* that described library services and new products. Exhibits in heavily trafficked areas were set up on special occasions such as National Library Week.

CONCLUSION

The AT&T-BL Library Network was the first industrial library network in the world. Both W. O. Baker (President of AT&T-BL) and W. K. Lowry (Director of the Library Network in the 1970s) were recognized for their influence on the library and information profession by being made honorary members of the Special Libraries Association. The above description covers what one might call the "glory days" of AT&T-BL, when it functioned like a major academic organization, conducting research that frequently had no obvious current application to its owners, but which often led to highly significant discoveries and gained major recognition for its staff. In such an environment, the Library Network expanded, thrived, and enjoyed a high reputation among its users.

Unfortunately, the AT&T Bell Laboratories Library Network no longer exists. However, many of its principles of operation, its professional management, use of management information, and the development of computer systems that enhanced a close attention and responsiveness to users' information needs were innovative and ground breaking. Even in the present days of universal access to information, they remain an example of how to design and operate a successful library and information service that earns the respect and high regard of its users.

EPILOGUE: 1983 AND BEYOND

External forces beginning in 1983 caused an enormous upheaval within AT&T and its subsidiaries, and ultimately led to the demise of the AT&T-BL Library Network. The painful process began when a ruling by the Federal Communications Commission required that the AT&T Information Systems division focusing on computer technology and telephone sales become a fully separated subsidiary of AT&T. The result was the creation of American Bell, Inc. (ABI), and the immediate effect of that action was that libraries primarily serving ABI technical staff were abruptly separated from the Library Network. In locations shared by AT&T-BL and ABI, the ABI employees encountered significant bureaucratic obstacles in using the libraries. It became necessary to launch clones of many Network services for use by ABI employees.

The Library Network was further challenged by AT&T's divestiture of the local telephone companies in 1984 and its subsequent deregulation. Deregulation allowed AT&T to enter competitive markets formerly closed to it, and although that resulted in a number of benefits, significant cost cutting became necessary. AT&T retained WE and AT&T-BL, but the character of the Library Network changed from that of a laboratory resource to a corporate resource (Hawkins 1985a, 199–206) with its activities viewed and operated as a business. As a result, a much greater emphasis was placed on electronic delivery of information through the "library" command. Cost structures for many services, previously provided without charge, were established, and these costs were charged back to requesters' departments. The most significant change was the charging of departments for the professional staff time spent on their requests. And in the new environment, a growing need for current marketing and competitive information resulted in the formation of a new unit of the Network specifically devoted to dealing with such requests.

After AT&T was restructured in 1984, the three entities, ABI, AT&T-BL, and WE were absorbed into AT&T and divided into several business units. The AT&T Technologies unit, which included AT&T-BL, was spun off from AT&T in 1996 and became Lucent Technologies, Inc., which was in turn acquired by Alcatel, S.A. of France in 2006, forming Alcatel-Lucent. Various vestiges of the AT&T-BL Library Network can probably still be found in that organization.

The Internet, of course, had a major influence on the Library Network as it did on virtually every other library organization. Many of the Network's services are now obsolete because of the direct user access that the Internet provides to information through a host of gateways, discovery services, online databases, and so forth.

REFERENCES

Brown-Woodson, Ina A. "Online Services to AT&T Employees." *Library Trends* 47, no. 1 (1998): 172–79.

Gertner, Jon. *Idea Factory: Bell Labs and the Great Age of American Innovation.* New York: Penguin Press, 2012.

Hawkins, Donald T. "Bibliographic Database Usage in a Large Technical Community." *Journal of the American Society for Information Science* 25, no. 2 (1974): 105–8.

Hawkins, Donald T. "Interactive Information Transfer in an Industrial Library Network." *IEEE International Conference on Communications, Conference Record* 2 (1976): 28-1-28-4.

Hawkins, Donald T. "Growth and Publicity of Online Information Retrieval in a Library Network." *Proceedings of the ASIS Annual Meeting,* 40th Annual Meeting, Chicago, 1977, 14.

Hawkins, Donald T. "Unconventional Uses of Online Information Retrieval Systems: Online Bibliometric Studies." *Journal of the American Society for Information Science* 28, no. 1 (1977): 13–18.

Hawkins, Donald T. "Crystallographic Literature: A Bibliometric and Citation Analysis." *Acta Crystallographica* B36 (1980): 475–82.

Hawkins, Donald T. "Management of an Online Information Retrieval Service." In *The Library and Information Manager's Guide to Online Services,* edited by, Ryan E. Hoover, 97–126. White Plains, NY: Knowledge Industry Publications, Inc., 1980.

Hawkins, Donald T. "Machine-Readable Output from Online Searches." *Journal of the American Society for Information Science* 32, no. 4 (1981): 253–56.

Hawkins, Donald T. "Library Networking at AT&T: New Information Needs and Technologies in a Competitive Environment." *Information Services & Use* 5 (1985a): 199–206.

Hawkins, Donald T. "Use of Machine-Readable Databases to Support a Large SDI Service." *Information Processing & Management* 21, no. 3 (1985b): 187–204.

Hawkins, Donald T., and Louise R. Levy. "Introduction of Online Searching to End Users at AT&T Bell Laboratories." In *National Online Meeting Proceedings, New York, NY,* edited by Martha E. Williams and Thomas H. Hogan, 167–74. Medford, NJ: Learned Information, Inc., 1986.

Hawkins, Donald T., B. A. Stevens, and Anton R. Pierce. "Computer-Aided Information Retrieval In a Large Industrial Library." In *Proceedings of the 1975 Clinic on Library Applications of*

Data Processing, edited by F. Wilfrid Lancaster, 31–55. Urbana-Champaign, IL: Graduate School of Library Science, University of Illinois, 1976.

Jackson, Eugene B., Ruth L. Jackson, and Robert A. Kennedy. *Industrial Information Systems: A Manual for Higher Managements and Their Information Officer/Librarian Associates*, 165–76. New York: Dowden, Hutchinson & Ross, 1978.

Kennedy, Robert A. "Computer-Derived Management Information in a Special Library." In *Proceedings of the 1982 Clinic on Library Applications of Data Processing*, edited by F. Wilfrid Lancaster, 128–47. Urbana-Champaign, IL: Graduate School of Library Science, University of Illinois, 1982.

Lowry, W. K. "Use of Computers in Information Systems." *Science* 175, no. 4024 (1972): 841–46.

Schipma, Peter B. "Design and Operation of a Computer Search Center for Chemical Information." *Journal of Chemical Documentation* 10, no. 3 (1970): 158–62.

Spaulding, F. H., and Robert O. Stanton. "Computer-Aided Selection in a Library Network." *Journal of the American Society for Information Science* 27, no. 5 (1976): 269–80.

Stanton, Robert O., "BELLPAY—Bell Laboratories Library Network Royalty Accounting System." *Proceedings of the ASIS Annual Meeting* 15 (41st Annual Meeting, New York) (1978): 326–29.

Talcott, Ann W. (former manager of the Murray Hill Library), personal communication.

Vollaro, Alice J., and Donald T. Hawkins. "End-User Searching In a Large Library Network: A Case Study of Patent Attorneys." *Online* 10, no. 4 (1986): 67–72.

Waldstein, R. K., "Library—an Electronic Ordering System." *Information Processing & Management* 22, no. 1: (1986): 39–44.

ACKNOWLEDGMENT

I thank Stephen J. Bell, Associate University Librarian, Temple University, for assistance in obtaining copies of some of the articles cited in the references, and Ann Talcott for her review of this chapter and the suggestions she made.

3

PREFACE: THE GLASS IS HALF FULL

JAMES M. MATARAZZO AND TOBY PEARLSTEIN

There is little, if any, substantive and sustained research and documentation on the causes of reductions and closures in corporate special libraries, studies that would help extrapolate a pattern of behavior or circumstances that could yield more than anecdotal lessons for these types of libraries in particular. For example, there are no statistics on the number of corporate special libraries and the number of openings, reductions, and closures affecting them over time. Such statistics would be invaluable for identifying trends that could guide practitioners in thinking strategically about their roles within their organizations. Library and information science (LIS) faculties interested in special libraries and corporate libraries specifically, as well as professional associations like Special Libraries Association (SLA), are uniquely positioned to collect and analyze this kind of data and bring it to bear for the benefit of our profession as a whole. Certainly the need makes potential projects like partnering with a corporate information professional to conduct some of this research a very attractive proposition.

LOOKING FOR THE LITERATURE

What is known anecdotally is that the current economic downturn, while unique in its severity, is not a first-time occurrence. How it is affecting corporate special libraries, however, may be a new twist. During the Great Depression of the 1930s, Day (1936, 329) noted that some special libraries had closed in the "past five years of depression." Interestingly, she wrote that untrained librarians had started those libraries that had closed. Unfortunately, she was not specific about these closures, other than noting that there had been only a few, though she also alluded to staff reductions and budget cuts. Day's opinion was reinforced by Alexander (1934, 62), who wrote, "Almost no special libraries had been discontinued during the [D]epression." The study of corporate library closures disappears from the literature after the Depression to 1963, when Woods (1963, 8) writes in the Directory of Special Libraries and Information Centers that "many company libraries are short lived, reflecting frequent administrative changes within business." The reader is left with the impressions that since administrative changes were generally normal to businesses, it would apply to the libraries that served them. Two articles in the 1970s reminded company librarians of their vulnerability during difficult economic times (Cupp 1970, 362; Strain 1970, 368–73). One described the approach to the search for employment elsewhere, while the other described the preparations needed to properly close a corporate library. The articles were not any more specific and did not even reveal the names of the firms. In one, the author even used a pseudonym. In 1972, Frank McKenna, the executive director of the SLA, commented on the economy and the loss of positions (McKenna 1972, 37). He specifically noted that defense and aerospace-related industries were being particularly hard hit. While written evidence documenting this in terms of numbers and locations of libraries affected is impossible to find in the special library literature, an article in the *1975 ALA Yearbook* provided insight into the prevailing conditions: "[A]nd almost every day—wondering if the widely publicized, improving economy of 1975 would permanently remove the long-lived—with threat of staff cutbacks, retrenchments in service, or even, going defunct."

By year's end the volatile nature of special libraries had, indeed, been reaffirmed with news and rumors of library mergers, cutbacks, folding; but, once again, volatility worked in both directions. In most cities, and special libraries tend to be a metropolitan phenomena, one could point to at least a few new organizations that were taking the special library or information center plunge (Strable 1976, 329).

In 1980, Matarazzo compiled a list of corporate libraries closed in a single metropolitan area (Matarazzo 1981). He found that the importance of these libraries was tied to the financial strength of their firm, that senior managers at the firms made the closure decisions, and that any real or perceived financial distress caused the companies to evaluate all expenditures. The ensuing management analysis established that these senior managers frequently found a company's library to be something that the firm could survive without. In fact, it was these findings that led Matarazzo to the development of the predictive model discussed later. The economy also suffered recessions in 1990–1991 and 1995–1996. Each time, some firms closed their libraries and/or reduced staff and expenditures. Matarazzo and Clarke demonstrated that there was growth in the number of vacancies in corporate libraries in 1991 compared to 2001 in at least one geographic area. Previous studies in 1985 and 1989 had demonstrated unsustainable growth in vacancies in New England. What differentiates these previous experiences from today is that during these earlier recessions and economic slumps, more new special or corporate libraries overall opened than were closed; there tended to be more "births" of special libraries than "deaths" (Matarazzo and Clarke 2008, 10–16).

So, while the profession during these periods may have bemoaned the many reductions or closures, there almost always seemed to be other jobs waiting in the wings for those who had been laid off. Today, casual observation indicates that the trend of cutbacks and closures appears to far outweigh the new jobs being created, even as information professionals demonstrate that their skill set can make greater contributions to an organization's success. While a body of literature has grown during the past 20 years to address the issue of operating benchmarks in corporate library management, little or no data has been gathered or analyzed concerning the health of this segment of the profession in terms of number of jobs, number of job seekers (successful or not), where jobs are located, how the jobs relate to their parent organizations overall, or whether or not these jobs are growing or reducing in number. Thus, there is no data from which we can hypothesize about cause and effect and/or see patterns from which we can learn how not to repeat past mistakes and learn about what has worked. Two recent projects provide examples of how information professionals and those who educate them might try to address the data gap in our understanding of reductions and closures. The first suggests a geographic approach. It is chronicled in an excellent and timely article in the July/August 2009 issue of *Information Outlook* describing the now familiar situation of bad economic times driving cutbacks in special libraries (Fletcher 2009). The authors of this article offer specific advice to prevent reductions or closures, their advice rooted in survey responses from a wide spectrum of types of special libraries and a couple of case studies. Even though the authors' survey is limited to the Washington, D.C., metropolitan area, it represents an attempt to document the impact of economic downturns on special libraries. These authors believe this combination of documented and case-based evidence can be a very powerful strategic planning tool for a library facing reductions or closure. The second effort is industry focused and is discussed in Chapter 4. Michelle Quigley's project, albeit by one individual with voluntary contributions of information, documents (admittedly not comprehensively) information services (IS) staff reductions and closures within the media industry. The data she has compiled (see the table in Chapter 4) provided a jumping off point to talk with both IS practitioners and end users, reporters, and editorial staff, about what was happening in their industry and how it might affect their in-house libraries or IS.

The chapter that follows here was researched and written in late 2007. The results of our review at the time left us concerned about a number of barriers to the conduct and use of empirical evidence-based research in the management of corporate library services. These barriers seem still to be in place and continue to give rise to a variety of challenges:

- The SLA research statement (2001) calls for relevant, practical research.
- SLA has limited funds for research and it lacks a referred journal, which sends most of what little research is done to other journals.
- Corporate library managers do not read the research produced and do not use research results.
- Corporate librarians do not have the time for research and lack the resources and rewards at their firms for conducting and publishing research results.
- Corporate library managers would need to have access to an array of resources in library, IS, and management literature in order to stay current with the literature.

Grants from professional associations along with those from academic institutions and publishers are the sources of most of the funding for research. In the current economic climate, these sources of funding are on the decline but they have not disappeared altogether. The goal of our 2007 review was "to provide a context for understanding why corporate library managers (and all special librarians) do not seem to have available to them a body of useful and usable research." Unfortunately, the context we reviewed now more than 5 years ago has not changed dramatically. Clearly, other types of libraries still have a much richer array of research and publication upon which to base practice.

SLA

Our original review of SLA research grant awards covered the period 1994–2006 (Special Libraries Association Research Committee 1994–2006). Since 2006, the following research grants have been awarded and results shared with the membership, with the exception of the 2009 grant which has just ended with results expected to be shared in late 2012 or 2013 (personal communication with the authors, July 2012, "Past SLA Research Grants" website).

- Understanding the value of corporate libraries in competitive intelligence practices (Awarded 2009)
- Experimenting Outside the Information Center: Non-Traditional Roles for Information Professionals in Biomedical Research (Awarded 2008)
  - "Librarians in Biomedical Research: New Roles and Opportunities" (Glenn 2010)
- Models of Embedded Librarianship: Final Report (Awarded 2007)
  - Models of Embedded Librarianship: Addendum (2011)—containing six case studies illustrative of the 2007 final report.

Another grant (related to developing SLA membership in Germany) was also awarded in 2007 but seems to have disappeared from the record.

The good news is that the reports on embedded librarianship have resonated with the professional community. As SLA members see possible new roles, these two reports are a very real service to the special library community. While our academic library colleagues appear to have seized upon the idea of embedding, which has resulted in many publications, our corporate library colleagues have come to this potential survival tool much more slowly.

The 2008 research grant led to the publication of findings related to new roles and opportunities for librarians in the area of biomedical research, and was very nicely summarized by Glenn in *Information Outlook* (Glenn 2010). These publications featured examples of librarians using their traditional skills to embed themselves into research teams aimed at developing innovative services. It is, in fact, a fitting complement to the previous study on Models of Embedded Librarianship.

The research report from the 2009 grant has only recently been received at SLA and will hopefully be published in late 2012 or 2013. This report will be the last result of SLA Research Grant Program for a while, since as of December 2011 the Association Board of Directors voted to deactivate the Research and Development Committee until such time as funding becomes available (SLA Board of Directors 2011).

The Alignment Initiative: Opportunities Remain for Further Analysis

In 2006 SLA's leadership undertook a major research study to prepare the Association and its members for the future. For 18 months, the respected firms of Fleishman & Hillard and Outsell, Inc. conducted a major research study with the assistance of Andy Hines, a futurist, with Social Technologies. This research cost hundreds of thousands of dollars and involved, in part, interviews with over 750 individuals from all facets of the information profession and those served by information professionals, and an array of focus groups. Those interviewed ran the gamut from library school students to C-level executives in the United States and Canada, Australia, and the United Kingdom. This was truly a significant data collection accomplishment.

The leadership of SLA repeatedly stated that this effort was about the future of the association and its members, and not about building a case for a name change for the association. However, it was only in 2011 that the membership has begun to see usable tools arising from analysis of the project's rich resources.

For a 2011 Annual Conference presentation to the membership of the Association's Business & Finance Division, Matarazzo and Pearlstein used some of the information from the alignment study to develop the following table. The takeaway from this was the significant gap between how information professionals perceived their roles in the organization (conducting research and managing a physical library) and how their customers wanted them to add value (more integration in management of internal content, close alignment or embedding with project teams and better integration of external content into work processes).

This is just a snapshot of what is available in the Alignment research results. Given the cost and the firms involved it is unlikely such a survey will be repeated. The data collected must be fully mined, and soon, if we are to realize the return on investment (ROI) of such an effort. Now, though, more than five years since the study was completed, how to best make operational this rich data is only beginning to be shared with the membership. The raw data itself needs to be made available for analysis on SLA's website. For example, to make practical the information found in the Alignment Project, Tchobanoff (2010) an Association Fellow,

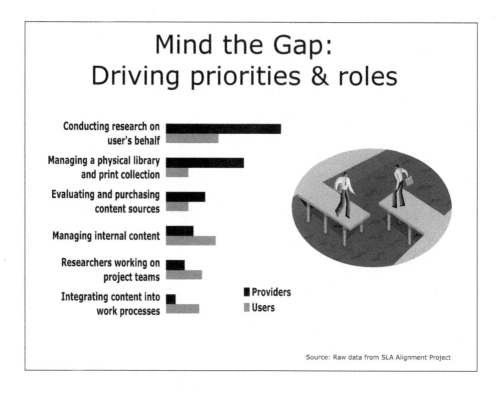

formulated the following three questions that could be applied immediately in any special library circumstance:

1. What are the top one or two current goals, objectives, priorities, and so forth of your parent organization and/or its major divisions?

2. What are you doing personally and as a department that helps your parent organization or division achieve its goals, objectives, priorities, and so forth?

3. How do you know that what you are doing personally or as a department is helping your parent organization or division achieve its goals, objectives, priorities, and so forth?

The Alignment Project data are just waiting to be more aggressively exploited.

SLA Portals

The Information Portals on the SLA website continue to have excellent potential as a way to keep members current on the literature. In order to achieve their potential they must be brought up to date and maintained.

Information Outlook

An excellent article, from a library manager's point of view, was published in *Information Outlook* (2009), entitled "Saving Special Libraries in a Recession." The authors, five students and a faculty member, surveyed special libraries in the greater Washington, D.C., area and received a 100 percent response rate (Flecter 2009, 37–42). Some 37 percent of the respondent libraries were identified as corporate. The survey was followed by four small case studies. The authors concluded that special librarians need to employ "business strategies in order to increase their chances of survival and success." Ongoing research and sharing of pragmatic lessons can be the foundation of such strategies.

Australia, New Zealand, and the United Kingdom

In the review below we highlighted the annual surveys published by *Business Information Review*. Their format has since changed and in 2010 and 2011 the surveys are now characterized as "in-depth interviews" with a much smaller sample of British corporate libraries. Both surveys note difficult conditions with reductions in budgets for content and for staff.

In a similar fashion we took note of the journal *Library Management*. However, most of this publication's articles now cover academic libraries and many deal with embedding librarians in an academic setting.

Other reports from the United kingdom as well as Australia and New Zealand are contained elsewhere in this volume.

Opportunities

With all the new faculty members at our LIS programs these gaps in research and data collection have to be seen as a genuine opportunity. At most institutions, small grants are available for research studies. Newly named Assistant Professors please take note: there is a need for your research skills in a field that requires serious investigation. You can have a significant impact using your university's small grant program alone or in combination with a special or corporate library. Take as an example William Edgar's study of the impact of a corporate library (Edgar 2004) published in *Library Quarterly*'s print journal followed by a second article in the electronic version. The corporate special libraries field needs you.

REFERENCES

Alexander, May Louise. "President's Page." *Special Libraries* 25 (March 1934): 62.

Business Information Review. London: Sage Publications.

Cupp, Bertha (pseudonym). "Fired." *Special Libraries* 61 (September 1970): 362.

Day, Mary Bostwick. "Special Libraries in Time of Depression." *Special Libraries* 27 (December 1936): 329.

Edgar, William. "Corporate Library Impact, Part I: A Theoretical Approach." *The Library Quarterly* 74 (2004): 122–51.

Flecter, Arlene, et al. "Saving Special Libraries in a Recession: Business Strategies for Survival." *Information Outlook* 13 (2009): 37–42.

Glenn, Emily. "Librarians in Biomedical Research: New Roles and Opportunities." *Information Outlook* 15, no. 10 (2010), http://www.sla.org/io/2010/10/934.cfm (accessed February 1, 2013).

Library Management. London: Emerald Group Publishing Limited.

Matarazzo, James M. *Closing the Corporate Library: Case Studies on the Decision-Making Process.* Washington, D.C.: Special Libraries Association, 1981.

Matarazzo, James M., and Joshua Clarke. "The Influence of Private and Public Companies on the Special Library Job Market." *Information Outlook* 12, no. 4 (April 2008): 10–18.

McKenna, F. E. "The Special Libraries Association." In *The Bowker Annual of Library and Booktrade Information*. 17th ed. New York: R. R. Bowker, 1972, 37.

Special Libraries Association, "Past SLA Research Grants," http://www.sla.org/content/resources/scholargrant/resgrant/pastresearchgrants.cfm (accessed July 23, 2012).

Special Libraries Association, "Research Statement," 2001, http://www.sla.org/content/resources/research/rsrchstatement.cfm (accessed July 23, 2012).

Special Libraries Association, Board of Directors. "Committee on Association Governance Report (1211-OM-A03)." *Meeting Minutes* December 1, 2011, https://www.sla.org/pdfs/boarddocs/2012/0112-EM-A01%20121511%20Board%20MinsWeb.pdf (accessed July 23, 2012).

Strable, Edward G. "Special Libraries." In *The ALA Yearbook*. Chicago: American Library Association, 1976, 329.

Strain, Paula M. "When a Library Job Ends . . . Find Another!" *Special Libraries* 61 (September 1970): 363, 368–73.

Tchobanoff, James. "Comments on the 23 Alignment Tools." Memo to the SLA Task Force members and the President of Special Libraries Association. Tchobanoff personal copy shared with authors. July 28, 2010.

Woods, Bill M. "Foreward." *Directory of Special Libraries and Information Centers*, edited by Anthony T. Kruzas. Detroit: Gale Research, 1963, 8.

A Review of Research Related to the Management of Corporate Libraries

JAMES M. MATARAZZO AND TOBY PEARLSTEIN

INTRODUCTION

The authors began this review of the research available on the topic of managing corporate libraries with the hypothesis that there has been a lack of funding for such research that in turn has limited its production. After reviewing the relevant research literature produced in the past three decades, however, the assumption of inadequate funding causing a lack of research on this topic could not totally be supported. As we sought to identify what funding was available, the literature suggested additional questions: How or if research on the subject of managing corporate libraries was encouraged and funded and by whom? What type of research would be most useful for corporate library managers? Finally, how research results were disseminated and whether the results had been put to use by practitioners? Here the authors are defining the topic of "managing libraries" in the broadest sense and occasionally delve more specifically into the topic of valuing library services. While we address corporate libraries in particular, most of our findings and commentary can be applied to special libraries in general.

In this chapter the authors explore the questions raised above by reviewing the body of literature reporting on research and activities on corporate library management (and in some cases generic library management) since the 1980s. Four major sources of this research were identified. These are the SLA serving corporate library members in the United States, Canada, Europe, and increasingly in Asia and the Middle East; and three active research environments covering the United Kingdom, Australia, and New Zealand.

Initially some assumptions about who might be impacted by research on corporate library management were made. There appear to be two major constituencies. First, little published

This chapter is adapted from Nitecki, Danuta A., and Eileen G. Abels, eds. *Influence of Funding on Advances in Librarianship* (*Advances in Librarianship*, Vol. 31), 93–114. Bingley, U.K.: Emerald Publishing Limited, 2008.

research by library school faculties, a significant source of research publications, can be found. This review concludes that this is likely due to a combination of inadequate funding and the discontinuation of SLA's refereed journal that offered a publication channel so critical for the promotion and tenure process.

The second constituency consists of corporate library managers. The literature suggests that they face significant challenges in being able to both undertake and share any research they do on their own and that this has resulted in a chilling effect on the creation of a body of knowledge that could be of use to their peers.

An overview of the research that has been done reveals some additional considerations. As one might expect, research seems primarily to be supported by grants from various professional library associations followed by academic institutions and publishers. Given that SLA is the major professional association for corporate librarians in North America, it was important here to fully review the Association's role in supporting research aimed at these members. When considering SLA's support, we came to believe that funding issues are part of a larger concern. The Association and its members seem to need a better understanding of what types of research will actually benefit corporate library managers so that the research that is funded can have a reasonable expectation of being useful to the audience. We were troubled by the question of whether or not the research generated is providing guidance that is pragmatic enough for the corporate library manager's needs. Finally, the need to re-engage with Library School faculty who are positioned to be a driving force for this research is essential.

The main goal of this chapter is to provide a context for understanding why corporate special library managers do not seem to have available to them a body of useful and usable research similar to that available to academic, public, and other types of special libraries. The conclusions and assumptions we put forward here are ripe for further analysis and we hope they will stimulate more discussion on how research can help corporate library managers cope with some of the challenges they face today.

Koufogiannakis and Crumley (2006, 324–40) point out that most areas of librarianship lack a solid evidence base and most practitioners do not incorporate research into daily practice. Why is this? Genoni et al. (2004, 419–60) suggest that this is due to a lack of funding overall and that what funding is available is made in rather small grants. In our review of SLA's research funding over the past 20 years, for example, we found that interest in research and consequently funding levels have been inconsistent. It is possible that with only small amounts of dollars for research, the researcher's time must be contributed for free or funded through other sources. We have not found much evidence of employers of corporate librarians eager to provide in-kind support for any research project. Our review indicates, though, that under-funding is not the whole reason for the disconnect found by Koufogiannakis.

The literature indicates that having the time to conduct research is also critical. Genoni et al. (2004, 419–60) have noted that those in practice do not have the time to conduct research.

Relevance of the research is also a concern. Practitioners may well find that the research literature lacks relevance for them. We would argue that while corporate library practitioners do not have the time or the support of their employers to conduct research on their own, they do want research available to them that applies to practical problems in their workplace rather than research that focuses on objective, verifiable data which are presented in scientific and technical terms. The literature reviewed reinforces this assumption.

The SLA Research Statement (SLA 2001) also calls for the corporate manager needing practical, relevant research and the more traditional scientific-based researchers to come together to share knowledge. This is quite a challenge. Practitioners seem not to either conduct or use research and if they do, their research is rarely published. LIS faculties conduct research but does this research result in something that can be implemented by the corporate library manager? For instance, Kantor and Saracevic (1995–1997) received funding from SLA to conduct a study on the value of special libraries and information centers. The resulting 60 plus page report, "Valuing Special Libraries and Information Services" (Kantor and Saracevic 1997), was intended to guide corporate library managers through the process of demonstrating the value of their libraries. Yet the vast majority of the report was devoted to a discussion of the study's methodology and taxonomy, and a technical review of the conduct of the research. In our opinion, it is doubtful that a practitioner would have taken away something from this report for practical implementation. We see this as symptomatic of the gap between what LIS researchers have received funding to do and what corporate library managers can use. While the SLA Research Statement advocates narrowing this gap, this review indicates that progress has been slow.

SPECIAL LIBRARIES ASSOCIATION

With more than 11,000 members representing a variety of disciplines and types of institutions SLA in 2007 is well positioned to drive the development and support of research projects relevant to the management of corporate libraries and information services. The following review of SLA funded research projects indicates that both the Association and its members continue to experience very real challenges in being able to provide or support research directed at answering the critical question of how corporate libraries can contribute most successfully to their parent organizations. While some research on special libraries in general has been produced, the work of several authors examined here suggests it may be lacking in applicability to corporate library managers. The impact of the 2007 launch of a new research funding effort awarded to study and report on the impact of "embedded librarians," a topic that seems very relevant to corporate library managers, remains to be seen.

Research Supported by SLA 1980–1990

Matarazzo (1981) investigated the need for research and its uses in special librarianship. His survey emphasized the role of the SLA and its commitment to research; the seeming lack of LIS faculty in the activities of SLA; the SLA research agenda and its relationship to research needs; the lack of funds for research; the low rewards for practitioners to publish; and a lack of evidence that the little research that does exist was applied to the management of corporate libraries. This review ended with a plea for SLA to join with other associations and organizations to more aggressively drive its research agenda. Much of the agenda, he felt, contained researchable questions which were broad and could benefit more than just special libraries.

From 1980 to 1990, LIS faculty were not involved in SLA by holding office, speaking, or publishing research in SLA's quarterly journal, *Special Libraries*. In fact, from 1980 to 1990, Tees (1989, 300) notes, "It seems clear SLA has not been blessed with a close relationship with library school faculty" (p. 300).

Tees's (1989, 298–304) study covering the years 1983–1984 to 1987–1988, found 0.5 percent of faculty had held any office in an SLA geographic chapter and only 4.1 percent had served on an SLA committee. For the years covered by her study, Tees counted 1,148 speaking opportunities at SLA's Annual Conferences. LIS faculty spoke at only 52 of these events. Tees also discovered that few LIS faculty published in what was then SLA's peer reviewed journal, *Special Libraries*.

In 1981 SLA's Research Committee had voted to dissolve itself (Tees 1989). It was not until five years later, as a result of a renewed interest in research, that SLA appointed a Special Committee on Research which recommended forming a standing committee as well as hiring an association staff member to support the work of the committee. By 1989, SLA had the Research Committee, a staff member, a research agenda, and funds for research. Of this renewed commitment, Drake (1989, 268) stated, "SLA has made a solid commitment to research." That very same year though, Tees, a past president of SLA, noted that the Association's "commitment to research has been at best, uneven" (Tees 1989, 302). Matarazzo (1981, 317) also warned "this heightened activity around and the desire for research may pass as quickly as it reappeared."

Research Supported by SLA Since 1990

The authors reviewed SLA's research publications since 1990 guided by the following three questions:

1. What impact on SLA funded research did the growing focus on evidence based research have?
2. Did SLA's renewed commitment to research, as evidenced by increased funding awarded during this period, result in research that was useful to corporate librarians?
3. Who was involved in the research projects funded by SLA (e.g., Library School faculty and/or practitioners)?

Focus on Funding and Sponsoring Evidence-Based Research

Matarazzo (1981) found that SLA's commitment to research seemed cyclical in nature. Celebrating its 10th anniversary as the group charged with "developing the research agenda for action by the Board of Directors," the Association's Research Committee in 1989 called for a revised research agenda. In 1999–2000, the Committee again sought to revise the research agenda by acknowledging that evidence-based practice had to become an integral part of the research program if it was to continue to meet the needs of the membership. Before 2000, the Committee had awarded a number of grants to fund research it believed was relevant to the membership. Why the Committee felt that funding research focused on "evidence-based practice" is a topic for a different review. The impact this change of focus had on grant applications and research produced is relevant for the purposes of this chapter.

In the new research guidelines accepted by the Board of Directors in 2001, "evidence-based practice" in the context of special libraries was defined as follows.

For special librarians, evidence-based practice refers to consciously and consistently making professional-level decisions that are based on the strongest evidence of what would work best for our clients. The areas in which decisions are made in library and information

practice are cited in our SLA competencies document: selection and acquisition of information resources; methods of information access; selection and use of information technologies; and management of library and information services (SLA Putting Our Knowledge to
Work 2001).

Research products resulting from this new agenda were to be directly related to the pragmatic needs of the membership, including corporate library managers.

As the following table illustrates, putting this evidence-based research agenda into
practice has been a challenge. From 1994 to 2000, prior to the evidence-based research
agenda, the Committee received between 7 and 20 grant applications each year for a maxi-
mum award of $20,000 during any given year and for no more than two projects and
usually only one award each year. From 2001 until 2006 (when SLA ran out of research
grant funds) applications dropped dramatically, never equaling that of the previous six
years. Between 2004 and 2006, less than five applications were received annually and
no awards were made. The body of literature to review since the implementation of the
evidence-based practice agenda is slim to nonexistent (SLA Primary Source Documents
1993–2007).

In 1991, the Steven I. Goldspiel Memorial Research Fund was established and named
in honor of the former president of Disclosure, Inc. In 1995, it was combined with the
Association's Special Program Grant Fund to become the major vehicle for providing grants
to support research (SLA Primary Source Documents 1989–2007). Three Goldspiel Grant
funded projects since 2000 led to publications covering topics such as organizing digital image
collections (Turner et al. 2002); changes in the profession (Barreau 2003); and applications of
evidence-based practice (Smith and Ruan 2004).

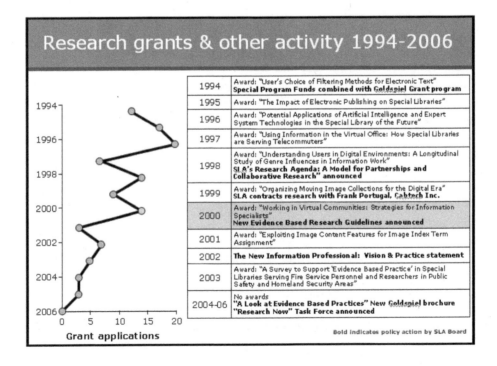

Disseminating Research

In spite of the decreased amount of funding and published research, SLA continues its efforts to serve the research needs of its members by linking them to research produced elsewhere and by encouraging members to participate in research efforts that will result in information of interest to the professional community. The SLA website (http://www.sla.org) links Association members to a significant amount of research that has been accomplished either with its support or in which SLA has encouraged its members to participate. These are reviewed subsequently.

Competencies for Special Librarians of the 21st Century, Library and Information Studies Program Survey, Final Report (SLA 1998).

This survey, done in conjunction with the Medical Library Association (MLA) and the Association for Library and Information Science Education (ALISE), sought to identify curricula in library science programs that "relate to the development of knowledge, understanding, and skills of special librarians and information professionals" (SLA 1998, 5). The object was to identify needs that could be satisfied through continued education (CE) programs offered by these participating associations. The results from this type of survey could help corporate library managers to better understand the skills and competencies of their potential employees as well as how to continue professional development of their existing employees.

Information Services Panel Surveys (Phase V Consulting Group Inc. 2000).

This series of surveys aimed to gather statistics relevant to the Association's members, including:

Financial and operating benchmark data, with comparative measures by size, sector, and topical focus

Technology environment and trends

Internet usage

Roles and responsibilities

Usage of products, services, and formats

The summary of the 2000 Survey contains a variety of statistics and trends useful to corporate library managers, both for strategic planning and in an operational context. For example, three years of data on what search engines are being used most frequently are helpful in conducting environmental scans for benchmarking.

Corporate librarians need information for purposes of strategic planning. Although they might not seek such data through formally conducted research, they turn to applied research that presents this type of comparative information. For example, Portugal (2000), created a "workbook" rather than a research product, although it draws on data from interviews with representatives from 125 corporations and organizations. As Portugal notes "this workbook presents four different approaches to the intangible valuation of information resources" (Portugal 2000, ix) by which corporate library managers could measure their organizational contribution. Unfortunately, Portugal confirms what other authors reviewed here found; all but two of those interviewed did not conduct valuations of their libraries and information centers. Nonetheless, the four methods he outlines (Return on Investment and Cost Benefit Analysis, Knowledge Value-Added, Intranet Team Forums, and Intellectual Capital Valuations) offer corporate library managers some very pragmatic language to use in thinking about ways to highlight the value of their services in very practical terms.

Coverage of this type of benchmarking data also can be found in the results of a partnership that SLA has formed with Outsell, Inc. Several reports highlighted below have either been prepared in conjunction with SLA or made available to SLA members through special arrangement with Outsell, Inc. These compile survey data that are useful to corporate library managers.

Information Management Best Practices: 2006 State of the Function (Outsell, Inc. 2006)

Information Management Best Practices: Fortunes Up For Information

Management Functions 2005—And With Fortune Comes Accountability (Outsell, Inc. 2005a).

Information Management Best Practices: Vendor Portfolio Management

Rationalizing Content For The Enterprise: 2004 (Outsell, Inc 2005b).

Changing Roles of Content Management Functions: 2004 (Outsell, Inc. 2004a).

Trend Alert: The Future of Libraries: Outsell's InfoAboutInfo Briefing (Outsell, Inc. 2004b).

Changing Role of the Information Professional: 2003 Outsell Survey (2003)

Compilations of practical information on timely topics are also found recently in a series of 10 Information Portals which the Association has begun to package through links to content at http://www.sla.org (Special Libraries Association Electronic Resources 2008). Not all the material compiled in these portals has been published in *Information Outlook*, the Association's monthly magazine, nor have all received funding or other support from SLA. Even if not all of the resources assembled (e.g., product reviews, case studies, web sites, monographs, etc.) could be technically defined as evidence-based or empirical research, this portal approach is another avenue to meet the pragmatic needs of corporate library managers seeking precedent, creative thinking, and best demonstrated practices to help them answer their management challenges.

The authors found that the mixture of sources covered in any one of these portals appears to be truly international and very timely. Using the LIS Research Portal (SLA—LIS Research Portal 2008) as an example, articles cited are from a variety of journals, including *Library and Information Science Research*, *Evidence Based Library and Information Practice*, *Library Hi-Tech*, *Journal of Information Science*, *Journal of the American Society for Information Science and Technology*, *Health Information and Libraries Journal*, *Law Library Journal*, *Journal of the Medical Library Association*, *Library Review*, *Library Management*, and *The Library Quarterly*. This suggests that there may be a fair amount of research activity of potential interest to corporate library managers that is not being sponsored or produced by SLA itself and may not be focused on the management of corporate libraries. Given that most corporate library managers would not subscribe to more than one or two of these titles, if any, this compilation by SLA becomes even more valuable.

Another SLA Information Portal, Management/Services—Outsourcing and Offshoring (2008a), offers an equally broad mix of sources. For example, its coverage includes Fast

Company, Library & Information Update, TechWeb, Money, Corporate Library Update, *Library Journal*, *Wall Street Journal*, *Information Management Journal*, *MIT Sloan Management Review*, and CIO.com.

All of the content compiled in this portal could be characterized as offering ideas or concepts possibly useful to corporate library managers facing managerial questions.

For more information on other Information Portals compiled by SLA the reader is referred to http://www.sla.org/content/resources/infoportals/index.cfm.

Do Corporate Librarians Either Produce or Use This Research?

This review of the literature concludes a partial answer to this question. The literature reinforces the conclusion that corporate library managers continue to need and seek pragmatic research to apply in their day-to-day activities, but that "not much" of this type of research is being produced through their primary professional association.

Dimitroff (1995, 256–64) attempted to find out if practicing special librarians conducted research and what interest they had in activities related to research. She reviewed research activity as reflected in the journal literature for special libraries, defined broadly to include law, medical as well as corporate. Of the 279 articles she found for the years 1993–1994, only 53 were reports of research; and academic health librarians wrote over half of these, likely the result of requirements for promotion and tenure. This study found only two research articles written by corporate librarians and six research articles written by LIS Faculty. Dimitroff characterized this small amount of research as "most startling" and observed that it showed no relation between research and what corporate librarians do every day (Dimitroff 1995, 263). Lack of time and lack of support from their management were the two most frequently cited reasons for not conducting research. Dimitroff further noted that while associations have tried to help with some funding, calls upon individual librarians to conduct and publish research have not been overly successful. It is not surprising, then, that corporate librarians face an enormous challenge to developing a culture of research from such a small base.

Powell et al. (2002, 49–72) found that better than two-thirds of SLA members did not conduct or publish research. In a survey of 1,400 members of various professional associations, Powell and his coauthors found that only about one-third of SLA members responded that they had time for research and only 20 percent of those thought some employer support for research was available. Furthermore, only 13 percent felt there was external support for research. When asked if they applied research results to practice, only 11 percent said they did, while 49 percent said never or seldom. Powell and his coauthors' findings confirm the point made at the beginning of SLA's current Research Statement (SLA 2001) that the connection between LIS research and the day-to-day problems faced by corporate librarians has not been made in the past.

Special Libraries was replaced by *Information Outlook* in 1997. The new publication has color, combines news and several topical columns, and has a few short feature articles in each issue. It is not intended to carry research articles and might not carry the same weight as a referred journal like *Special Libraries* when brought to a university promotion and tenure committee. This does not necessarily diminish the usefulness to corporate library practitioners of articles published there, albeit that usefulness might be at a less granular level than a full research study would offer. So we might conclude that a journal like *Special Libraries* was equally important to practitioners who want to read about research at a deeper level and possibly apply it to practice.

Even when a journal similar to *Special Libraries* is taken into account, though, it is still not clear that corporate library managers are taking advantage of the research found there. Edgar (2004, 122–51) examined the topic of the impact of a corporate library on its parent organization. He presented the theoretical framework in an article in the journal's print version, and followed with a second article in the electronic version of the same publication where he provided the methodologies that could be used to measure impact. Only two articles have cited Edgar's work in the past three years and neither was written by or for corporate librarians or corporate libraries. If others put Edgar's articles into practice, they have not published their experiences.

That corporate librarians are still struggling with defining what type of research will be most useful to them is evident in two recent efforts by SLA to further define relevant research topics and activities as well as to provide funding for undertaking them: the SLA Research Now Task force (SLA Research Now Task force 2006) and the most recently revised Research Grant Guidelines (SLA Research Grant Guidelines 2007).

The Task force set out to accomplish two objectives:

1. Define subjects for research that will best serve SLA's strategic plan by demonstrating the information professional's value to the organization and

2. Take one or more of these topics and conduct a research study with results available for the June 2006 conference (SLA Executive Summary Document 2006).

Toward these ends, the Task Force conducted an exploratory research project focused on stakeholders and their perceived value of the information professional and the role of personal networking. The findings of this project suggested the following:

- Timeliness and the ability to locate information are the service attributes that matter most to stakeholders.
- Stakeholders believe the major purpose of the information professional is to provide critical information that helps in making business decisions or solving business problems.
- Conducting research and knowing where to find information are the information services that are most valued.
- IS save time and money, and allow other staff to be more productive.
- The knowledge and skills for which information professionals are most valued are their expertise in accessing and retrieving reliable information and for their strategic awareness or knowledge of issues of interest to the company or organization.
- Proactive networking by information professionals with other staff helps to further the goals of their organization.
- Stakeholders value librarians who keep knowledgeable of current issues or projects so they are ready to provide information and resources to support their work (SLA Research Now Task Force 2006).

In its summary report, the Research Now Task Force expressed some of the same "lessons learned" that have been discussed elsewhere: the difficulties of conducting underfunded research, the challenges of addressing the needs of a broad segment of the special libraries population, and the challenge of getting volunteers to take the time needed to engage with the research. In fact, a review of the Task Force recommendations offers insights on the relatively recent appearance of Information Portals on the SLA website as well as the ongoing focus on finding and disseminating relevant research produced beyond the Association sponsorship. The report highlights the following insights:

- Continue to focus research on the value of the information professional to the organization.
- Utilize other related research results conducted by other organizations such as OCLC's (Online Computer Library Center) Perceptions of Libraries and Information Resources and Bersin & Associates' research study of the amount of time executives spend searching for information.
- Provide time slots at the annual conference for presenting research results of interest to the entire membership (SLA Research Now Task Force 2006).

The Task Force even recommended that this might be accomplished by partnering with other library or information professional associations and/or research companies or by providing funding for research by one of three possible means: SLA funded, SLA partnering with other professional associations, or nonprofit organizations, or SLA negotiating funding support from one or more information-related companies.

Within a year of the report of the SLA Research Now Task Force (SLA 2006), the Association announced new Research Grant guidelines (August 2007) that began to provide at least some structure of support for research. Two types of grants were offered; one focused on evidenced-based practice as outlined in the Research Agenda with awards up to $25,000 and another for projects that directly benefit the operations of SLA and its units by furthering scientific, literary, and educational purposes for which the association is organized and operated with awards up to $10,000. Two recipients were chosen in December 2007; "Impulse for Growth! Laying foundations for SLA membership acquisition and growth in Germany for 2008," Michael Fanning ($10,000) and "Models of Embedded Librarianship: A Research Proposal," David Shumaker and Mary Talley ($25,000).

Other funding sources are also attempting to fill some of the gap for research support in this area. There is some overlap between American Library Association (ALA) and SLA in intent, if not practice, especially in the form of ALA's RUSA (Reference and User Service Association) and BRASS (Business Reference and Services Section) groups. For example, in October of 2007 Emerald Group Publishing disseminated an email message throughout ALA which was subsequently also sent to the SLA Business & Finance listserv via a member who belonged both to SLA and BRASS. The "call for grant applications" encouraged readers who had a "business information research idea" and needed financial help to carry it through, to apply for a Review of Research Related to Management of Corporate Libraries Emerald Publishing Group $5000 grant award (Pearlstein 2007). This effort by a private publisher to encourage research that would be of interest to corporate library managers is one example of other efforts than SLA sponsorship that are available.

While Drake (1989) made a cogent case for research and its relationship to practice, those in practice do not appear to have been convinced. Perhaps the source of the intermittent quality and lack of pragmatism in SLA's research program to date is in part the responsibility of the membership. Their apparent lack of interest in research and in producing or using research seems clear, at least in North America. In a review of publications in Australia, New Zealand, and the United Kingdom, however, the authors found a somewhat more robust body of research publications.

AUSTRALIA, NEW ZEALAND, AND THE UNITED KINGDOM

Research and publication on corporate libraries in these three countries is frequent and very well executed. While there are more corporate libraries in North America, there appears to be more literature on the subject of corporate libraries in these countries. One reason for this might be that company librarians in Australia, New Zealand, and the United Kingdom tend to belong to their national library associations which actively encourage research relevant to them and provide adequate resources and interest for this research on par with that for other types of libraries. It is our contention that the opposite seems to be true in North America, with company librarians more likely to be members of smaller organizations (e.g., SLA, MLA, American Association of Law Librarians, etc.) with more narrowly focused interests and correspondingly less interest or resources to fund research.

Not only is research on corporate libraries being actively supported in these countries, it is focusing on those topics that seem directly relevant to corporate library managers. Special librarians in a corporate setting tend to be more pragmatic than their academic or public counterparts when it comes to the type of research findings they need to support them in demonstrating their value to their parent organization. A review of research activities in these countries illustrates this difference.

Measuring "Value" in Australia

Greenshields (1997, 55–56) reports that in the 1990s the Australian Library and Information Association (ALIA) concluded that the major threat to corporate business libraries was the lack of knowledge about the contributions these libraries made toward corporate goals. As such, ALIA was going to embark on an explanatory study to determine the perceived value of librarians and libraries in Australia's top 100 companies. This research was proposed to add an Australian perspective to studies completed a few years before in the United States.

The American studies had shown that it was necessary to demonstrate the value of the librarian and the services provided. The Australian study was begun to counter a perceived lack of empirical data on value as measured by the opinions of senior managers at 100 companies. The results would not only be of value to managers of company libraries, but also to library education programs seeking to prepare graduates to work in the corporate sector.

The next year, Walsh (1998, 6–7) reported most Australian company libraries judged measuring number of requests as a measure of value. Other survey results mirrored a set of earlier research reports conducted in the United States. It is interesting to note, however, that 25 percent of the Australian respondents felt that library resources did not meet the needs of users. A much longer report of the same survey results by Walsh and Greenshields (1998, 59–101) appeared in *Australian Special Libraries*.

McCallum and Quinn (2004, 27–31) presented an overview of research reports on the economic value of libraries. While their review addressed the value of both public and special libraries it also discussed reports from the United States, Canada, and Australia on public libraries and the United States and Australia for special libraries. The authors argue that public and special libraries are difficult for financial managers to understand, while users were seen to appreciate the services provided. Since special libraries have to demonstrate value, they found that research that has been completed, shared, and replicated would enable Australian libraries to state objectively their economic value.

That same year, Leavitt (2004, 95–97) noted in an editorial that one of the hallmarks of a profession is genuine research that underpins both theory and practice. He went on to lament the lack of published research from the many master's and doctoral degree recipients in LIS. In fact, Leavitt speculated that "those who complete these research reports are so burnt out by their projects, they each lack energy or interest to publish the results and share their work with the profession at large (95)."

Missingham (2005, 142–56) undertook a review of the past decade of research on the value of library services in a variety of settings. She reviewed research in Australia, as well as the United States, United Kingdom, Canada, and New Zealand and found that demonstrating the value of LIS had been a theme of library research in these countries for decades. In discussing value, she identified three waves of activity: (1) Efficiency or output oriented studies aimed at proving that libraries are operating efficiently. (2) Studies of financial return to the organization equated the success of the library with the organization's financial success. These studies involved using techniques that allowed the customer to place a monetary value on the service. Missingham found, however, that these studies "did not seem to fully convince managers . . ." (144). (3) Studies that seek to value libraries by establishing their value to managers through data collected on the number of requests, time and money saved, and value-added services provided. The reader is referred to Missingham's original review for a more in depth look at these three waves of research activity.

New Zealand

The New Zealand Library and Information Association (LIANZA) has taken a different approach to supporting research on corporate libraries. In 1998, LIANZA engaged Coopers and Lybrand to conduct a study of the library at the New Zealand Dairy Board. At the time, this library had a budget of $300,000 and 3.75 staff members. To accomplish this study, Coopers and Lybrand charged a discounted rate of $21,000 ($19,000 was contributed from the New Zealand Dairy Board and $2,000 from LIANZA). Had it not been discounted, the cost of the study would likely have been closer to $28,000 (LIANZA 1998). The report states that the study required 146 hours of an analyst's time, 30 hours of supervision, and 69 hours of the library manager's time. The end result was a short report that estimates a return on assets of 13 percent but projected this likely is higher, in the range of 19–20 percent since some services could not be assigned a value. The report suggested that the New Zealand Dairy Board spend $28,000 annually to continue the study.

In 1997, LIANZA worked with PricewaterhouseCoopers International Limited on a "value added library methodology" (LIANZA 1999) for the Parliamentary Library. This methodology calculates the return on investment in terms of the value libraries add to information. It measures library usage, services and resources using a top-down and bottom-up approach. The "topdown" approach measures the value of information in the context of what a buyer would pay for it, the time saved by using the library, and the cost of replacing the library and its services, if they did not already exist. This result is compared to the "bottom-up" approach which compares the library to other businesses in order to calculate the return on investment in the library's assets.

This research was completed at a reduced cost of $15,000. The market rate would have been about $32,000 (150 hours of analyst's time, 34 of a supervisor's time and 23–90 hours of library staff time). The report concluded that library services were valued at 2–20 times budget and showed a net benefit for all services provided of 9.8 percent and 16.4 percent regardless of how measured.

United Kingdom

Whitehall (1995, 3–11) provides a review of the literature on measuring value in library and information management in all types of libraries—with a majority in corporate settings—in the United Kingdom. This review was completed to provide evidence for libraries to use when they face the harsh reality of the allocation of resources at any organization. It includes a discussion of use, value addition, how to measure the value of information, value of service, and many more topics with an extensive bibliography. "The consequence of our focusing on the cost of providing services without being able to demonstrate their value and quality is that we leave the initiative to people whose chief concern is cost control or profit" (Whitehall 1995, 10).

Marshall (1993) published an excellent study of libraries in the financial sector in Canada and their contribution to these types of firms. This study was replicated in the United Kingdon by the Strathclyde Graduate Business School in the area of retail banking and four other types of organizations and pulled information from all five sectors into one article (Grieves 1998, 78–85). The conclusions from all five studies place a high value on information especially as used for better decision making. Differences between the UK studies and the Marshall study were pointed out as were the differences between the other sectors studied. The author warns that these were short-term studies with small samples but nevertheless could give useful insights.

Another study by the staff at the Strathclyde Graduate Business School (Reid et al. 1998, 86–109) takes an in-depth look at the role and value of information in the decision-making process and the impact of the corporate library in the UK banking sector. Managers in the banks studied the evaluation and on the whole agreed that information affected how decisions were made. The information they reviewed came not from the company library but from other sources. In those banks with libraries, information was seen to be used in decision making. In fact 79 percent of the corporate managers said their libraries "saved them considerable time" (Reid et al. 1998, 97) The Strathclyde Study warned that libraries need to be proactive about promoting the existence of their services and the kinds of information they can provide. Also of note is the caution that corporate librarians must be familiar with the business of which they are a part. Libraries, they wrote, also need to analyze information for value and relevance to the organization.

Measuring value perceived and received by actual users is challenging. Libraries have nonusers too; however, research on nonusers has been sparse. Brick's (1999, 195–205) research used a combination of questionnaires and interviews with a small sample of 12 corporate managers which was geographically limited to greater London (p. 15). She found corporate managers were not high users of corporate libraries except in the area of business consulting. Lack of awareness of the library's services was most often given as the reason for nonuse. In reviewing older studies, she states that the library level of nonuse remains about the same as do the reasons. She reports that 70 percent of corporate library managers interviewed have not tried to solve the problem of nonuse (Brick 1999, 203).

Foster and Foster (2003, 5–24) published the 13th survey on Business Information Resources. Sixty-two percent of respondents were from financial, legal, property, and consulting firm libraries, making up the largest number of all respondents in the corporate sector. Company library respondents overall stated they were "adding more value and providing more in depth analysis" (Foster and Foster 2003, 22). They appear to be focused on providing a high-quality product, improving competitor intelligence, and the overall quality of services. These libraries were also adding electronic access to annual reports and journals. In general, the survey revealed company libraries were seeking greater recognition of their services, promoting the value of information, developing a knowledge management policy, and wanted a greater role in business development, while also coping with change. The 2003 survey also revealed more work on portals, containing costs, and increasing the number of staff to cope with heavy workloads. Respondents were also facing end-user training issues to help some employees do more research for themselves.

Broady-Preston and Williams (2004, 5–10) conducted a series of interviews with a range of small to large law firm libraries to establish how they use information to create value. The respondents all felt that information is perceived to be a valuable asset in law firms. It was, however, difficult to offer any quantitative measure of demonstrating value. The authors assert that "Law is an intensive profession in which there has traditionally been a great reliance on external information" (Broady-Preston and Williams 2004, 9). Those interviewed saw information services as adding value to the business, improving service delivery and customer service.

Library Management in 2007 began a new column, "Theory, Research, and Practice in Library Management" (*Library Management* 2007). The column will select key management subjects and examine the topic from the viewpoints of theory, research, and practice. The plan is to discuss management issues by moving to an evidence-based model that coincides with a movement to evidence-based library practice. This follows a similar trend toward evidence-based research adopted by SLA in 2001; a trend that unfortunately does not seem to have resulted in an increase of pragmatic, sharable, repeatable research projects for the benefit of corporate libraries.

CONCLUSION

This chapter on the impact of research funding and support for corporate library management intends to raise interest on the part of both LIS faculty and corporate library managers to look for ways to address the questions posed at its outset.

How or if research on the subject of managing corporate libraries was encouraged and funded, and by whom? Various attempts to fund such research were made by the SLA, but were not sustained over time. Colleagues in other English-speaking countries (Australia, New Zealand, and United Kingdom) appear to have more support by national associations to conduct such research.

What type of research would be most useful for corporate library managers? Research falls into two categories for corporate library managers. Theoretical research about the activities involving corporate libraries is of little interest, except for the emergence of evidence-based research related to decision making. Pragmatic, problem-solving research results or more simply, data gathered for a purpose such as strategic planning and corporate advocacy, are welcomed by practitioners in the corporate library sector.

How research results are disseminated and whether the results had been put to use by practitioners? SLA previously published research in its peer-reviewed journal, but over time this practice was replaced by maintenance of online portals where links are offered to potentially relevant reports and to articles published in a range of other professional publications.

Given limited resources for corporate librarians to purchase publications for internal applications, this referral role shows signs of being helpful to the SLA membership. In other countries, there may be a more active culture of producing and utilizing research than is found in the United States among corporate libraries.

There is no question that professional associations, especially those in the United States, United Kingdom, Australia, and New Zealand have a role to play to engage in research about and for corporate libraries on several levels. For example, associations could conduct the following activities: advocate a research agenda that is practical and of interest to their membership; provide sufficient funding to fully support research so that LIS faculty are attracted to participate; provide channels for distribution of research results that serve the needs of both faculty and practitioners; and investigate further ways to provide guidance to corporate librarians in how they can contribute to a shared knowledge base without compromising their organization's confidentiality or other proprietary requirements.

Leavitt (2004, 95–97) maintains that one of the hallmarks of maturity in any profession is research and its contributions to theory and practice. Practitioners do not appear to be convinced, however, of the relationship between research and practice. Perhaps that is the problem corporate library managers are really facing: that the profession has not yet reached maturity.

REFERENCES

Barreau, D. C. "The New Information Professional: Vision and Practice." Research funded by the Special Libraries Association, Stephen I. Goldspiel Memorial Research Grant, August 7, Final Report. Washington, D.C.: Special Libraries Association, 2003.

Brick, L. "Non-use of Business Libraries and Information Services: A Study of the Library and Information Managers' Perception, Experience and Reaction to Nonuse." *Aslib Proceedings* 51 (1999): 195–205.

Broady-Preston, J., and T. Williams. "Using Information to Create Business Value: City of London Legal Firms, a Case Study." *Performance Measurement and Metrics* 5 (2004): 5–10.

Dimitroff, A. "Research for Special Libraries: A Quantitative Analysis of the Literature." *Special Libraries* 86 (1995): 256–64.

Drake, M. A. "Research and Special Libraries." *Special Libraries* 80 (1989): 264–68.

Edgar, W. "Corporate Library Impact, Part I: A Theoretical Approach." *The Library Quarterly* 74 (2004): 122–51.

Foster, A., and P. Foster. "Empowering the End-user: Business Information Resources Survey." *Business Information Review* 20 (2003): 5–24.

Genoni, P., G. Haddow, and A. Ritchie. "Why Don't Librarians Use Research?" In *Evidence-Based Practice for Information Professionals*, edited by A. Booth and A. Brice, 49–60. London: Facet Publishing, 2004.

Greenshields, S. "The Value of Corporate Libraries." *Australian Special Libraries* 30 (1997): 55–56.

Grieves, M. "The Impact of Information Use on Decision Making: Studies in Five Sectors-Introduction, Summary and Conclusions." *Library Management* 19 (1998): 78–85.

Kantor, P. B., and T. Saracevic. "Valuing Special Libraries and Information Services." Washington, D.C.: Special Libraries Association, 1995–1997.

Koufogiannakis, D., and E. Crumley. "Research in Librarianship: Issues to Consider." *Library Hi Tech* 24 (2006): 324–340.

Leavitt, J. "The Nature, Utility and Essential Unknowability of Research in Our Disciplines: An Editor's View." *Australian Library Journal* 51 (2004): 95–97.

LIANZA Executive Summary of the N Strategy Methodology. Library and Information Association of New Zealand, Wellington, 1998.

LIANZA Parliament Library VLM Trial. Library and Information Association of New Zealand, Wellington, 1999.

Library Management Theory, Research and Practice in Library Management: New Column. *Library Management* 28 (2007): 63–164.

Marshall, J.G. "The Impact of the Special Library on Corporate Decision Making." Washington, D.C.: Special Libraries Association, 1993.

Matarazzo, J.M. "Research Needs and Issues in Special Librarianship." In *Library and Foundation Science Research: Perspective and Strategies for Improvement*, edited by C.R. McClure and P. Hernon. New York: Ablex, 1981.

McCallum, I., and S. Quinn. "Valuing Libraries." *Australian Library Journal* 53 (2004): 27–31.

Missingham, R. "Libraries and Economic Value: A Review of Recent Studies." *Performance Measurement and Metrics* 6 (2005): 142–58.

Outsell, Inc. "Changing Roles of Content Management Functions, Executive Summary." 2004a, http://www.sla.org/pdfs/2006OutsellIMFunctionExecSumm.pdf (accessed March 5, 2008).

Outsell, Inc. "Trend Alert: The Future of Libraries." *InfoAboutInfo Briefing*, 2004b, http://www.sla.org/pdfs/2006OutsellIMFunctionExecSumm.pdf (accessed March 5, 2008).

Outsell, Inc. "Information Management Best Practices: Fortunes Up for Information Management Functions 2005-and With Fortune Comes Accountability." 2005a, http://www.sla.org/content/resources/research/researchlinks/isp99.cfm (accessed March 5, 2008).

Outsell, Inc. "Information Management Best Practices: Vendor Portfolio Management Rationalizing Content for the Enterprise." 2005b, http://www.sla.org/pdfs/2006OutsellIMFunction ExecSumm.pdf (accessed March 5, 2008).

Outsell, Inc. "Information Management Best Practices: 2006 State of the Function, Executive Summary." 2006, https://www.sla.org/content/resources/recindreps/imbp2006/ index.cfm (accessed March 5, 2008).

Pearlstein, T. Personal email correspondence: SLA Business and Finance Division Listserv, October 10, 2007.

Phase V Consulting Group Inc. "State of the Market 2000, Results from the Information Services Panel Survey," 2000. Readers may link to summary results of this survey at http://www.sla.org/content/resources/research/researchlinks/isp99.cfm (accessed March 5, 2008).

Portugal, F.H. *Valuing Information Intangibles: Measuring the Bottom Line Contribution of Librarians and Information Professionals.* Washington, D.C.: SLA, 2000.

Powell, R.R., L.M. Baker, and J.J. Mika. "Library and information science practitioners and research." *Library and Information Science Research* 24 (2002): 49–72.

Reid, C., J. Thomson, and J. Wallace-Smith. "Impact of Information Corporate Decision Making: The UK Banking Sector." *Library Management* 19 (1998): 86–109.

Smith, L.C., and L. Ruan. "A Survey to Support 'Evidence-Based Practice' in Special Libraries Serving Fire Service Personnel and Researchers in Public Safety and Homeland Security Areas" funded by 2003 SLA Steven I. Goldspiel Memorial Research Grant, Special Libraries Association, Alexandria, VA with Additional Support Funded by the 2004 Campus Research Board Award. Champaign, IL: University of Illinois at Urbana-Champaign, 2004.

Special Libraries Association. Battaglia, R.D. to Associate Executive Director, SLA. Original letter re: Steven I. Goldspiel Memorial Research Grant, June 6, 1993.

Special Libraries Association. Primary Source Documents Collection, 1989–2007.

Special Libraries Association. "Putting Our Knowledge to Work: A New SLA Research Statement, 2001. The Role of Research in Special Librarianship," 2001, http://www.sla.org/content/resources/research/rsrchstatement.cfm (accessed March 5, 2008).

Special Libraries Association. Latham, J. R. List of Grants awarded from 1991–2004, April 16, 2004.

Special Libraries Association, Association for Library and Information Science Education, and Medical Library Association. *Competencies for Special Librarians of the 21st Century, Library and Information Studies Program Survey,* Final Report. Washington, D.C.: Special Libraries Association,1998.

Special Libraries Association (SLA)—LIS Research Portal, 2008, http://www.sla.org/content/resources/infoportals/research.cfm.

Special Libraries Association Management/Services Outsourcing and Offshoring Portal, 2008a, http://www.sla.org/content/resources/infoportals/contract.cfm.

Special Libraries Association Research Agenda Document A89–72, 1989.

Special Libraries Association Research Committee, Annual Reports to the Board of Directors. (1994–2006: April 29, 1994, May 3, 1995, May 9, 1996, May 1, 1997, April 29, 1998, May 2, 1999, May 8, 2000, May 6, 2001, May 3, 2002, 2002/2003 (undated), 2003/2004 (undated), May 5, 2005, May 4, 2006).

Special Libraries Association Research Committee, Meeting Minutes, June 6, 2005.

Special Libraries Association Research Committee/Endowment Grants Committee, Coordination meeting minutes, Houston, TX, January 20, 2006.

Special Libraries Association Research Grant Guidelines, 2007.

Special Libraries Association Research Now Task Force, Recommendations, Executive Summary Document A06–48, May 8, 2006.

Tees, M. H. "Faculty Involvement in the Special Libraries Association." *Journal of Education for Library and Information Science* 29 (1989): 297–304.

Turner, J.M., M. Hudon, and Y. Devon. "Organizing Moving Image Collections for the Digital Era: Research Results." Research report from the project of the same name funded by the Special Libraries Association under the Steven I. Goldspiel Memorial Grant for 1999. *Information Outlook* (August 14–25, 2002).

Walsh, V. "ALIA Explores the Value of Corporate Libraries." *InCite* 19 (1998) 6–7.

Walsh, V., and S. Greenshields. "The Value of Libraries and Library Professionals to Australia's Top 100 Companies: Draft Report of the Study Conducted by the Australian Library and Information Association." *Australian Library Journal* 31(1998): 59–101.

Whitehall, T. "Value in Library and Information Management: A Review." *Library Management* 16 (1995): 3–11.

FURTHER READING

Information Center's Resources Website is a clearing house for all information resources available to SLA members, through SLA's own library, http://www.sla.org/content/resources/inforesour/index.cfm (accessed March 2, 2008).

Information Portals Website links to articles, Web sites, books and other resources on 40 topics including corporate and other special library management, http://www.sla.org/content/resources/infoportals/index.cfm (accessed March 2, 2008).

Recent Industry Reports Website contains reports on information industry issues http://www.sla.org/content/resources/recindreps/index.cfm (accessed March 2, 2008).

Research and Surveys Website for assistance with benchmarking and strategic planning http://www.sla.org/content/resources/research/index.cfm (accessed March 2, 2008).

Research Grants Website provides background and additional information on SLA's grants process, http://www.sla.org/content/learn/scholarship/researchgrant/index.cfm (accessed March 2, 2008).

Resources Website. Provides access for SLA members to both SLA sponsored and SLA recommended information and research covering management and other topics, http://www.sla.org/content/resources/index.cfm (accessed March 2, 2008).

Special Libraries Association electronic resources. http://www.sla.org (accessed March 2, 2008).

PART II

STRATEGIES AND TACTICS FOR SURVIVAL
INTRODUCTION

JAMES M. MATARAZZO
AND TOBY PEARLSTEIN

In Part I of this anthology you will have seen how important it is not only to collect data about what you do but to also translate that data into measurements and actions that demonstrate your contribution in a language that your boss understands.

In Part II, the focus is on several tools including the Predictive Model, Alternate Sourcing, Professional Association membership, and Scenario Planning among others that can be used both strategically and pragmatically to further ensure that your information services are aligned with and contribute directly to the mission of your parent organization. Your survival and sustainability are dependent on this critical alignment.

4

STAYING AFLOAT IN TURBULENT WATERS

JAMES M. MATARAZZO AND TOBY PEARLSTEIN

WITH LYNNE PALOMBO, LEIGH MONTGOMERY, AND ELAINE RAINES

Quite a bit has been written about the fate of newspapers and magazines and the staffs that support them with respect to creating new publishing business models. Weaning the industry away from a model based on print advertising alone in order to arrive at a successful Internet-based business model seems to be the overriding challenge. As recently as January 2010, the *Financial Times* (*FT*) reported that Alan Rusbridger, the editor of *The Guardian*, "described the financial effects of the Internet on his newspaper . . . [as] sometimes quite scary" (Gapper 2010, 9). In discussing the viability of pay walls such as the *FT* itself now uses and was implemented by *The New York Times* in 2011, the author points out that even if only a small percent (6 percent is quoted from an Outsell, Inc. study) of U.S. readers will pay for online news sites, this number alone could mean profitability and could provide enough data about subscribers to enable more targeted and therefore more sellable online advertising (Gapper 2010; Gapper refers to an Outsell, Inc. research report that quoted this number). The kicker, if you will, is that specialized business publications such as the *FT* and *The Wall Street Journal* have a better chance of survival because their business focus draws corporate customers. For the general newspapers to be saved, they will have to "take the plunge" and find a new way of doing business.

NEWSPAPER AND MEDIA LIBRARIES

In thinking about survival lessons for newspaper and media libraries, the metaphor of the "newspaper morgue" kept coming up in the process. The "morgue," the traditional name for a newspaper's archive, is a critical source of knowledge for reporters and the public, as

This chapter was adapted from an article that originally appeared in *Searcher Magazine*, Volume 18, Issue 4, Pages 14–18, 46–53, May 2010.

well as an important repository of the history of the paper's interaction with its community. Access to this source is frequently managed by an information professional, and, increasingly the skill set of librarians is brought to bear in projects to digitize and index this archive to increase its value to the organization.

On the other hand, there is the recent, oft-reported "death" of newspaper libraries sometimes along with the newspapers themselves, although often just the library. Here the morgue metaphor has a much more devastating meaning and one that may be misleading. It is time for a new metaphor that better reflects how newspaper and media librarians work thoughtfully every day to help their services and their organizations stay afloat in these turbulent economic times. In choosing to be optimistic rather than fatalistic about survival, in choosing to aggressively figure out more effective ways to "row and bail" rather than listening to the band play "Nearer My God to Thee" as the ship goes down, newspaper and media librarians will do all that is possible to ensure themselves at least a place in the lifeboat.

WHAT'S HAPPENING WITH NEWSPAPER AND MEDIA LIBRARIES TODAY?

Michelle Quigley of the *Palm Beach Post* (Florida) began keeping her list of "News Library Layoffs and Buyouts" around 2005. The authors cannot help but wonder if the more than 70 publication or media outlets currently on the list indicate that something more library-centric is going on in the news or media business, specifically causing such a large number of closures or reductions in news libraries? Also troubling in this context is a significant decline in the membership of the Special Library Association (SLA) News Division, which has seen an almost 46 percent drop in membership since 1994 (Campo 2009). While this decline could be driven by many factors and while the authors cannot equate a dropped membership with a closed library, the question must be posed: Are these libraries simply victims of circumstance or is something larger going on that has led to their near or total demise?

A variety of studies from both within and outside the publishing or media industry show that newspapers are in dire economic straits (Kirchoff 2009). As the Congressional Research Service reported to Congress recently, "advertising revenues are plummeting . . . while readership habits are changing as consumers turn to the Internet for free news and information." Publishers in all media struggle with the fee versus free dilemma, as well as with challenges to the fundamental definition of journalism with the advent of the blogosphere and the notion that everyone with a cell phone, Facebook, or Twitter account is now a "journalist."

Some have suggested that the actions of corporate executives have led to the huge debt loads that have resulted in reductions throughout organizations in order for the debt loads to be repaid. Dan Kennedy (2009), professor of journalism at Northeastern University, as well as a columnist and commentator on media issues, told us flat out: "The real culprits are mergers and acquisitions and corporate greed." Referring to *The New York Times'* purchase of *The Boston Globe*, Kennedy noted: "*The Times* bet half the company on the *Globe* purchase. Think about it: the *Times* was worth $2.2 billion at the time and spent in excess of $1.1 billion on the purchase." In his view, reductions experienced in news libraries, and throughout the organizations, are more a function of this kind of deal rather than librarians having failed in their mission.

Organization	Effective Date	Cut	Remain	Notes	Organization	Effective Date	Cut	Remain	Notes
ABC News Research Center (Washington, DC)	June 2006 and 2009	13	0	Research Center dismantled and the collection dispersed. See memo, etc.	Newsday (Long Island, NY)	Mar-08	1	11	Staff reduced from 23 through attrition since 2002.
Albany Times Union (Albany, NY)	July 2008 and 3/2009	2	1		News-Gazette (Champaign, IL)	May-08	1	1	
Arkansas Democrat-Gazette (Little Rock, AR)	May 2009	1	3		Newsweek	1/2006, 12/2007, 2008, 2/2009	7	3	
Atlanta Journal Constitution (Atlanta, GA)	April 2009	15	0	Research discontinued, archiving outsourced.	The Oregonian (Portland, OR)	2007 and 2008	5	2	
Baltimore Sun (Baltimore, MD)	Apr-09	1	2		Orlando Sentinel (Orlando, FL)				
Capital Times/Wisconsin State Journal (Madison, WI)	June 2008 and September 2008	2	2		Ottawa Citizen (Ottawa, ON, Canada)	2006 and 2008	2	2	
Charlotte Observer (Charlotte, NC)	September 2008	3	2		The Palm Beach Post (West Palm Beach, FL)	8/12/2008, 9/2009	8	2	
Chicago Tribune (Chicago, IL)	2008, February 2009	9	5		The Patriot Ledger (Quincy, MA)	2/2008 and 11/2008	2	1	
Cincinnati Enquirer (Cincinnati, OH)	July 2009	1	1	Remaining position is part-time	The Patriot-News Company (Harrisburg, PA)	Nov-08	1	1	

(Continued)

Organization	Effective Date	Cut	Remain	Notes
Columbus Dispatch (Columbus, OH)	June 2006, March 2007, June 2007	3	4	
Corpus Christi Caller-Times (Corpus Christi, TX)	Spring 2007	2	1	
Daily Camera (Boulder, CO)	Jun-07	1	0	Archiving automated.
The Daytona Beach News-Journal (Daytona Beach, FL)	June 2008, September 2009	4	1	
Denver Post (Denver, CO)	Jun-07	1	4	
The Des Moines Register (Des Moines, IA)	2/2008, 12/2008, 5/2009	4	1	Archiving automated.
Detroit Free Press (Detroit, MI)	6/22/2009	3	0	Research discontinued, archiving automated.

Organization	Effective Date	Cut	Remain	Notes
Pittsburgh Post-Gazette (Pittsburgh, PA)				
Plain Dealer (Cleveland, Ohio)		4	5	
Portland Press Herald/Maine Sunday Telegram (Portland, Maine)	Jun-09	1		
Providence Journal (Providence, RI)	Oct-08	2	1	
Reno Gazette-Journal (Reno, NV)	Jul-09	1	1	Part-timer will be brought in to replace long-time librarian.
The Republican (Springfield, MA)	1/12/2009	2	2	
Richmond Times-Dispatch (Richmond, Virginia)	Apr-09	8	2	Need verification on numbers.

Newspaper	Date			Notes
Entertainment Weekly	November 2008	2	1	
Florida Times-Union (Jacksonville, FL)	November 2008	2	4	
Forbes	January 2009	2	1	
Fort Worth Star-Telegram (Fort Worth, TX)	6/2008 and 3/2009	5	1	
Fortune	Spring 2008	4	2	Business Information Center serving Fortune, Money, FSB and various Time Inc. corporate departments eliminated.
The Free Lance-Star (Fredericksburg, VA)		1	2	
The Fresno Bee (Fresno, CA)	June 2008	1	2	
Rocky Mountain News (Denver, CO)	Feb-09	1	1	Newspaper closed. Archives to Denver Public Library and Colorado Historical Society.
The Royal Gazette/Mid-Ocean Newspapers (Bermuda)	7/29/2008	1		
San Antonio Express-News (San Antonio, TX)	10/2007 and 3/2009	2	4	
The San Diego Union-Tribune (San Diego, CA)	12/2006–5/2009	13	3	Includes 5 cuts through attrition.
San Francisco Chronicle (San Francisco, CA)	12/2008 and 3/2009	4	2	
San Jose Mercury News (San Jose, Calif.)	11/2005–6/2008	6	2	
Seattle Post-Intelligencer (Seattle, Wash.)	3/18/2009	2	0	Newspaper ceased operations.

(*Continued*)

Organization	Effective Date	Cut	Remain	Notes	Organization	Effective Date	Cut	Remain	Notes
The Globe and Mail (Toronto, ON, Canada)	April 2009	6	8		Sporting News	Jul-08	1	0	Research center closed.
Hartford Courant (Hartford, CT)	July 2008 and March 2009	2	2		St. Louis Post-Dispatch (St. Louis, MO)	2008–2009	7	4	
Houston Chronicle (Houston, Texas)	November 2007, November 2008	11	2		St. Petersburg Times (St. Petersburg, FL)		2	12	
Knoxville News Sentinel (Knoxville, TN)	June 2007	1	0	Archiving automated, other library functions eliminated.	The Star-Ledger (Newark, NJ)	5/2006 and 12/2008	6	4	
Lexington Herald-Leader (Lexington, KY)	May 2009	4	1		The State (Columbia, S.C.)	1/2006–2/2008	3	0	Library positions eliminated through attrition. Archiving automated.
Los Angeles Time (Los Angeles, CA)					Sun-Sentinel (Fort Lauderdale, FL)	7/2008, 4/2009, 5/2009	4	3	Library dismantled.
Miami Herald (Miami, FL)	2008	4	3		Syracuse Post-Standard (Syracuse, NY)	2005, 2006, 2009	4	2	
The Morning Call (Allentown, PA)	1/2008 and /2008	2	2		Tampa Tribune (Tampa, FL)	5/27/2009	5	3	
NBC InfoCenter (New York, NY)	April 2009	4	3	Two other positions lost through attrition in 2004 and 2007.	Time, Inc.				

Publication	Dates			Notes
New York Daily News (New York, NY)				
New York Times (New York, NY)	2007, 2008	13	7	The NYT still has additional part-time positions.
News & Observer (Raleigh, NC)				
News & Record (Greensboro, NC)	January 2006, June 2007, January 2009	3	1	
Times-Herald Record (Middletown, NY)	5/15/2009	1	1	
USA Today	12/2007 and 12/2008	9	4	
Vancouver Sun / The Province (Vancouver, BC, Canada)	12/2008–2/2009	4	6	
Wall Street Journal (New York, NY)	Mar-09	2	0	
Washington Post (Washington, DC)	2006, 2008, 2009	9	7	Includes 2 positions lost through attrition

For most recent information see

https://docs.google.com/document/pub?id=11G5CxLF_lyjzaYu400ATYvrrlcgTv1uzEgHR-FrWoEY last accessed December 3, 2012

While not heaping blame on news librarians for any failure to reposition themselves in a rapidly changing environment, Kennedy also feels that news librarians have been "made utterly obsolete by technology!" "Yes, media outlets have had some decline in audience," he continued; they have suffered catastrophic declines in ad revenues. Reporting in these new and much smaller papers has changed from investigative to shorter stories that do not require as much research.

With questions of how much information readers are willing to consume, on what platforms, and at what prices plaguing the newspaper and publishing industry as a whole, what does this mean for librarians working in newspapers and other media organizations?

As newspaper revenues have declined, management has had to make reduction decisions that have affected every facet of the business, including their libraries. However, in interviews with news librarians, they say that it is not just this decline in revenue that has affected them. Two technical advances have also had serious consequences for their work, both related to their end users' desktops. First was the ability of reporters to access the Internet and the World Wide Web directly, including basic aggregated research tools such as Factiva or Nexis. The second and related advance was when a newspaper's archive itself could be similarly accessed. Together these advances reduced the number of basic information requests coming into the library. Exacerbating this decline has been a steady drop in both investigative journalism and other types of long, in-depth stories, which has likewise reduced the opportunity for more sophisticated and collaborative research support. It would be telling only part of the story to stop here and say that financially complex and risky mergers and acquisitions, reductions in advertising revenues, and the ability of reporters to do some of their own online and archival research alone have reduced the work of librarians and their staffs or have led to outright closures. The decline of the industry as a whole reminds us of how closely the life of the corporate library ties to the life of the business itself. Our experience tells us that Kennedy's belief that technology has made news librarians obsolete, along with the belief of many librarians themselves that giving end users access to research resources at their desktop and training them to use these resources efficiently is tantamount to doing themselves out of a job, is really only a very small part of the story of reductions and closures. Often such deployments have meant that the librarians' skills could now be applied in other ways. John Cronin (2009), chief librarian at the *Boston Herald* from 1976 to 2006, put it this way:

> The amount of work in the library did not decrease. Rather it changed; a great deal of time was now spent on formatting the paper for the database aggregators. This included coding for headlines, notations for photographs, pagination, etc. The photographs were not digitized at that time and these had to be filed manually.

Interviews with other news librarians noted similar reductions in reference questions and related reductions in staff, which coincided with other staff reductions at their papers, and a focus of the remaining library staff on preparing the paper for submission to the database vendors. Surely, though, preparing their paper for submission to database vendors is not all that newspaper librarians have left to do. First of all, not all newspapers have deals with the aggregators, and, increasingly, those that do deploy customized software packages to do the majority of the preparation.

SO WHAT ELSE DO NEWS LIBRARIANS DO NOW?

A recent article in *Wired West: The Newsletter of the Special Libraries Association Western Canada Chapter*, described the role of librarians at the Pacific Newspaper Group (*Vancouver Sun* and *The Province*) as trainers for newsroom staff. The author, Kate Bird (2009), noted: "Technological change in a work environment such as ours, where staff are required to adopt new technology and workflow while publishing a newspaper six days a week, presents a unique training challenge." Not only did they continue to train staff on library applications, but they also took on the role of trainer for nonlibrary applications in conjunction with the information technology department. Bird pointed to the practicality of using librarians as trainers in this way. After all, these were their customers, relationships with them already existed, and the librarians knew the strengths and weaknesses, as well as the varying needs, of the reporters. Unlike outside trainers, the librarians were also available for follow-up.

To get some idea of just what other kinds of tasks newspaper or media librarians do, we monitored the SLA News Division listserv (*Newslib* 2009) for 6 months. Postings are found on a dazzling array of operational issues that give some insight into what these folks currently do and think about. (Three experiences reported later in the chapter describe specific activities and/or changes in how news researchers operate. They highlight ways in which you might inoculate yourself against catching something fatal.)

Overall, the range of a myriad of activities is incredible. One recurring theme is helping to figure out new revenue streams for their organizations. Others include figuring out how to use new technologies to enhance productivity and increase existing revenue sources, including everything from digitizing text and photos (current and archival), marketing network stock footage, fielding research inquiries from the public, using wikis as the backbone for an intranet, repurposing blogs in print, using social media sites as research resources (e.g., *The Journalist's Guide to Facebook*), using nonprofessional staff on the "help desk," all the way to thinking about ways to reform copyright laws as they apply to "free riders" who "divert readers and advertisers" from the newspaper that originally created the content (Sims 2009). The experience reported by Elaine Raines of the Arizona Star, for example, describes her success in creatively bridging her research role with that of being a content provider for her paper.

FROM SUPPORTING CONTENT CREATION TO CREATING CONTENT

by Elaine Y. Raines, Director, News and Research Services, *Arizona Star*, 1982–2009.

As the number of online news sources grew and local resources shrank, the news focus of the *Arizona Star* began shifting to an even stronger emphasis on local news. Everyone, including library staff, was asked to contribute content to the print and online products. The library had always contributed to the *Star*'s news content, providing research, timelines, and history boxes, but now the department was being asked to increase that effort and to quantify our contributions. For many local stories that meant writing Did You Know? sidebars and Local Angle boxes for national stories.

Did You Know? sidebars are short, highlighted items containing information on the subject such as something of historic interest or a little-known fact. Local Angles provide a Tucson angle to a national article, such as when the subject of an obituary had visited Tucson. For years, the library staff had written a column called Critter of the Week. In 2007, these items were compiled into a database. This allowed the popular column to once again become available to readers. It is often included as an online link to local wildlife stories. Also, in 2007, a new feature began in the paper and online called Tucson Timecapsule. Each day, a *Star* photo from that date in the past was selected to run in the paper. The photo was chosen from the *Star*'s detailed photo logs going back more than 35 years. Caption information included not only the original information, but often provided updates on the subject matter. The library was responsible for the selection, researching, and writing of this feature. The Timecapsule was well read, and readers were encouraged to upload their old Tucson photos to an online gallery. As an extension of this focus on historic Tucson, a history blog was started. Tales From the Morgue was a perfect platform for providing more information and photos from Tucson's past. It was a place to showcase an interesting article or advertisement gleaned from old pages of the *Star* or to recount a historic Tucson event. The blog was very popular and always in the top 10 of the most accessed *Star* blogs. To demonstrate the contribution of these efforts, hits were very closely monitored. From the beginning, the Timecapsule received good online numbers, and there were letters to the editor and calls regarding the print version. As space became tighter, it would occasionally get cut from the paper. That meant it also didn't run online. The managing editor sent out word that the Timecapsule should not be cut from the paper and it was always to run on StarNet.

Tales From the Morgue grew out of the Timecapsule's success. The numbers for the blogs were very closely monitored, and it became a competitive thing. Tales From the Morgue was always right up there with the University of Arizona sports blogs and the Hollywood gossip blog. It was frequently promoted on the homepage using one of the photos from the day's entry. The library director also received an employee of the month award once when it had really big numbers. Critters was submitted by the *Star* to the Arizona Newspapers Association *Best Practices* publication, where successful ideas that other papers used to build readership were presented.

The Local Angle and Did You Know? boxes were monitored monthly, and editors were required to meet a specific number for each of them.

What the activity on *Newslib* (2009) (which also includes subscribers who are not members of SLA) illustrates is a very vibrant community of loyal and skilled employees working as hard and as creatively as they can to contribute to their employers' survival by using their significant set of information professional skills and the very substantial power of professional networking to share knowledge. These activities underscore an equally diverse array of job titles ranging from information editor to research editor to the most common, news librarian (or news researcher) to the esoteric durable content coordinator. Nonetheless, the fact that usage of their libraries is not growing is somewhat "old news" for this group of librarians. Paul and Hansen (2002, 44), for example, in a splendid article in *Library Journal*, described the situation very well (also see Hansen et al. 2003). They surveyed librarians, journalists, and managers (usually editors) hoping to understand their attitudes toward information use and management within their organizations and to see if their responses yielded any solutions to shrinking usage and substantial cuts in newsroom staff. They found some interesting disconnects that certainly should have informed the strategic thinking of anyone concerned with news libraries. For example, "Some 54 percent of reporters and 58 percent of librarians [believed] the most important role of the librarian is as information retrieval expert. Only 39% of managers agreed." In the context of the authors' predictive model, the disconnect between the value reporters placed on librarians and the librarians' own perception of their value versus how editors who held the purse strings viewed them indicates the onset of a disease that may yet reach plague proportions (for more information on disconnects between information professionals' views of their value/role and that of their customers, see data on SLA Alignment Project).

An example of getting out in front of this potential disconnect is the case of *The Oregonian*, where researchers moved from the library to the newsroom floor in early 2001. The events of 9/11 and the ease of access to these researchers embedded in the newsroom created a much more symbiotic relationship between reporter, librarian, and management than might ever have happened if the researchers had operated in the "relative isolation and quiet of the library" (Bramucci 2002). The article describing the success of these "embedded researchers" appeared in a journal whose readers are investigative reporters and editors (i.e., end users). It offered several tips for this group on how to make best use of their librarians. Here were news librarians reaching out to their organizations to show how, in a pressure situation, their work in the trenches contributed to successful coverage of these events. Getting in front of their audience in this way is something special librarians need to do much more often.

 THE EMBEDDED RESEARCHER

Lynne Palombo, News Researcher,
The Oregonian (Portland, Oregon)

In 2000, *The Oregonian*'s news research department consisted of 12 people working from a semi-secluded library one floor below the main newsroom. By 2009, the library was gone and the news research department was a one-person team. I am it. A lot has changed in the intervening years—in my position obviously, but also at my paper and, more broadly, across the industry. I have done my best to adjust, adapt, and move forward. But moving forward means letting go too. Looking back now, the first transition was a big one. During the summer of 2001, a decision was made to split the five news researchers off from the archivists and photo librarians and move them into the main newsroom. It was a bit jarring for some: The library was a cozy and secluded place. Then came 9/11, which was an all-hands-on-deck story in which our hands were not only needed but a visible part of the news team. After that, I think everyone (researchers, reporters, and editors) was much more aware of how vital we could be to day-to-day coverage. Our workflow changed once we were integrated into the newsroom, of course. Before the move, we were working off a traditional question-and-answer model. And our newsroom training was a lot more formal. Our new location provided the opportunity to develop closer relationships with reporters and editors and to make many of the processes less formal. There was much more collaboration on projects. And our integration increased our visibility, which in turn brought us new "customers." We had several good years working under this new model, with a staff to do it well. Then the industry-wide downturn crept into our daily lives and *The Oregonian* started offering early retirements and buyouts. Other positions were left vacant. All of us had to learn to do more with less. By the fall of 2007, only two news researchers remained.

But even more change was still on the horizon. I soon left my desk next to my colleague in the news research pod and joined the breaking news/online team. This move was bittersweet. At first, I missed having a department, but then I realized I was missing our old department news team. The managing editor and I believed I would provide the best value by becoming a part of the online/breaking news team. I was still responsible for providing reference services to the rest of the newsroom and for doing administrative tasks. But now I was looking at ways to be more efficient with my new team. Fast-forward another year and the newsroom research staff had shrunk again, making yours truly the only one still standing. The library support staff has also left.

Some of my previous goals and tools have been jettisoned as part of this transformation. I am much more focused on deadline reporting, for example, than I was before. We just don't have the luxury any longer of assigning someone to work the big breaking news story of the day while others handle longer-term investigative and feature stories. So sometimes I have to put things on hold and juggle more than I would like to, but I've decided that my first and best use is as a resource to reporters on fast-moving, breaking news stories. Another downside to being a one-person department is that we just have fewer hours of coverage (which means more calls to my home). I also need to be selective about projects I can help with, which frustrates me at times when I'm forced to turn down projects that would be interesting and helpful. My outreach and training have slowed considerably too, although everyone knows I am available for training if there is anything specific that people need help with. I also miss the time (and money) to test out and experiment with new products. Professional development is also difficult. As a solo librarian, it can be hard to get away from the building for professional events, although I've tried to take advantage of opportunities as they arise. (I was able to attend a local ORSLA-Oregon Chapter of SLA, event recently on my day off and I am taking an online continuing education course in a few months.)

With all the changes in our industry, it is easy to lose confidence and feel lost. But that isn't a productive way to spend my day. It is my responsibility to show my skills to my coworkers and/or our readers. I have found that it is much more productive to keep my goals in line with the general goals of the newsroom. Even in hard times, there are opportunities.

Creative thinking. Creative thinking should be cultivated. Otherwise, you risk feeling like a drone. Plus, creative thinking sparks enthusiasm, and enthusiasm is contagious.

Self-directed work. Being more empowered to take actions that resolve day-to-day problems is a good feeling. It is also a lot easier to plan, control, and improve your workflow when you only have your own personality to consider.

Increased relationship building. I think embedded and solo librarians tend to have more interactions with the people they help. Increased interactions change the dynamics of a service relationship and can put you in a position of having more insight over the work you perform. Relationship building also feeds creative thinking and self-direction.

Flexibility. Most importantly, I have learned that we need to stay flexible!

Reporters and editors were interviewed for their views on news librarians. Based on the Paul and Hansen (2002, 44) survey findings, it was no surprise to us that reporters were very positive regarding librarians and their helpfulness in researching and especially their institutional memory. When layoffs affected librarians among others, the reporters expressed sympathy. However, there was also either relief that it was not one of them or explanations that this was the news business, where people come and go regularly. The editors each mentioned how much they liked their libraries. Kevin Convey, editor-in-chief of the *Boston Herald*, said that he could not imagine the paper without its library and saw the library as needing to step up and play a strong role in the paper's technology advancement (Convey 2009). He definitely saw some technology advances (such as automated archiving) as likely changing the role of the library and the number of librarians needed. Right now, according to Martha Reagan (2009), the *Herald* chief librarian, the staff spends about 80 percent of its time preparing the paper for the database aggregators and the rest of the time in a mix of activities including research support, manually filing photographs, and negotiating contracts for desktop databases such as Factiva and LexisNexis. It was clear that Convey valued the library's past contribution and would look to it for future contributions. Reagan's role at the *Herald* is not unusual. Another chief librarian, this time at a Midwest newspaper also reported (Chief Librarian 2009) that she, like Reagan, has one assistant and together they spend a great deal of their time getting the paper ready for the aggregators. They have a hard time juggling their tasks to find time to answer questions from the editorial staff. Unfortunately, because their customers know how busy the library staff is, they are reluctant to ask questions. In fact, in the past, this chief librarian had even attended budget meetings, which led to numerous research queries (which one would think a good thing). However, with staff reductions from small layoffs over time, she could no longer attend these meetings and that very beneficial avenue of insight into the paper's operations has gone away.

John Yemma (2009), editor at *The Christian Science Monitor* (*CSM*), represents the other end of the spectrum from Kevin Convey and the *Boston Herald*. *CSM* is the first major newspaper to go totally virtual (with the exception of a Friday-only print magazine). In the past, Yemma told us, 95 percent of the paper's resources went toward print; everything was geared to the print deadline. *CSM* has changed its entire approach to the process of publication, becoming more nimble and creating a structure more conducive to the Web than the old industrial structure. Nonetheless, he felt the role of the library has not radically changed. It is still needed on a daily basis to support reporters and editors as stories develop and to do more introductory research for the weekly print magazine. Yemma commented that his librarian understood the fiscal implications of the changes in the paper and made commensurate changes. He also noted the preeminence of the library when it came to "knowing databases." He felt the paper had to have someone "out there fishing on the frontier" and helping to build the *Monitor's* community online. While it was very early into the *Monitor's* five-year plan to make any judgments about how things were going, it was clear to us that Yemma felt the library's database expertise (along with design and coding ability), in addition to its usual role in research support, made them a partner in the potential success of this new business plan.

 THRIVING ON TURBULENCE: THREE QUESTIONS TO HELP KEEP YOURSELF GROUNDED

by Leigh Montgomery, Librarian,
The Christian Science Monitor

After celebrating its centennial in 2008, *The Christian Science Monitor* became the first national newspaper to go to a web-first publishing schedule and drop its daily print edition; news would be reported not only online, but also in the most appropriate format. This included two subscription-based editorial products—a weekly print magazine and a PDF daily digest. As the *Monitor*'s librarian, I have a decade of experience in adapting to changes in media while working in a field with some of the most demanding production cycles of any industry. I saw early on in my career the advantage of welcoming change since it is always a learning experience. I also knew that convergence was roiling in the media industry. It was clear that the rising costs and cumbersome delivery of putting the news on paper—as well as daily deadline pressures—would mean that a move to where the readers were, as well as developing the flexibility to reach them right when they were looking for information, would be happening soon. One of the ways in which we tell stories now is through the use of lists. Here's a list of a few questions for news librarians—or information professionals in other fields—to ask themselves in order to best support their enterprise in these turbulent times.

1. What are my strengths? What do I bring every day? We rarely ask ourselves these questions voluntarily. Now is the time to evaluate yourself regularly. In my case, I had a digital career whose arc began when the *Monitor* rode the waves of media change. It was one of the earliest newspapers to have an online edition; first to offer audio for its website, first to offer RSS feeds. I bring a dedication to accuracy in every piece of information I obtain or analyze for our journalists. Accuracy is still paramount, perhaps even more so with so many more voices telling the story but with varying degrees of journalistic credibility or ethics. I can say with confidence I have never had a correction or clarification attributed to anything I have done. That continues, though we now produce more content than ever. I am also responsible for managing our digital asset management system. We have three new formats to archive—our weekly pages, the PDF digest, and born-digital content—in addition to our photos and cartoons. Since I have also been managing the electronic and print resources for the newsroom, and training our staff on how to use them, I am well practiced in evaluating tools and changes in the information business as a researcher as well as a manager and trainer.

2. What do I need to learn as our business changes? Ask yourself this question regularly and ask your manager periodically. When I asked this question of my manager (our managing editor), he replied that content and its production would be "less traditional." This was even before our transition to the new multi-platform publishing model. We both acknowledged that there may not be the usual production-line chain of handling, or by as many intermediaries, and editors might be performing different functions. Deadlines, would, of course, be fluid for the web-first content. We would be more "scattered" as far as teams were concerned, and a common editorial pool would contribute to both the online content and the print content, each with very different production schedules. I saw

this as a need for flexibility as well as the responsiveness that our staff has come to expect, particularly as they have to react faster to each news event. As with many companies, the librarian here is also seen as the in-house expert in that broad category known as "archives." Our own content is arguably the most valuable asset we possess. It has taken on new importance with the ability to serve up related information as additional context without having to write it into the story. In addition to maintaining an encyclopedic back file in my memory, developed through both researching the stories and archiving them post-publication, I have also noticed a trend toward more intelligent ways of indexing, classifying, and arranging information. When information is outside the printed page, it can move from being static to dynamic. While this is exciting, it requires planning a taxonomy for site users as well as external agents. I quickly found a continuing education course and learned all I could about this in the time I had. I have also been an active participant in many conversations about the future of journalism. These have been taking place off and online, and I've become a volunteer in an organization that holds these sessions to teach people about ways of doing journalism online.

3. How am I connected to business development? What more can I do to contribute to it? Most media organizations traditionally contributed to the information economy: a huge and complex business, difficult to understand, and now in the midst of massive change. Some activities within this context have been handled by librarians who have been involved, as I am, in maintaining data quality for their organizations' archives, as well as sending large vendor databases of news content to aggregators—not my responsibility. Or maybe they have been involved, as I am, in photo sales or syndication or an "information store" of some scale. The newspaper business has to diversify its revenue streams or find totally new ones, since depending on the individual subscriber paying for a newspaper to land in their driveway at 6 a.m. is a vestige of the 20th century. Today, new ideas are much needed and welcomed. Since librarians are aware of the many information sources available and not only use them directly but also negotiate contracts for their usage, there are many ways they can use this knowledge to support business development. One of the activities I do is evaluating how our own content is arranged on any third-party service, as well as suggesting other places, whether commercial or on the open Internet, where it would be an appropriate fit. With so many more contributors, journalism has a vibrant future and, therefore, so do information professionals working within the media industry. Many of the newer entities may not have the infrastructure to archive and

syndicate content or there may be a learning curve in the ethics and practices of research and storytelling. Existing media organizations may not be fully aware of the many contributions that librarians make, particularly related to off-page elements, metadata, and taxonomy. In my opinion, the science of information is more important than ever. I've found that by regularly asking myself these three questions, I can continue to change with and contribute to my organization as it changes. If your organization is not on the brink of total shutdown, you can at least try some things to both showcase how you can contribute and to position yourself for a seat in the lifeboat.

KEY TAKEAWAYS

No one questions the fact that the newspaper industry and perhaps all of media and publishing is going through a significant transition, not only in terms of interactions with their traditional customers, but also in regard to their overall business models as well. The *CSM* has taken the risk of going all electronic, with the exception of a weekly in-depth news magazine. The jury is still out on this experiment; it is both too early to tell how it will pan out and, with the significant financial backing offered by the Christian Science church, it is a relatively unique situation. Whether or not suggestions such as changing the copyright laws or reducing the number of times a paper is printed, even making newspapers into nonprofit entities (something Convey of the *Boston Herald* felt would never work due to lack of funds), or putting content behind a pay wall will materialize also remains to be seen.

Many newspapers, some considered "too big to fail," to use a now familiar euphemism, have either gone out of business entirely or drastically cut back on operations to the point of being shadows of their former selves. The idea of a "one-paper town" in a city like Boston, unthinkable a year ago and certainly not desired by anyone, is within the realm of possibility. Many are scrambling to understand how to change the business paradigm of newspapers that has seen them almost totally dependent on advertising revenue. The publishing industry overall is facing their own business paradigm challenges in the form of e-books, self-publishing, and price wars with big box stores.

Certainly this is not the first time in their history that newspapers have experienced the kind of downturn they now face. The Great Depression saw newspapers hurt by the introduction of the radio, advertising revenues plummeted, and many papers had significant layoffs or closed entirely. Every decade since, there have been consolidations, chain buy-ups, closures, and so forth. Kirchoff (2009) writes: "[T]he key challenge for newspapers [today] is to hold on to lucrative print readers, while finding ways to make more money from a growing online audience that generally reads the paper for free." An analysis of the lessons to be learned from this history is left to the economists and newspaper publishers.

Amid all of this, then, how can news librarians hope to cast or recast themselves in the role of asset rather than liability? One thing for sure is that in some instances, no matter how good you are, no matter how well aligned with your parent organization, no matter how much those with the purse strings appreciate what a library can do for their business, if the whole enterprise is going under, there is nothing to do but package yourself to be ready for another opportunity. However, if your organization is not on the brink of total shutdown, you can at least try some things to both showcase how you can contribute and to position yourself for a seat in the lifeboat.

Three librarians have shared their experiences. Following publication of this article, Elaine Raines reported to the authors that the library staff at the *Arizona Star* was eliminated. These experiences provide important key takeaways and reinforce two major themes: (1) Take action to inoculate yourself to try to ward off a fatal illness, and (2) even when very positive action is taken, sometimes there is no antidote.

REFERENCES

Bird, Kate, "Librarians as Technology Trainers—A Dispatch From the Front." *Wired West: Web Journal of the SLA Western Canada Chapter*, 12, no. 4 (2009), http://units. sla.org/chapter/cwcn/wwest/vl2n4/arti cle_bird.shtml (accessed November 27, 2009).

Bramucci, Gina, "News Researchers Play Key Role in Fast-Strike Terrorist Coverage." *The IRE Journal* 25, no. 1 (2002): 26.

Campo, Charles. *Virtual Veranda.* *Newslib* posting, October 2, 2009, http://www.ibiblio.org/slanews/

Chief Librarian, *Midwest Newspaper*, Interview October 9, 2009.

Convey, Kevin. Interview. August 2009.

Cronin, John. Interview. September 22, 2009.

Gapper, John, "Charge for News or Bleed Red Ink." *Financial Times*, January 21, 2010, 9.

Hansen, Kathleen, Nora Paul, and Betsey Neibergall. "Survey of Large Newspapers Studies Information Practices." *Newspaper Research Journal* 24, no. 4 (Fall 2003): 36–48.

Kennedy, Dan. Assistant Professor of Journalism, Northeastern University, Interview. September 15, 2009.

Kirchoff, Suzanne M. "The U.S. Newspaper Industry in Transition," *Congressional Research Service*, July 8, 2009.

Krueger, J. "Special Libraries Job Postings at Simmons College." *The Boston Chapter News Bulletin* 54 (1985–86): 16–20.

Paul, Nora, and Kathleen A. Hansen. "Reclaiming News Libraries." *Library Journal* (April 1, 2002): 44, http://www.libraryjournal.com/artJcle/CA201862.html (accessed November 2, 2009).

Reagan, Martha. Interview. August 2009.

Sims, Damon. "Tighter Copyright Law Could Save Newspapers: Connie Schultz." *Cleveland.com*, June 28, 2009, http://www.cleveland.com/schultz/index.ssf/2009/06iighter_copyright_law_could_sa.html (accessed November 2, 2009).

SLA Alignment Project. http://www.sla.org/content/SLA/alignment/portal/index.html.

Yemma, John, ed. *The Christian Science Monitor*. Interview. August 26, 2009.

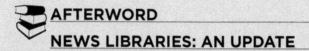

AFTERWORD
NEWS LIBRARIES: AN UPDATE

Leigh Montgomery

A news library at a Connecticut news outlet is not only open to all the journalists on staff—but also to the public. Another librarian, about to depart the news business for a public library, is recruited for a newly launched program. More news librarians have a divided, "slash" title—librarian/content manager, where they curate information as well as create content. Another, a recent master of library science graduate, and after multiple internships, is hired for a contract position at a television network. News librarians are still doing essential work in media. Many have survived numerous organizational restructuring efforts, physical moves, declines in staff with corresponding increases in demands; and all are shifting with changes in the news ecology.

Since the last report on news librarians, one certainty must be affirmed: change is a continuum. It isn't just a shift from a print to a (mostly) digital reality, but is, in fact, a constant. This is as it was previously, but there is now much more ambiguity which is nearly impossible to predict.

INVESTIGATIVE JOURNALISM

Accountability reporting is a core mission of journalism. Long-term projects should have a librarian or a researcher on the team. For example, this past year news researchers were cited as finalists and in the winning category for investigative journalism series by the organization Investigative Reporters and Editors, which focuses on improving the quality of investigative reporting.

Data journalism, whether analyzing and filtering datasets or preparing statistics for visualization in graphical presentation, is attracting new enthusiasts among reporters, open government advocates, and computer scientists. News librarians have participated at this intersection of computer science and journalism for many years now, and are partners in acquiring, synthesizing, and hosting data. A few, such as Kelly Guckian of the *Atlanta Journal-Constitution*, become database specialists, with a concentration in analysis of public data and hosting these repositories for colleagues and increasingly, for the public to access from the news organization's online edition.

Again, any research should have a librarian on the team, and usually does; though they generally do not have the luxury to work exclusively on a project, and the journalists may not either. Librarians are usually doing this work in addition to the many demands of a news organization from training staff, archiving content, managing information portfolios, and building internal and external informational services.

HIGHER VOLUME

Broadcast outlets, magazines, and newspaper entities are now digital media platforms, producing and posting more content online in the process. News articles are numerous and shorter, as more users are accessing news on their mobile devices. Networks are flexibly responding to these changes as well: one veteran news librarian at a 24-hour cable news outlet segued from work in a centralized library area to embedded work within a program unit at the network.

CONTENT: CREATION AND CURATION

With more information being created and circulated, a critical function for librarians is to interpret and present content from many sources that is relevant to the audience or community. Lu-Ann Farrar, a librarian from the *Lexington Herald-Leader*, is now an Online Content Editor, writing a daily column including news relevant to citizens in Kentucky throughout the day for *Kentucky.com*, a property of the *Lexington Herald-Leader* newspaper.

ARCHIVING

Publishers are finally seeing archives as assets. They are being used to augment contemporary journalism, have been revived on social media outlets, and syndicated to other companies. News librarians have worked with such archives for years, and many gained their first bylines by writing about this material.

OPPORTUNITIES

Data journalism is being championed by the media and technology sectors as the new frontier for accountability and authenticity. This is something that news librarians, since the days of CDs and the early Internet, have been closely involved with.

This trend is also occurring parallel to one in the scientific community with the advocacy of open data, which allows the underlying data in research to be accessed by other researchers or the public to examine or even append. Media are doing more of this as well, hosting public datasets for citizens to search. These require a librarian's knowledge in obtaining, hosting, interpreting—as well as promoting.

Curation—the act of collecting, describing, and presenting information on the proper platform about a topic, is emergent. Drawing from the best online informational sources, even produced by other media, is not only more common but also a reader service.

Taxonomy and the prospects for linked data are likewise becoming popular in the digital environment. Librarians understand this, have managed ontologies and other metadata for various news formats for many years, and this will considerably aid in connecting news content with other informational sources—and when coupled with the vast amount of information being generated and more powerful computing power, more relevant news will more easily be found amid the noise.

CHALLENGES

An information industry—which could be any industry, since just about every company is a media company of sorts—needs a librarian. Many publishers have retained librarians because they are creating more content, and have demonstrated that the news librarian dramatically impacts the outcome of essential projects. There should most assuredly be more of them.

Unfortunately, the contraction of the media business continues and the news library staff, which is usually small, is not readily replaced. One publisher realized this after their last librarian retired, and then was compelled to approach the city library for assistance in archiving their daily product. This was in response to concerned readers, who could not find recent content on the newspaper's website. More evidence that news archives need to be preserved for future citizens, scholars, and others, in addition to the fact that they are a revenue source to sustain the operation.

Another troubling indicator is how internal content is managed and accessed within companies—of all kinds, but in the news in particular. A recent global benchmark study called the *Industry Information Index*, by SmartLogic and MindMetre research (*CMS Report* 2012), was conducted in a range of industries. No industry scored over 50 percent, meaning that knowledge management needs improvement everywhere. At the very bottom of the list: Media & Publishing. In a way this is unsurprising: there is so much emphasis on the daily product that knowledge management is an afterthought. The media business is full of unstructured information, from news articles, blog posts, comments and alerts, to e-mail newsletters and it is in disarray. The industries that were atop the list tend to have access to and produce more structured information, such as transactions, forms, and proprietary reports, that are easier to centralize. Upon review of the industries leading the list (Oil/Gas/Mining, Retail, Law, Charity, Food & Drink), this could be due to the nature of their enterprise, profit motives, or legal requirements. A correlation between corporate viability and information professionals demands further attention and study.

THE NEW PROFESSIONALS

The good news is that librarians in media are changing along with the news ecology, as they have always done. Success in news coverage demands compelling reporting that reaches the reader wherever they are, and convinces them to refer to that source regularly. There is a closely watched trend toward paid and premium content, which has to be accurate and accessible on demand. The kinds of careers on this horizon involve the intersection of information and computer science: developing applications, data visualizations, and analyzing statistics. It also acknowledges that the news can come from and be circulated anywhere.

For all of the above reasons, and the continuing need for strong journalism that people can take with them to improve their lives, we need journalists who are librarians. It is clear that they are needed, that they are involved in every aspect of the operation, and evidently strengthen the juncture between technology, research, and preserving all digital products for the future.

REFERENCE

Smartlogic and MindMetre. "Benchmarking study shows information industries among the worst at leveraging knowledge assets." *CMS Report*, http://cmsreport.com/press/2012/03/benchmarking-study-shows-information-industries-among-worst-leveraging-knowledge (accessed June 15, 2012).

5

CORPORATE LIBRARIES: A SOFT ANALYSIS AND A WARNING

JAMES M. MATARAZZO AND TOBY PEARLSTEIN

When a library closes or suffers drastic reductions, is it suicide or murder? And what happens to the survivors? This chapter looks at case studies of corporate library reductions and closures and what you can do to minimize your chances of becoming a victim. When the Internet as a popular research tool began affecting the lives of librarians and information professionals and their clients, accountability for contributing to the mission (i.e., bottom line) of one's parent organization, whether a for-profit or not-for-profit, became the most critical driver behind the survival of corporate libraries. If corporate library managers had not already realized this, they now found themselves confronted with a clear mandate: Contribute demonstrably to your organization's success or risk becoming marginalized and an easy answer to the question, "Where can we cut costs?" Increasingly during the past 5 to 10 years and especially in this recent volatile period across major segments of the financial services industry, library managers have either been asked to find or have proactively sought ways to make their services integral to their organization's survival. The authors are deliberately not characterizing this as "finding ways to save their libraries," but rather finding ways to integrate their services and skills with essential organizational functions. Sometimes these efforts are the same, but be prepared to think of them as very different strategies. Views vary widely about the causes of downsizing and closures of corporate libraries. Corporate libraries and librarians have been affected even in environments with a strong tradition of library support, but as traditional library services are vanishing so are traditional practitioners. What should alarm us is that more companies don't recognize the utility of their libraries during times of downturn. Too often, the library is seen as a liability. Whether as a result of consolidation, outsourcing, off-shoring, economic realities, or

This chapter is adapted from an article that originally appeared in *Searcher Magazine*, Vol. 17, Issue 6, Pages 14–17, 52, June 2009.

just plain naïveté about the Web's capabilities, there is no question that the closure of many corporate libraries and attendant job losses are having an effect, not only on corporate librarians but on their organizations as well (Matarazzo and Pearlstein 2007). In today's tumultuous environment, self-defense is the best offense if you want to survive. With its focus on case studies in different types of organizations, this book attempts to glean from library reduction and closure experiences any lessons that might help others take steps to ensure that they are in sync with their organization's most fundamental information needs. That may mean adapting to new ways to use our skills. Special librarians need to ask themselves some hard questions. Are the librarian's skills valued enough in these organizations so that even though the library is closed or reduced, their skills can be repurposed elsewhere to support good decision making? In other words, can the librarian survive even if the library does not? In his recent special report "Prospects for Specialized Libraries: Comments from Colleagues," Guy St. Clair (2008) identifies a

> new working environment managed by information professionals who see themselves as knowledge thought leaders providing information, knowledge, and strategic learning support for non-library affiliated knowledge-centric organizations, businesses, or other types of research-focused environments.

By highlighting skills such as "research asset management" or "knowledge asset management," St. Clair reinforces the idea that "it is imperative for us to describe to non-LIS managers and enterprise leaders how our skill set relates to the organization's larger mission."

How do decision makers in organizations that have significantly downsized or outright closed their libraries continue to get the information they need to make good decisions? This constitutes a directly related issue, the exploration of which proves much more challenging to research. Unfortunately, there is not much research done on what, if anything happens to an organization when their library is reduced or closed. However, it is possible to draw on findings from research done recently on the perceived value a specialized library brings to decision makers in an organization, especially those in upper-echelon positions. This line of research is followed throughout this book.

LESSONS FROM THE PAST

Corporate library closures were last studied in depth in 1980 (Matarazzo 1980). At that time, Matarazzo found several common elements in situations in which libraries were either closed outright or severely cut back. It is not too farfetched to propose that the existence of these conditions can be considered a "predictive model" of sorts. In reviewing these case studies, readers are encouraged to also review their own situations with this model in mind.

- Was the decision made at the top, without consultation of those who used the services?
- Was there a reduction in the number of customers?
- What is the availability of outside resources?
- Was there a lack of evaluation of library services?
- Was there evidence of financial crisis in the parent organization?

THE CASE OF THE DIVISIONAL LIBRARY
AT CAVEAT PUBLISHING CO.

In the spring of 2008, Caveat Publishing Co.'s corporate management engaged a leading consultancy to study overall operating expenses and to recommend ways to reduce costs and increase revenues. One of the consultant recommendations was to close one of the several divisional libraries and lay off the four librarians and a staff assistant. The consultants further suggested removing this one library's collections and renting the 1,000-plus square-foot space to another organization, despite the fact that the space had recently been remodeled at considerable expense. While this division had had library services for decades and served four different Caveat publications as well as two corporate-level departments, difficult economic times now demanded drastic actions. Closing this divisional library, while retaining the services of the head librarian, would save hundreds of thousands of dollars. The closure was implemented immediately on instructions from corporate upper management with no time or chance to offer alternatives.

Was the Handwriting on the Wall?

The division's head librarian, an experienced and respected corporate practitioner, had been recruited by Caveat from another firm several years ago. When she started at Caveat, this divisional library had a staff of 10, including the head. Over the ensuing five years, there were ongoing budget restrictions. So as librarians left their positions voluntarily to pursue other opportunities, these positions were not filled. Nonetheless, the head librarian and the remaining four professionals kept the library open each workday from 9 a.m. to 9 p.m. using staggered shifts. If overtime was needed, the librarians, who were very well compensated, received additional compensation. While this divisional library had originally been designed to serve four of Caveat's publications and two corporate departments, two of these publications were subsequently eliminated at the consultant's recommendations because these titles failed to contribute to the bottom line of the division. Shortly thereafter, the remaining four librarians were given two months' notice, with no severance package, to find employment elsewhere. The head librarian was asked to stay on at Caveat, along with her staff assistant, for four additional months.

No Time to Defend the Library or Its Staff

This left no time to defend the library, its space needs, or services in the face of these final cost reductions. Other departments in the division who also lost staff and space were treated the same way. In fact, the head librarian had previously worked out an evaluative system for the library and its services with the financial person in the division. This system had worked very well during five years for three of the four financial managers with whom the librarian worked. However, as the budget situation in the division deteriorated, the fourth and final financial manager seemed less than interested in her evaluative reports. Interestingly enough, the two remaining publications the library supported still made money for the division. The two eliminated had historically only provided about 20 percent of the library's operating budget via a service agreement. This was apparently not considered in the reduction decision.

Decision Made at the Top: Resistance Is Futile

While the manager to whom the library reported was supportive, he made it clear it was useless to resist; the decision had been made. The librarian was told that the collection including books, periodicals, and reports would be shipped to another floor and put in storage. The new "library space" would be her office, period. The thousands spent on the recently completed renovations did not matter, her manager made it clear that the division had to meet its new budget goals and no alternatives would be entertained. As noted, the library also supported two corporate-level functions at Caveat: Strategic Planning and Finance. In fact, a member of the Strategic Planning Department had told her that the closure decisions had been made at the top, above her bosses. "Nothing could stop the reorganization," he said.

New Duties for the Head Librarian

The librarian's role now became one of training the publication staff to meet their own information needs by using the databases arrayed on their desktop. As she set out to train the writers and reporters, she found she had to do it one-on-one in order for it to be effective. Some of the young staff members had learned to do some searching, but "others have difficulty logging into their computers." Many others want her to do the searches and prepare research packages for them as needed. However, she is now on a 9 a.m. to 5 p.m. schedule, with no overtime compensation available. In retrospect, she noted, "my boss was supportive. He understands libraries and even has a relative who is a librarian. It is very sad. Sales and revenue are down. Business is bad. We had to downsize."

Her Qualities and Skills Assured Her Retention

The head librarian has always been respected for her skill in negotiating database contracts for use in the library as well as on division desktops. She is also admired for her people and relationship skills, which were described by her boss as "exceptional." From the time she reported to her new position, she had handled all staff requests in a professional manner with anyone in the areas she served. Her personality was such that she was able to develop relationships with many division and corporate staff members. She was also admired for being a good manager of people and resources in the library.

So Now What?

Where are the information users in this division of Caveat Publishing to get their information going forward? As with any specialized library, there were external research resources that Caveat had used from time to time. Unfortunately, an industry library that Caveat used had also recently closed its doors. This eliminated one of the obvious alternative sources for information. At this writing, there does not seem to be any coordinated plan to use any other outside resources, most of which are themselves facing reductions or cannot provide the level of service a publication with tight turnaround deadlines and high-quality expectations requires. Reporters and writers at Caveat (and at most, if not all, publications) do have access to some databases at their desktops, but, although available for quite some time, usage has never been high. The librarian's assumption is that management expects the writing staff and other employees to step up and take whatever training exists to become better versed in the information tools they have and then to use them. Yet, as another publishing industry information professional told us, "writers have their own jobs." Is it reasonable to expect that they can do the job of a researcher as well? One writer expressed this in another way. He especially appreciated "that the librarian got to know him and how he worked and could be very proactive with him." He "liked bouncing ideas off of the librarian and getting their perspective on the story." The reality, however, seems to be that the writers, as with employees in other organizations where library services have been cut or eliminated, will have to adapt to a different way of doing their jobs. Perhaps, as one senior writer said during the survey, he "can always find someone to do the research for him." Who this someone is or what their research skill level might be remains unknown. Realistically speaking, what may be found is that writers simply will not do as many "in-depth" stories as they once did. Not only is there less interest in this kind of piece, but also less resources (i.e., researchers/librarians) to assist in doing the research needed.

In similar publishing environments where the library has been cut, one writer noted that he never heard anyone say it was a good thing to cut the library. Nonetheless, no one was in a position to protest, "The whole industry was contracting and this was one of the many bad consequences. People were worried about their own positions as well." Speaking cynically, he added, "other things sell magazines besides quality."

The Way Ahead

Caveat's senior corporate management had hired the outside consultants to evaluate the use of resources and to make recommendations for economies. Since they never asked for any data from the library manager, one can presume they were asked to make recommendations for economies "regardless" of how or if the library was being used. While the librarian had established a system for performance measures that interested her previous managers, her current financial manager did not appear similarly interested. In any event, it is easy to understand how reporting to four different managers in five years presented enough challenges for the head librarian, who had to adapt to the different styles and interests of each.

Recommendations went to Caveat's senior managers without consultation with customers or with the department managers in question. Furthermore, the loss of two of the four publications reduced the number of customers for the library's services overall. At least four of the five elements of the "predictive model" (Matarazzo 1980) discussed above seem to have been present in this case. In a recent article, John Latham reminds us that library managers are responsible for understanding the finances of their department and company (Latham 2007). At Caveat, the head librarian knew that business was bad, and, in fact, had already experienced a reduction in staffing through attrition and budget restrictions. She was nonetheless at least a little surprised that her operation became a victim of the exigencies being experienced by the overall business. In this economy, we all need to pay very close attention to the bottom line of our organizations and be prepared for the unexpected. Latham states: "If you know that the organization is experiencing financial difficulties, be prepared for some cost-cutting exercises, remembering that information centers, together with R&D, are often the first areas axed. Being prepared is not just the motto of the Boy Scouts!" Have there been other warnings to the profession? In 1992, Davenport and Prusak (1993, 411–12) warned corporate librarians:

> The library was created at a time when information access and usage was a more leisurely activity. We might want to return to those days, but they have not been present for a long time in the corporations we study and work with. To adapt to current and future information environments, radical changes must be undertaken in corporate libraries.

More recently, Matarazzo and Pearlstein (2007, 43) offered the following:

Views vary widely about the causes of downsizing and closures of corporate libraries. Corporate libraries and librarians have been affected even in environments where a strong library foundation has been traditional. But as traditional library services are vanishing, so are its traditional practitioners.

No one would argue with the statement that good decisions depend on good information. In the case of Caveat, the authors have been told, "editors knew there was value in the library even if they didn't use it directly." Yet in a recent Outsell, Inc. briefing, Joanne Lustig (2008, 4), writes: "When asked to identify the most valuable service offered by their institutional libraries or information centers, 82% of executive respondents . . . said their organizations did not have such a function." Perhaps there was a disconnect between the library and the divisional heads or their bosses at Caveat that made it easier or at least less controversial for them to drastically reduce library services. It is also likely, given the way in which the cuts were made overall, that by the time the consultants were called in, nothing could have saved the Caveat library and, in fact, Caveat itself still fights to remain a viable publisher. The librarian's role now became one of training the publication staff to meet their own information needs.

REFERENCES

Davenport, T.H., and L. Prusak. "Blow Up the Corporate Library." *International Journal of Information Management* 13 (1993): 411–12.

Latham, John. "Understanding the Finances of Your Department and Your Company Is a Key Responsibility." *Information Outlook* 11, no. 9 (2007), http://www.sla.org/io/2007/09/285.cfm (accessed January 2013).

Lustig, Joanne. "What Executives Think About Information Management, Information Management Service." *Briefing, Outsell, Inc.* 11 (2008): 4.

Matarazzo, James M. *Closing the Corporate Library*. New York, NY: Special Libraries Association, 1980.

Matarazzo, James M., and Toby Pearlstein. "Corporate Score." *Library Journal* 132 (February 1, 2007): 43.

St. Clair, Guy. *Prospects for Specialized Libraries: Comments from Colleagues*. SMR Special Report, 2–3. New York: SMR International, 2008.

COMPANION ESSAY

A Warning from the UK

Sylvia James

The demise of the information professional and by implication the corporate library had long been predicted in the UK. The "Doomsday Scenario" (Lewis 1977) was a very controversial paper predicting the end of the information professional. Written by Dennis Lewis, then a well-known British corporate librarian, this 1977 report still resonates today. The message of the paper in one phrase was that "there won't be an information profession in AD 2000." It was a startling contention for those days and at the time, was much discussed and debated. Lewis went on to leave his corporate environment to head the UK special libraries information association, ASLIB (now known as the Association for Information Management), in the 1980s. ASLIB represents both corporate and academic libraries, both are classified as "special libraries" in the UK to distinguish them from public libraries.

The prediction had really come true to a certain extent during the 1990s in the UK, even before the impact of the Internet and the expectation that everyone in any corporate environment had the time and expertise to do their own competent research using the World Wide Web. Corporate research and information services were mainly print-based desk research. Scientific and technical publishers and just a few token business information databases dominated online information services.

Through my advisory consultancy working for a range of large industrial and service companies, it was my experience in that exciting climate of using and introducing new types of automated information services to end users, that the corporate library was usually left out of discussions on developing information services in companies. Often, when I enquired why the corporate librarians were not being involved in a project, I was told that they were too inflexible, had no real idea of the business needs for (electronic) information, and that all they did was purchase and administer and circulate book and journal collections. Few of the libraries had access to electronic information services, whose use in the business was usually the subject of my consultancy. I had no real answer to this widely held view of why they should not participate in an information project, so did not press the point any further for their involvement. It was not a good feeling to ignore my fellow professionals in their already doomed, obsolete, unused, and unloved corporate libraries, but I felt that I needed to respect my client's wishes in order to develop a good rapport and do the best work I could on the consultancy. On some projects I was invited to include the corporate library in my interviews of corporate information users and found that many of the "librarians," were not in fact qualified in any way, but had come to the positions as promoted administrative assistants, secretaries, or even long-serving staff whose original job had long since disappeared, and no one in the human resources department could think of any other role for them in the corporation. It was no surprise that these units, headed by a totally unsuitable manager, who had no idea of the professional approach to running and developing a state-of-the-art corporate library, were so disregarded by the up and coming front-line managers.

In his gloomy prediction, Dennis Lewis had been writing and speaking about just this type of corporate libraries that he knew well, which were certainly seen by all those in the profession as the backbone of the special library sector in the United Kingdom. These services, generally expensive to maintain as corporate overhead, were run from a corporate central budget, making them ideal targets for cost cutting. Online database usage had then hardly made any impact on their work. Dennis Lewis was right about the special library that dominated at that time in the United Kingdom. Corporate information centers and special libraries run as a central resource had disappeared by 2000.

My observation from over 40 years of working in corporate research was that there is still no lack of demand for an excellent information service for any sized corporation and that these fossilized corporate libraries of the 1990s really missed the opportunity to develop the right service at the right time.

Today, I rarely come across a corporate library in Europe in the course of my consultancy work. Few and far between, they are notable when I do find them and often have a really good lesson in survival for other corporate libraries. They are invariably very specialized and tend to be confined to scientific, technical, and legal work, with a few units in other professional ser-vices, such as management consultancy and financial services. One strong and overwhelming common factor for their survival, I have noted, has been the need for complete confidentiality in their corporation. Many of these current "libraries" are sited in high security units, their staff embedded, working alongside the highly qualified professionals they support.

A good example is a remarkable unit based in the Netherlands, staffed by qualified scientists (none have any library qualifications) working on the information needs required to develop new diet products. They had been charged with providing a new expertise in corporate research in Asia, as senior management wanted to expand into the region. They had rarely ever been responsible for business information and sought a high level of train-ing in corporate research, so they could justify management's confidence in their ability to be an important part of the expansion. The work they did on the scientific side was highly confidential and the laboratories they worked alongside were very highly security protected. I often feel that the confidentiality aspect of the corporate librarian's work is missed as a really vital element in retaining the unit and should be highlighted in any decisions to close them. The business information they were charged to develop was also highly confidential and there was no question of outsourcing. All work had to be done in-house by permanent staff.

Here is a very good example of survival and not being phased by being required to switch to a new type of information work. Perhaps it was precisely because none of the corporate library's staff were qualified information professionals that they saw no barrier to embracing the new challenge.

Amazingly, the predictions of Lewis's paper are still being actively discussed. What of the other type of special librarians, the academic librarians, especially the academic subject librarians (that can be most closely associated with corporate librarians in the type of work they do) that were included in the Doomsday Scenario? According to Graham Pryor on the DCC website blog (Pryor 2012), academic librarians have successfully reinvented themselves and have metamorphosed, managing to rise to all the challenges presented in the 21st century. Making an even broader statement that these librarians have always been able to transform themselves "across the centuries to meet cultural and technological change," he then refers to the Dennis Lewis paper and the predicted demise of the information professional by the year 2000. Far from disappearing, Pryor further describes the academic librarians as "these highly sustainable professionals [who] transformed themselves into digital and systems librarians, [and] learned how to teach information literacy to students of the digital age and they became the stalwarts of institutional repositories."

But even in these most rosy views on the future of academic librarians, Pryor admits that there is still much to be done and that the "Subject Librarians" (rather the digital and systems librarians) face a great challenge in supporting academic staff and need to redefine their role in the academic institution very quickly. Either that, he concludes, "or the Doomsday Sce-nario may yet just catch up."

REFERENCES

Lewis, D. E. "There Won't Be an Information Profession in 2000 AD." In *The Information Worker; Identity Image and Potential.* London: ASLIB, 1977.
Pryor, Graham. "Reskilling for Research—Observations on a RLUK Report." Digital Curation Centre (DCC) Blog. http://www.dcc.ac.uk/node/9351 (accessed July 25, 2012).

6

ALTERNATE SOURCING: A CRITICAL COMPONENT OF YOUR SURVIVAL TOOLKIT

JAMES M. MATARAZZO AND TOBY PEARLSTEIN

By rigorously evaluating the advantages and disadvantages of all information service activities in terms of "buying" rather than "making," library managers can take a leadership role and put themselves in a position to, if not control the decisions, at least not get caught by surprise.

RESEARCH BACKGROUND

In 1942, Harvard University's Graduate School of Business Administration, Bureau of Business Research published the case study "Make or Buy: A Consideration of the Problems Fundamental to a Decision Whether to Manufacture or Buy Materials, Accessory Equipment, Fabricating Parts, and Supplies." The study was written by James W. Culliton, a professor of business management at Boston College's School of Business Administration (Culliton 1942). Culliton's thesis was that "every economic entity, whether it be a family, a business, or a government, frequently must decide whether to make or to buy the things it needs" (Culliton 1942, 3).

At the time, Culliton noted that "despite the frequency with which make or buy alternatives arise in business, there is little in business literature to tell how businessmen make the choice, and there is even less dealing with the way in which businessmen should proceed when faced with the alternative of making or of buying" (Culliton 1942, 1). He called for the development of a more systematic procedure than simply listing the possible advantages or disadvantages for discovering whether, in a specific instance, making or buying could be expected to bring the greater advantages. Culliton recognized that labor problems, quality considerations, and potential savings were fundamental to this decision-making process and that the decision was actually quite complex, with multiple variations possible. Ultimately,

This chapter was adapted from an article that originally appeared in *Searcher Magazine*, Volume 17, Issue 8, Pages 32–39, September 2009.

though, the objective was to determine the "best source from which to obtain the materials and supplies needed in a business" (Culliton 1942, 5). More recently, this objective has been characterized as capability sourcing, the "process of gaining access to best-in-class capabilities for all activities in a company's value chain to ensure long-term competitive advantage (Armacost 2005). Today, more than 67 years after Culliton's groundbreaking work, the make-or-buy decision that he found so fundamental to any business and so in need of a systematic process remains a challenge to many organizations around the globe. In his survey of British business information managers, for example, Foster (2008, 1) reported that "off-shoring information and research work has not expanded significantly, but more companies are considering this option." For those firms that do outsource, he found the trend is to use this to "build some contingent capacity" (Foster 2008, 20). Off-shoring, on the other hand, is described as a much more radical strategy in that it transfers work to another country. Approximately 20 percent of those surveyed had an off-shoring presence. Some firms, especially investment banks, were pleased with their off-shoring operations, while others, especially large legal firms and management consultancies, were less comfortable with it. However, Foster concluded, one thing was very clear: Whether research was outsourced or off-shored, the process was driven by senior management and not by the corporate information manager. Four reports from the British legal field indicate that outsourcing and off-shoring have been at the forefront for some time. All agree that the banking industry has led the way on this matter, driven by financial pressures to lower costs. Law firms also feel pressure from their clients to lower costs. At one conference, Colley reported a speaker who stated: "Process driven intellectual work is not sustainable from expensive locations" (Colley 2008, 55). Another speaker at this same conference claimed that information professionals who perform basic research will disappear in the United Kingdom in three to four years. Diggle (2008, 115–17) claims that outsourcing a whole range of functions is inevitable. He maintains that the savings and benefits will become clear as time moves on. If you understand all of this and if you consider all the risks, as an information manager, you can think more strategically. Fahy (2008, 104–9) is convinced that outsourcing the management of information in the legal profession is here to stay. She suggests that information managers see this as an opportunity to increase the value of the remaining in-house staff while providing an outline for successful outsourcing. Worley (2008, 109–14) on the other hand, describes the outsourcing process in the context of knowledge management (KM). She maintains the legal profession is risk-adverse and, as a result, has been slow to embrace outsourcing. However, she speculates about the potential and the issues involved in any outsourcing of KM. In their report of the results of interviews with 11 libraries, Goody and Hall (2007, 36–42) confirm that asking the right questions is critical. These interviews provide a wealth of actual experience with outsourcing. The authors recommend several questions that anyone who is considering alternate sourcing should ask. For example: What are the benefits and risks? Is outsourcing good for everyone? What will happen to the traditional careers of information professionals if research is outsourced to a greater extent? How do you handle any diminished quality of service for those who use the outsourced resources? Goody and Hall also note the large amount of time necessary to manage any third-party operation. Failure to adequately understand the time needed to get a third-party operation up and running is a key theme repeated in almost all the outsourcing literature. Discussion of outsourcing beyond the United States is not unique to the United Kingdom. Van der Ligta (2007, 132–34), for instance, discusses the outsourcing to Bangalore, India, of a portion of a patent search department in the Netherlands. His step-by-step how-to article concludes that, with proper management, outsourcing can be both successful and cost-effective.

So regardless of whether you are an information manager, and certainly if you are in a professional services, financial services, or legal organization, the make-or-buy decision manifests itself in the question of whether or not to outsource, alternate source, in-source, in-shore, or off-shore some or all of your work processes. For purposes of this chapter, this myriad of "buy" alternatives is referred to as outsourcing or capability sourcing.

CONTEXT

Remember the predictive model we discussed previously. When some or all of the model's conditions exist, library reductions and/or closures (or outsourcing) are usually not far behind.

- Decisions made at the top, without consultation of those who use the services
- Reduction in the number of customers
- Availability of outside resources
- Lack of evaluation of library service
- Evidence of financial crisis in the parent organization

These elements are interrelated. Obviously, if your parent organization is experiencing a financial crisis, there is increased likelihood that ways to operate more cost-effectively will dominate management thinking (strategic or otherwise). Getting out ahead of "crisis thinking," being a thought leader, and using your normal services evaluation process (and anyone who does not have such a process in place is encouraged to get one fast), shows that you too are looking for ways to "help the bottom line." Using alternative resources (among other tools) may well contribute to your survival. Unquestionably, "outsourcing" became a mantra for information services in the late 20th century and remains so today. This is not surprising. Any information professional in the past 50 years would be hard-pressed to find a public, academic, or special library that has not outsourced one or another of its activities on a regular basis. How else would you characterize the common library services you now "buy" from someone else: interlibrary loan, cataloging, serials subscription services, book jobbers and publisher approval plans, and head hunters, to mention a few? Yet we seem to have minimized, if not totally ignored, the contribution that these decisions have made to our organizations. Information services (IS) professionals have consistently led when it comes to finding more effective, efficient, and usually less-costly ways to provide the services employers need. Your experience in this is a competitive advantage as special librarians vie for resources within their organizations. Likewise, this experience positions them to provide strategic and operational input to any make-or-buy decisions under consideration, both inside information services and throughout our host organizations. Perhaps the scope of today's make-or-buy decision and its consequences are more complex (and often much less obvious) than in the post–World War II period of Culliton's study. If so, one could argue that these decisions need to be put in more of a strategic context for our organizations than ever before. Further complicating what should otherwise be a dispassionate evaluation is the more recent trend of "shoot from the hip" decisions to close entire in-house IS operations all together (thereby *de facto* outsourcing them to Google) or jump on the India (or China or Philippines or Idaho . . .)

bandwagon and search for someone else, anyone else, to do the job as long as he or she can do it cheaper. How the "job" is defined and what constitutes "cheaper" are the very elements of the make-or-buy decision process that we can contribute to, but often it is these elements that special librarians, as information professionals, have the least influence over. To examine a typical professional services firm as an example of the context in which a corporate library manager would use the make-or-buy evaluation as soon as the manager has sensed that the elements of the predictive model have become apparent within the organization, the authors have created the fictitious Wells Incentive Capital (WIC). Even though WIC is set up as a for-profit services firm, many key takeaways from how the make-or-buy challenge is handled can readily be extrapolated to academic, public, and other types of special libraries.

THE CASE OF WIC

Here is the background about WIC. WIC is a global professional services firm head-quartered in Houston, Texas, and has historically served energy and related industries. WIC currently employs roughly 7,000 people worldwide. The firm's IS have grown along with its analyst staff and client base, and today, 50 professional researchers support its global invest-ment teams from four research centers located in Houston (HQ), London, Singapore, and Dubai. Within any 24-hour period, a WIC analyst can interact with a researcher in whatever information centers are open. WIC's "follow the sun" IS model has worked well and has continued to perform responsively as, over time, the firm's energy-related practices have di-versified to cover disparate industries. Integral to WIC's success is its remaining nimble and responsive as a firm in order to win and service clients. WIC professional researchers have also done whatever it takes to repurpose their skills and expertise as macro changes in the firm have occurred. IS customer evaluations have consistently been high, and IS has always been viewed globally as a contributor to the firm's success. Recently, however, WICs fortunes have taken a dramatic downturn. For the past year, the firm has aggressively sought ways to work more efficiently (i.e., cut costs), including reducing its analyst recruiting targets, rethinking previously liberal travel and training policies, exploring new markets for its ser-vices, and generally thinking about how to do more with less in order to keep the firm viable and positioned for the economy's resurgence. Everyone's been talking about first-time ever layoffs and the possibility of closing or consolidating some of the offices outside of the United States with small client bases. WIC's IS manager, Thatcher Greenstreet, is responsible for all the company's research professionals and negotiates for and is the content manager of all da-tabase and other contractual relationships IS undertakes. Since he first stepped into this role seven years ago, Greenstreet has prided himself on being in tune with what's happening in the firm. He regularly has coffee with one of the senior partners and encourages his researchers to be very proactive in keeping in touch with the analysts they support. He also keeps up with the library and business literature and knows well that alternative sourcing and outsourcing in particular has become something of a panacea to many for reducing costs without substan-tially affecting services. In fact, WIC's corporate finance department has recently undertaken a regional "in-shoring" pilot to test if consolidation of certain common tasks now handled by each office on its own could be removed to a lower-cost U.S. location, thereby accomplishing the tasks more cost effectively and with reduced head counts. Greenstreet has already had several conversations with the Controller, sharing lessons learned from the IS literature and his network of Special Libraries Association colleagues that relate to issues around training, quality control, churn, and other very real challenges faced in this version of the make-or-buy decision. He knows what he's been learning from the Controller's experience will come in handy in the not-too-distant future. Because of the ubiquity of the talk of alternative sourcing at WIC, Greenstreet has been preparing for the inevitable when he too will have to answer the question, "Why not outsource?" Greenstreet is pragmatic enough to know that no one in the firm is immune to cost cutting. He remembers the worry he heard in the senior partner's conversational tone when they last met. He has been thinking of how his department might be impacted and what he can do to help the firm (and his team) remain competitive. He knows he must be courageous and move quickly to more aggressively evaluate all the services WIC IS offers, not only to better identify those to which his team adds the most value (those WIC IS should continue to "make"), but also to identify those of less value that could either be stopped outright or "bought" less expensively/more efficiently from an alternative source. Moreover, in order to prepare himself and his team for the tough times ahead, Greenstreet has taken on the role of devil's advocate and begun evaluating his department's operations through the eyes of firm management, trying to understand management's perspective, rather than simply assuming that his team's past success will guarantee its future within the organization. Greenstreet has determined he must do three things relatively quickly. First, he must review and further document those aspects of his budget and processes for which he has already taken action to contain costs by "buying" services from a third-party provider, rather than increasing his overhead or headcount. Some lessons he's learned he can share with other departments. These include using a subscription service to consolidate ordering, billing, and claiming of journal subscriptions; turning over some common research tasks directly to analysts by contracting for basic databases at their desktops; reducing the real estate his various research hubs occupy by limiting print collections; and using third-party document delivery services to obtain materials on demand. Second, Greenstreet knows he needs to further capitalize on his previous alternate sourcing experience. Just as he had to decide whether or not to have a professional researcher or a third party manage all the subscriptions, or whether to use document delivery services rather than attempting to buy everything an analyst requested to support client work, he now can use the same evaluative processes when considering some of the research-related and other IS technical services tasks. To do so, he must determine if these tasks remain necessary in their current form, and if so, whether the tasks can be accomplished more economically. Greenstreet knows that head count will be a prime focus of the cost reduction efforts. He is sure management will ask why, if the analysts have databases and the Internet at their desktops, WIC still needs 50 researchers in four different locations. Likewise, he realizes that management rarely sees a distinction between what analysts can find on their own and what professional researchers can find for them. He knows trying to convince management otherwise at this stage will be counterproductive and simply look like a desperate effort to save IS. Rather, he decides to take the laborious (and sometimes painful) step of taking his usual monthly macro-service evaluation to the next level and review what each of his researchers is doing at a micro level to seek out any obvious opportunities for savings in time or dollars. Further complicating the decision, particularly relating to the use of third-party contractors for certain types of research, are the overarching considerations of confidentiality and the handling of proprietary information. This has most recently been widely discussed with respect to outsourcing work that is related to medical records; it also has specific concern for the types of professional services firms mentioned above: legal, patent, and investment. When deciding to make or buy, any organization must squarely face the challenge of how to protect its intellectual capital in a third-party situation that could well involve competitors using the same contractor's services; churn of employees who, having left your contractor, are no longer bound by confidentiality agreements; loss of control over mission-critical client data; and so forth. In addition to quality control, confidentiality and control of intellectual capital are critical decision factors in the make-or-buy decision process.

WHAT WIC INFORMATION SERVICES ACTUALLY DOES AND GREENSTREET'S NEXT STEPS

In his review Greenstreet finds that of the 50 researchers, 35 handle more than 80 percent of the research requests submitted. Spot-checking the topics of the requests, he also learns that roughly 20 percent of these could have been done by the analysts themselves. The other 15 researchers, several of them very senior, do a combination of tasks beyond typical research, including some requests that analysts should do for themselves (after all, the firm has been committed to a significant investment in desktop resources for several years); "special projects," during which the researcher is excused from taking requests for significant periods of time; developing training materials and conducting training classes for end users; supporting the WIC Intranet; and a variety of technical services and back-office tasks, such as checking and paying invoices, cataloging, and so forth. When WIC was doing well during the past several years, it always seemed that the researchers were "fully booked." In fact, capacity was often scarce, with many researchers routinely working a 50-hour week despite the "follow-the-sun" model. And, in light of the fact that WIC IS typically recovers about 70 percent of its costs from client charge-backs (the other 30 percent being a mix of client development costs that do not convert to billings once a client is sold and other non-billable activities), a macro monthly evaluation has sufficed to keep management informed of IS activity and to support budget requests. Greenstreet has, however, always collected a variety of monthly metrics from his global team, much of which, to date, have not be used. Recently, though, he has increasingly seen what he knows will become a red flag for management. At any given time, at least 15 well-paid researchers are "busy" but not doing "billable" work in support of the firm's revenue generation. He knows management will not see that most of the tasks these 15 do are non-research activities necessary to keep WIC IS running effectively and support the firm's ability to use information fully. Or so he had always thought.

Greenstreet decides to rank these non-billable tasks and find out how to accomplish them more economically. After doing so, he must face the hard question of whether or not the size of his professional research team is "must have" or "nice to have," especially given the economic realities and the firm's commitment to and investment in end-user desktop research. Thinking strategically about head count, his goal is to strike a balance between the following:

- Research that only professional researchers can do
- Research that analysts can do on their own
- Research and tasks that can be "bought" outside of WIC IS
- Tasks that do not need to be done at all

In taking these three actions, further documenting and sharing what he has already done to contain costs, reviewing each of his department's processes in terms of a make-or-buy decision, and rigorously analyzing what each of his team members does on a daily basis and tying each one to the firm's bottom line, Greenstreet will challenge WIC IS to demonstrate to management how his team will contribute to the firm's ongoing viability.

As he goes back to the library and general business literature, some of which we have discussed above, for guidance on the topic of alternate sourcing and its applicability to his needs, Greenstreet focuses on reviewing all the "watch outs" experienced by IS professionals who have chosen to "buy" one or more services. He finds some certainties and a lot of "wait and sees." Given the immediacy with which WIC could be making decisions about its operations, his thinking and actions must be simultaneously strategic and operational if he is to exercise credible thought leadership. Only then can he create a successful path forward for WIC IS.

ALTERNATE SOURCING: IF YES, THEN WHAT, WHEN, WHERE, AND HOW?

First, and most importantly, Greenstreet defines the parameters of his make-or-buy evaluation in the WIC context. Based on his experience, readings, and discussions with colleagues, he sees two possibilities for alternate sourcing that could present opportunities for WIC IS to push its strategic thinking to the next level:

- Outsourcing or hiring non-WIC employees to perform certain tasks
- Off-shoring (or in-shoring) by "hiring" WIC employees in "lower-cost" locations to perform certain tasks

He knows, however, that it is not as simple as choosing neither option (i.e., determining that there is no benefit in "buying" more than what there already is), one option only, or a combination of both. Whatever his choice, it will have significant implications. Pearlstein (2005) outlined four typical goals of the decision to make or buy:

- Cost reduction
- Supplementary capacity
- Increased service quality
- Increased expertise

In 2005, alternate sourcing was a hot topic. For IS professionals, it was clearly a situation of accepting the reality that host organizations were avidly pursuing it, learning about it, and being prepared to discuss and possibly implement it or becoming marginalized. Around the same time, Outsell (Strouse 2005, 7) found off-shoring by information mangers still in its infancy, with those who did buy services finding the choice a "huge time-sink to manage the relationship," low satisfaction with the work of off shore agencies, and verdicts of "too early to tell" if it brought any real savings.

Although the goals had not changed, they were being expressed a bit differently, and by 2007, outsourcing was seen "as diverse as business itself," providing the following:

- Cost savings
- Access to capabilities (human talent, process excellence, sheer physical resources)
- Strategic benefit ("freeing up one's own resources," improving flexibility, etc.)

Outsourcing as a general business practice was considered a "major competitive advantage" by the 226 customers and 66 vendors PricewaterhouseCoopers (2007, 2–3) interviewed. By 2008, in the face of an increasingly precipitous economic downturn, corporate executives were counseled to take an even more strategic approach and to "realize that cutting jobs in [IT, finance, human resources, and other back office functions] was not a sustainable approach, unless the underlying work activity is also redesigned or eliminated." Decision makers were urged to "adopt a structured approach to evaluate and implement suitable alternate service delivery strategies" (PricewaterhouseCoopers 2008, 2).

Our man Greenstreet will want to measure each of WIC IS's tasks and services through the lens of how well-accepted alternate sourcing has generally become in business in order to determine if any of them are a suitable candidate for the "buy" decision. A few important conditions must also be present for "buy" rather than "make" decisions.

- "Scalability" (defined as having enough work for the alternate source to make the investment worthwhile)
- Compelling cost savings (defined over time rather than just at start up) including the following:
  - Cost of shifting designated tasks to a lower-cost location
  - Additional training as needed
  - Ongoing management and quality control of new processes
  - Need to later re-create any experienced researcher positions if some are cut now as a result of the "buy" process
  - Acceptable level and quality of services
  - Ability to find qualified specialists in an alternate source location
  - Cost of access to needed sources
  - Fit of alternate source with WICs culture and business model (Pearlstein 2005)

It is generally accepted in the recent literature of outsourcing that "cost reduction" should never be the sole factor driving the "buy" decision. It is simply too difficult to accurately predict upfront costs and cost savings over time; and as outsourcing achieves one of its theoretical goals, namely to raise up the work force in emerging markets, pricing differentials, while still present, are rapidly diminishing.

Overall, in the context of WICs new circumstances in the marketplace and in light of his review of all of the research and other tasks his team is handling in their four locations, Greenstreet has the opportunity to propose some far-reaching changes that could totally recast how IS can contribute to WICs resurgence. By conducting an unfettered analysis, that is, by considering all possible solutions, no matter how uncomfortable, Greenstreet and his team can make some hard decisions about what is "adequate" versus what is "ideal" in terms of the level of support WIC analysts require from professional researchers and from where that support is provided. Only after this full analysis will he be able to present the most effective case to management should the decision be to utilize one or a combination of the alternate sourcing tools. No question that, under the right conditions, the "buy" decision can be of great benefit and can potentially reveal or create opportunities and flexibility for both the organization as a whole and IS in particular.

KEY TAKEAWAYS

- Be prepared to participate in any "make-or-buy" decision processes in your organization, not just in your own department
- Be smart on the subject and share your knowledge with others
- Conduct regular audits of your IS functions
  - Pressure-test against a "make-or-buy" decision
  - Identify which, if any, might be ripe for alternate sourcing
- Reinforce your alignment with your host organization's business goals
- Have or put processes in place to minimize need for new head count
- Network proven alternate source relationships
- Load-share across your existing team as needed
- Position yourself to drive the decisions related to your department, especially those related to make or buy.

REFERENCES

Armacost, Robert. Bain & Company, Inc. "Capability Sourcing Overview." Presentation delivered at SLA Annual Conference, Toronto, 2005.

Colley, Annabel, "Courage under Fire: The Impact of Outsourcing." *Library and Information Update* 7 (2008): 55.

Culliton, James W. *Make or Buy. A Consideration of the Problems Fundamental to a Decision Whether to Manufacture or Buy Materials, Accessory Equipment, Fabricating Parts, and Supplies.* Boston: Harvard University Graduate School of Business Administration, Bureau of Business Research, 1942.

Diggle, Jack, "Outsourcing Information Management—Why, Where and How?" *Legal Information Management* 81, no. 2 (2008): 115–17.

Fahy, Sarah, "Outsourcing Know-How in Law Firms—Strategies for Success." *Legal Information Management* 8, no. 2 (2008): 104–9.

Foster, Alan, "Business Information Survey." *Business Information Review* 25 (2008): 1, 20.

Goody, Melanie, and Hazel Hall, "Better Out Than In?" *Business Information Review* 24 (2007): 36–42.

Pearlstein, Toby, "Alternative Sourcing: Decision Making Process and IS Client Service Model at Bain." Presentation delivered at Special Libraries Association Conference Toronto, Canada, 2005.

PricewaterhouseCoopers International Ltd. *Outsourcing Comes of Age: The Rise of Collaborative Partnering.* 2007: 2–3.

PricewaterhouseCoopers International Ltd. *Confidence in the Face of Turmoil: Making Sourcing Decisions in an Economic Downturn.* 2008: 2.

Strouse, Roger. "Information Management Best Practices: Navigating Outsourcing and Offshoring," *Briefing*. Vol. 8 of *Information about Information Briefing*, 7. Outsell, Inc., 2005.

Van der Ligta, Gerard, "Establishing a Search Department in Bangalore, India." *World Patent Information* 30 (2007): 132–34.

Worley, Loyita, "Examining the Long-Term Impact of Outsourcing Know-How." *Legal Information Management* 8, no. 2 (2008): 109–14.

7

RESUSCITATED: THE EPA LIBRARIES' NEAR-DEATH EXPERIENCE

JAMES M. MATARAZZO
AND TOBY PEARLSTEIN

In February 2006, the U.S. Environmental Protection Agency (EPA), facing its preliminary 2007 fiscal year budget, announced a series of library closures intended to save the agency money. The Bush administration's proposed FY 07 budget for EPA regional libraries was $500,000, an 80 percent reduction from the previous year's $2.5 million funding (this funding applied to just 10 of the 28 EPA libraries). The agency's reaction, to move for immediate closures and reductions in service, was considered by many within and outside the agency (to give it the most kindly characterization) as precipitous. After all, the budget had yet to go through the congressional approval process that could have provided oversight for how to implement such a significant reduction. Many believed the congressional process would also have offered an opportunity to make a case for restoring some of the funding. What ensued was more than two years of advocacy and intervention by agency employees and their unions, information industry associations, and congressional committees aimed at forestalling or reversing these closures in the interest of two critical constituencies: the public with its need for access to government information supporting public health and environmental issues and EPA's own employees needing to perform their jobs efficiently, effectively, and therefore at less cost. In October 2008, even presidential candidate Barack Obama entered the fray. In a letter to the president of the American Federation of Government Employees, Obama shared his views on "inadequate funding for the EPA" and stated, "I strongly oppose attempts . . . to eliminate the agency's library system" (Obama 2008).

Thanks to the tireless and sometimes very public efforts of the stakeholders, more than a little success has been achieved in restoring access to critical materials and services, but challenges remain. For example, a recent series of articles in the *Milwaukee Journal Sentinel* on the dangers of toxic chemicals in day-to-day products present to the public health and a similarly themed Government Accountability Office (GAO) report focused on the EPA's failure to gather even basic information (Rust and Kissinger 2008). Both pieces attribute this failure to

This chapter was adapted from the article that originally appeared in *Searcher Magazine*, Volume 17, Issue 5, Pages 12–15, 47, 2009.

weaknesses in the agency's chemicals management and risk assessment programs. The GAO report specifically notes "the EPA lacks adequate scientific information on the toxicity of chemicals that may be found in the environment—as well as on thousands of chemicals used commercially in the United States. . . ." (U.S. GAO 2009). It might not be surprising to find out, then, that the EPA's Office of Pollution Prevention and Toxics (OPPT) Chemical Library is "non-existent," with "its staff, collection, and services placed in the main EPA Headquarters Library" or dispersed to other libraries in the agency during the process of closing and then re-opening the EPA Libraries in 2007 (Stoss 2009). Fortunately, in a March 2008 report to Congress, the EPA stated that the Chemical Library—among others—would be reopened, which it was in late Fall 2008 (EPA National Library Network 2008).

Those interested in a detailed chronology of the "EPA Library Affair" to date, as well as links to background documents, should go to the update compiled by the Special Libraries Association (SLA) Public Policy staff at http://www.sla.org/con tent/SLA/advocacy/EPA/epaupdate.cfm and the American Library Association's compilation of related materials at http://www.ala.org/ala/aboutala/offices/wo/woissues/governmentinfo/fedlibs/epalibraries/epalibraries.cfm.

THE STRUGGLE TO QUANTIFY THE LIBRARY CONTRIBUTION

The pressure to reduce budgets is constant. In the EPA's case, as early as 2003, budget pressure took the form of requiring that the libraries present to management "a business case" for their existence. However, the resulting report only extrapolated the costs and benefits of maintaining libraries at each EPA regional facility. Part of the challenges the EPA libraries faced in quantifying their value consisted of how they were, and continue to be, administered. Beginning in the early 1980s, as with services in many other federal agencies, the EPA libraries were privatized; the provision of services in the regional libraries was contracted out to nonfederal employees. Furthermore, each region was allowed to develop its own contract specifications and budgets. So the size of staffs, services provided, purchase decisions, and costs were within the purview of each region; only rather recently were any agency-wide minimum standards set. While decentralization and contracting out for services are not in themselves negative activities, the way the EPA administered them seems to have exacerbated the context in which the closures and reductions were even harder to counteract.

As one former EPA employee told us, the regional libraries did not have specific budgets; they were funded from a pool of money distributed to the regional assistant directors for use at their discretion and, therefore, what the libraries actually cost was extremely difficult to calculate. Furthermore, no consistency existed across the regions in terms of purchasing, staffing, and even what services to support. For example, some regions supported the regional law library while others did not (Pearlstein 2009).

More than 20 years ago, in an attempt to quantify benefits, the EPA libraries conducted an analysis to calculate the "value of studies read" by their users as one possible metric to tangibly express the value of the libraries (Huffine 2005). The resulting dollar amount, they felt, could be pointed to in business terms as a contribution by the libraries to the agency's mission. The two value studies only represented a variety of attempts during the past three decades to establish benchmarks for the EPA libraries to use in understanding costs as well as the value being contributed. With each attempt, however, the variables studied were not comprehensive in terms of the five functions that the libraries themselves had put forth as key components of the service provided:

- Perform research and interpret results
- Distribute information and bibliographic resources
- Select and acquire information products (electronic and paper resources)
- Provide access to other information
- Manage and administer

While a cost–benefit approach is certainly relevant, the approach used here limited its focus to the "as is" state of the libraries, failing to address the critical questions of possible improvement through centralization of services or a closer alignment with the mission and goals of the agency. Perhaps a better approach would have taken the number of reference questions, searches, and resources supplied and estimated the number of hours of staff time saved in each of the libraries, correlating this with a cost per hour of the customer's time. The multiple could have led to "savings" in number of dollars with dollars aggregated as net benefit and divided by the cost, yielding a ratio. For example, for every dollar spent operating library services, $2 in benefit might be realized. This analysis could be done across all the libraries regardless of location, thereby creating a benchmark to serve as a standard for all to meet. Finally, in demonstrating any kind of contribution, one must include client valuations. How do the customers view the services? How have client needs changed? It is absolutely vital to answer these questions in order to build a more cost-effective, value-added service—the goal of any business case! While we know that the clients of the libraries were ultimately very vocal about the value of the services, the vociferousness of the input came after the reductions and closures. One wonders if such input had been collected regularly, whether the eventual course of events would have been different. A more significant issue in EPA's approaches to library valuation was the failure to determine what services contributed to the organization's ability to meet its mission. Limitations in the cost to benefit analyses were rooted in assessment of an "as is" nonstrategic setting. In our view, any business case evaluation must provide answers to the following questions:

- What is the current alignment of the information/library services to the present mission of the organization being served?
- How does this need to be changed, if at all, and what are the opportunity costs and benefits to adopting a more strategic focus and direction?

If you agree that your library could benefit from a better business case, please see some recent studies by Jacobson and Matarazzo (2001, 47–53) and Jacobson and Sparks (2001, 14–20) for a full description of how to conduct such a study. If you need a better sense of strategic focus and its benefits, please take note of a benchmark study of 25 information centers in the pharmaceutical and medical device industries. There, the author notes:

> As libraries transition from books to bytes, successful benchmark partners create a strong niche in their corporations through a process of identifying 'unique and critical' aspects of the business, determining where the information center can play a significant role, creating a mission around that role, and aligning library resources with the mission. (Best Practices LLC 2003)

Some have suggested that the closures and resulting employee, public, and information industry outcry may have caused an indirect benefit to the EPA libraries. Having struggled with what, in retrospect, seems a very dysfunctional organizational and budgetary structure, the agency's regional libraries—or at least those that closed and then reopened—are perhaps presented with an opportunity to become more creative and rethink how services are provided in an agency-wide context. No one would argue that the pain and disruption caused by the events at the EPA was good. Being able to see the opportunity offered by any reduction or even closure, though, may well mean the difference in long-term survival for any library or for any librarians.

In a *Library Journal* article, we recently called on library managers to provide leadership and "show the companies we work for that our services are essential" (Matarazzo and Pearlstein 2007, 42–43). On the other hand, a recently completed review of the literature relating to the management of corporate libraries notes an absence of research, either theoretical or pragmatic, on this subject in the United States (Matarazzo and Pearlstein 2008, 93–114). It is hard to know where to look for guidance in these uncertain times. Nonetheless, your survival is at stake and you must act now. Be a leader, prove value, or become a footnote in the history of libraries.

AFTERWORD

In February 2009, another example of a major library closure in the news industry occurred with the announcement that *The Wall Street Journal*'s news library would close in the spring (Strupp 2009). So the ongoing saga of the EPA libraries in many ways represents a bright spot in what seems otherwise to be a litany of service reductions and closures both in the public and private sector and across all types of libraries, public, academic, and special.

More to the point for our purposes, though, is what we can learn from the EPA experience and how we each can apply these lessons to our own environment. We see the key takeaways from the EPA experience as follows: Verify the realities of savings touted by those recommending reductions and/or closure. If possible, counter them with hard figures of your own about savings generated by maintaining services. State these savings unequivocally in terms directly relevant to your organization's bottom line (e.g., hours saved and monetary equivalents, business opportunities identified, clients won, etc.). Generate ongoing, focused advocacy (even protests) by users across all target groups crucial to describing your "relevancy" and your contribution. We stress here the value of "ongoing advocacy." Don't wait until after the door is locked to ask your users how valuable you were to their work product. Follow the model used by information industry associations such as American Library Association and Special Libraries Association in advising Congress. Supply a list of questions for your management to use in evaluating any closure/reduction recommendations. Put these questions in meaningful, relevant business—not library—terms. This can help get management to at least stop for a minute and think about consequences in a very directed way.

Always have one or more potential strategies in place (regularly refreshed based on changing circumstances) so you have a clear vision and plan describing your role in the organization's success. Think in terms of "minimum," "adequate," and "ideal" and their related ramifications to accommodate any obvious compromises. Know in advance the arguments you might likely face and be prepared to respond. Keep usage statistics, such as the elusive term "value," in context. Create one relevant to your organization and understandable to nonlibrary users. Use benchmarks from your competitors to differentiate the contribution you make. Watch out for clear dangers. For example, EPA was criticized for lack of communication, having no strategy in place either pre- or post-reorganization, and for lack of centralized leadership and oversight in carrying out plans. Review successful past efforts to enhance efficiencies, respond to business changes, and continue alignment with business needs and goals. Be ready to cite specifics of where the library has contributed. Finally, face the political realities. Even if you are not in a public organization, politics remains a reality you must address and may well explain what is happening to you. Certainly politics and self-interest typically play roles in the positions advocated by various stakeholders. In the case of the EPA libraries, it is likely that many of the decisions made were a direct result of the politics of President George W. Bush and his appointees. The unions had their own bargaining positions that impacted how quickly plans to reopen the libraries could be pursued. Even the information professional associations had a stake in taking full advantage of this opportunity to visibly act as advocates for their memberships.

One of the most important lessons to learn from the EPA experience is to make sure you understand who all the players are in your organization, who your champions are, and how to use informal as well as formal channels to make sure the benefits of your services are made known on an ongoing basis (Davenport et al. 1992).

In the past, most often in difficult economic times, one frequently heard about special library closures or reductions. Recently, however, the pace of these cutbacks seems to be increasing, fueled by the erratic economy and unprecedented corporate bankruptcies, mergers and acquisitions, and, sometimes in the case of government agency libraries, by calls for reduction in the cost and complexity of government itself. The EPA "library affair" explores a near-death experience and subsequent resuscitation in a government agency. These life-threatening challenges are faced by other segments of the special library community, including financial services, publishing, and healthcare. We hope to help you better understand whether, in the current environment, the cutbacks or even deaths of libraries result from organizational homicide or some form of suicide. The corollary question also arises as to whether organizations ordering cutbacks or closures have plans for meeting their information needs going forward that include the skill set of information professionals, even if it does not include what we traditionally define as a "library." In other words, do these organizations realize they need librarians even if they don't need a library?

AFTERWORD: EPA LIBRARIES IN 2009

The EPA National Library Network consists of three repository libraries, 10 regional libraries, five specialty libraries, and nine research laboratory libraries. Three of these regional libraries, Region 5 (Chicago), Region 6 (Dallas), and Region 7 (Kansas City), had closed due to the budget cutbacks and some, if not all their collections, were disbursed. The headquarters library in Washington and the Chemical Library had also closed. As of January 2009, the three regional libraries reopened and are well into reestablishing their collections and services. The Headquarters Library and the Chemical Library have been combined and also reopened, though some concern remains about the Chemical Library collection. The agency has promulgated new operational standards for the National Library Network where none had existed before; reporting lines have been more firmly established. For example, at a minimum, the regional and Headquarters libraries must be open at least four days per week on a walk-in basis or by appointment during core business hours. Questions remain about how quickly the agency will proceed with digitizing resources given budget and copyright issues. Nonetheless, during 2009, a much more robust strategic planning effort is underway by EPA's chief information officer that includes all stakeholders. The EPA libraries website (http://www.epa.gov/natlibra) is encouraging the public to provide input on current library services as well as on the future of the Library Network.

REFERENCES

Best Practices, LLC. "From Books to Bytes: Creating Effective Corporate Libraries m the Digital Age." (2003), http://www3.best-m-class.corn/bestp/dornrep.nsf/Content/6C4BFAACF239 AD2D85256DDA0056B53E!Open Document (accessed March 3, 2009)

Davenport, Thomas H., Robert G. Eccles, and Laurence Prusak. "Information Politics." *Sloan Management Review* 34, no. 1 (1992): 53.

EPA National Library Network. *Report to Congress* (2008): 3–4.

Huffine, Richard. "Making the Business Case for Information Services." Paper presented at Special Libraries Association Conference, Toronto, Canada, June 6, 2005.

Jacobson, Alvin L., and James M. Matarazzo. "Corporate Bunker or Cyber Café. Rethinking the Strategic Role of the Library in the Corporation—A Case Study." *An Information Odyssey.* Papers presented at the SLA Annual Conference, San Antonio and published by Special Libraries Association (2001): 47–53.

Jacobson, Alvin L., and Joanne I. Sparks. "Creating Value: Building the Strategy Focused Library." *Information Outlook* 5, no. 9 (2001): 14–20.

Matarazzo, James M., and Toby Pearlstein. "Corporate Score." *Library Journal* 132, no. 2 (2007): 42–43.

Matarazzo, James M., and Toby Pearlstein. "A Review of Research Related to Management in Corporate Libraries." *Advances in Librananship* 31 (2008): 93–114.

Obama, Barack. *Letter to John Gage.* National President American Federation of Government Employees, AFL-CIO, October 20, 2008.

Pearlstein, Toby. Personal Conversation, March 2, 2009.

Rust, Susanne, and Meg Kissinger. "Chemical Fallout: A Journal Sentinel Watchdog Report." *JSOnline, Milwaukee Journal Sentinel* (2008), http://www.JSOnline.com/watchdog/ 34405049.html (accessed March 3, 2009).

Stoss, Frederick W. Email, to the *Newslib* Mailing List newslib@hstserv. unc.edu, Subject: "GAO: EPA Lacks Information to Evaluate Chemical Risks; Jackson Promises Reform" (2009): January 27, 9:41 a.m.

Strupp, Joe. "Wall Street Journal Librarian Laments Shutdown." Editor & Publisher, February 11, 2009, http://www.editorandpublisher.corn/eandp/news/article_display.jsp?vnu_content_ id=1003940607 (accessed March 2, 2009).

U.S. Government Accountability Office. "EPA Needs to Ensure That Best Practices and Procedures Are Followed When Making Further Changes to Its Library Network," *Report to Congressional Requesters, Environmental Protection* (2008): GAO-08-304, http://oversight.house.gov/docurnents/20080313092521.pdf (accessed March 3, 2009).

AFTERWORD REDUX

EPA LIBRARIES AT 40—LOOKING TOWARD A BRIGHT FUTURE

Deborah Balsamo,
National Program Manager,
EPA National Library Network

For the U.S. Environmental Protection Agency (EPA) National Library Network, turning 40 in 2011 was an extraordinary milestone to be celebrated. Continuing the positive strides of recent years, EPA's libraries commemorated this milestone in unprecedented ways. The Network invested in its future by publishing a strategic plan, enhancing service offerings, upholding its mission of providing information services to EPA staff and the public, and extending access to Agency information. EPA's libraries garnered additional attention by being named Federal Library of the Year for its many recent accomplishments by the Federal Library and Information Center Committee (FLICC) at the Library of Congress.

While much has been written about the past, current evidence indicates that EPA's libraries are very much alive and thriving. The Library Network is composed of libraries and repositories across the Agency, all of which are accessible to the public and have onsite professional staff. A Library Network policy and accompanying procedures, issued by EPA's Chief Information Officer, establishes baseline standards and brings consistency to library services at all locations. The procedures enable collaborative Network efforts and establish formal methods for collecting and reporting service data and customer feedback to inform decision making.

Over the past six years, Network libraries have contributed to projects and enhanced services for both the public and staff. EPA's libraries continue to facilitate digitization efforts by evaluating and providing Agency publications from their collections. EPA's digital repository of Agency publications has grown to over 55,000 documents freely available to the public via the Internet, ensuring future access to environmental information.

New services implemented for EPA staff provide virtual access to the libraries and extend the reach of librarian expertise. The Network's live chat reference service—*Ask a Librarian: Real Help, Real Fast!*—was launched in 2009 and pools coast-to-coast service desk hours of library staff to offer live chat to employees during extended hours. In 2010, the Network developed a National Training Program to expand access to library training opportunities for EPA staff and further leverage the expertise of the librarians across the Agency. This award-winning training program, recognized by EPA's chief information officer for innovative efforts, offers locally developed library classes to an agency-wide audience via remote instruction technologies. Feedback on both services confirms that EPA libraries are responding to user needs in effective ways.

Building on positive momentum, in 2011 the Library Network developed and published a three-year strategic plan that sets the foundation for the future and provides library customers with a picture of where the Network is going. The *EPA National Library Network Strategic Plan FY 2012–2014* offers a roadmap for building a robust network of libraries to serve the information needs of EPA staff and the public. Through its implementation, the Agency expects to improve library services, manage collections effectively, help ensure ongoing and consistent funding for the libraries, and make sure EPA staff is informed about the availability of services.

While a lot of focus has been on changes to enhance and strengthen EPA's Library Network, the all-important task of communication remains constant to help ensure long-term viability into the future. The Network seizes every opportunity to engage with and inform all stakeholders, from library users to EPA senior management, as well as outside interested parties. The Library Network ensures that communication channels are operating in every direction and that the message of the value the libraries bring to the Agency is loud and clear.

While EPA's libraries are vibrant and strong today, are the worries over? No. Do we still have concerns about the future? Like all libraries, always! But one thing is certain—EPA libraries are stronger and more resilient than ever. The Network makes sure people know what the libraries can do to help them work smarter. And with a collaborative nature and a strategic roadmap, EPA libraries know where they are going and have a plan to get there.

8

EDUCATING SPECIAL LIBRARIANS: "THE PAST IS PROLOGUE"

JAMES M. MATARAZZO
AND TOBY PEARLSTEIN

A "special library" is not an entity; it exists as an integral part of a highly special-ized kind of organization whether it be an industrial corporation, research, or service institution, a trade association, a government agency or a museum. Since it exists to serve the members of that organization, it is necessary to provide in the training pro-gram an orientation to the structure, functions and activities of the varying types of organizations.

—Ruth S. Leonard (1950, 157)

Addressing survival lessons for special libraries brings up more questions than answers. What we have learned is that there is no one "right way" to be successful as an information professional in a corporate or other type of special library. Frankly, though, it was pretty straightforward to come up with several wrong ways that make being successful even more of a challenge. Arriving at the right ways to succeed and thereby ensure survival is more difficult. Nonetheless, we do firmly believe there is one generic formula that makes success more likely, strategic alignment with your parent organization or potential employer. How you go about "doing the math" depends totally on figuring out how to achieve that align-ment. It might be useful to "peel back the onion," and look at the roots of how someone who wants to be an information professional in a special library would achieve that goal. This led us to review some of our initial questions about the likelihood of special library or librar-ian survival in the context of library education, basically going back to the source of how information professionals learn about the profession and how to pursue it specifically when working in a specialized environment (corporate, medical, government, legal, etc.). Here is where we might find the root cause of many of the obstacles to success with which special libraries and the information professionals who work in them struggle. This discussion about

This chapter is adapted from an article that originally appeared in *Searcher Magazine*, Volume 19, Issue 2, Pages 30–39, March 2011.

library education refers to graduate level library or information programs accredited by the American Library Association (ALA) and resulting in a master's degree or the myriad similar degrees related to information management currently being offered (ALA 2010).

DEJA VU ALL OVER AGAIN (WITH APOLOGIES TO YOGI BERRA)

Writing in the journal *Special Libraries* in 1910, John Cotton Dana had already realized the challenge faced by the profession in formulating a definition of a special library. He characterized an early definition, "the library of the modern man of affairs," as not sufficiently inclusive. Even his beloved Modern Businessmen's Branch in the Newark Public Library, though it had proved itself of great value as a "useful tool for business firms of all kinds in the city," was still considered "far from being a typical special library of men of affairs" (Hanson 1991e, 53). Dana found there was already such a variety of special collection of books, reports, and other printed materials that no definition could satisfactorily include them all. He predicted an even wider and more rapid development of all kinds of special libraries.

By 1914, when the number of special libraries had grown, Dana described the driving force behind this growth:

> One can only say that managers of scientific, engineering, manufacturing, managerial, commercial, financial, insurance, advertising, social and other organizations, including states, cities, government commissions and the like, are . . . coming every day in increasing numbers to the obvious conclusion, that it pays to employ an expert who shall be able, when equipped with proper apparatus, to give them from day to day news of the latest movements in their respective fields. (Hanson 1991d, 62)

From the special librarians' perspectives, the role of providing "day to day news of the latest movements in their respective fields" is simply another way of recognizing the value of special librarians who are aligned with their employer's mission. By 1919 Dana was being even more explicit:

> [The special library] contains all the useful things in all aspects of the organization which maintains it, and can obviously contribute to that organization's success; and it contains much, very much, that can help the men behind the organization–the "workingmen." . . . His library does not only tell the owners of the enterprise, for which it exists, how to prosper, it tells the same to those who labor for the owners. It is . . . an informative, thought-provoking, habit-disturbing, ambition-arousing library [which is] eagerly sought and used by all the men and women on the organization's job. (Hanson 1991c, 66)

By 1929, Dana could enumerate more than 1,000 special business libraries in the United States alone and the existence of a British Association of Special Libraries and Information Bureaux. In his opinion, this increase was driven by three factors: the explosion of business literature, the increases in communication and transportation facilitating the exchange of information, and the "increased interest in the professional development of workers [i.e., librarians] in the field" (Hanson 1991a, 67).

What of this "professional development of workers in the field"? As early as 1893, the Denver Public Library noted, "It is believed that a year in an active library would prove to many, more valuable than a year in the best of colleges for women" (Hanson 1991b, 97).

Chauvinistic sentiment notwithstanding, we see even this early in the profession, the sense by an employer that hands-on work in a library might well provide a more valuable education for the aspiring professional than a year of college courses. Throughout Dana's writings, his expression of the value of the librarian as someone who is able to characterize and categorize a rapidly growing body of printed information, knowledgeable about his or her clientele and whose role is defined as someone who connects that clientele to a vast array of available information recurs.

Fast-forward to 1950. The May–June issue of *Special Libraries* featured two articles that directly addressed the challenges faced by special librarians during and since Dana's time: How to be educated to be a special librarian and how the role of a special librarian *vis-à-vis* his or her employer should be defined.

Ruth Leonard (1950), writing about education for special librarianship, identified three prevailing views of how one could become a special librarian. The first thesis was that special librarianship could not or need not be taught; training could only be acquired properly through experience. Others, she wrote, believed that intensive academic preparation in subject fields (e.g., law, chemistry, music, etc.) plus a general library education would be adequate. Finally, there were those who "see in special librarianship a distinctive relationship to business, industry or the professions which requires 'special' content and method in the training program" (Leonard 1950, 157).

Leonard found few library science (LS) programs of the day prepared to train their students for a career in a special library. She noted the lack of textbooks on special library administration and "very little organized literature on the characteristics and philosophy of special librarianship" (Leonard 1950, 157). She felt that few schools offered courses devoted to organization and administration so that students could be specifically trained in the variety of administrative and professional operations that librarians of industrial corporations, nonprofit associations and institutions, and government agencies must know. She contrasted this overall situation with the master's program that had been on offer at the School of Library Science at Simmons College since 1940. The uniqueness of the Simmons' approach was that it offered a program (graduate program in special librarianship), not simply an elective course, in special libraries. Fully one-half of the required 40 semester hours were devoted to courses carefully integrated to make a balanced preparation for special library positions.

The other critical components of Simmons' training of special librarians at the time was a two-week period each spring devoted to specialized experience in the field, provided through the cooperation of special libraries in the Boston area, and a requirement that any students who did not already have professional experience in a special library undertake a "six week in-service training in a well-organized and capably administered library. There, students would be given sound experience under the guidance of a qualified special librarian." Students were also able to take eight semester hours of graduate courses in their respective fields to strengthen their subject preparation.

One of the most prescient points Leonard makes, though, is one we feel still holds true today. "Successful development of special library education," she wrote, "is also impeded by the fact that the library educator and the special librarian continue in their failure to understand each other" (Leonard 1950, 157). The training and experience of library educators was "general" compounded by little contact with special libraries, while the special librarians often failed to see beyond their own organization and had little in common with the experience of the library educators.

Writing in the same issue of *Special Libraries* as Leonard, Samuel Sass described the challenge facing special librarians being asked to undertake tasks that he felt were beyond their
training and, moreover, beyond what he saw as their appropriate role in the organization
(Sass 1950, 160). Sass saw the role of the special librarian as a bibliographer, someone who
knew the sources of information within a specific industry. He felt strongly that it was not
the role of the librarian to abstract or synthesize or translate or in any way be an expert in
the field (of the organization). While the special library might house those whose task it was
to translate materials or to synthesize information and this would be a good thing for the
visibility of the library, these individuals would not be librarians who had enough to handle
doing their own jobs.

Almost 50 years after the founding of the Special Libraries Association (SLA), Sass wrote
about the value and role the special librarian could play within a business organization. Yet
these two major issues—how to educate someone for working in a special library, and the appropriate role of the special librarian within an organization—remained the object of much
discussion and no resolution.

Almost 50 years later, Marion Paris (1999, 12) would take up these questions again, illus-
trating at least to some, that these issues remain the core of discussions around the survival
of special libraries and the information professionals who work in them.

WHAT IS THE GOAL OF GRADUATE EDUCATION IN LIBRARY SCIENCE?

Plainly stated, the hypothesis of the authors is that if you want to be an information professional in a specialized environment (e.g., medical, legal, government, museum, records
or knowledge management, competitive intelligence) rather than in a public, school, or undergraduate academic library, or a scholar of library and information science, most master
of library science (MLS) programs provide little or at best inadequate preparation. Graduates, therefore, especially in times of economic downturn, are left with a significant gap in
relevant marketable skills that prospective employers in specialized organizations will find
compelling.

To place this in context, an analysis of for-profit positions advertised in New England
between 1997 and 2009 (Matarazzo and Pearlstein 2010, 12–14) illustrated how the use of
data gathered over time can provide insights into the viability of pursuing a career in special libraries. The study demonstrated a significant downward trend in the number of jobs
advertised across a variety of organization types. While this represents only one geographic
area, it does show the value of gathering such data on a wider basis to better inform the
development of library school curricula, as well as offering a way for potential information
professionals to determine how to focus their MLS studies to make the most of opportunities for employment. Once again, organizations such as SLA, which are uniquely positioned
to collect this kind of data on behalf of their membership, are urged to do so in a systematic
and ongoing way.

With only a couple of exceptions, most MLS programs focus on the core LS skills. When
anything like a "track" is offered whereby students could customize their learning or training, it typically focuses on school library media center certification preparation, which is
regulated very specifically by the state in which the individual wants to work. Preparation
for any other kind of information-related employment is almost always left to students and

their advisors to cobble together a program of courses that address a specific environment. A student must hope that enough courses will be taught related to this specialty during the course of their matriculation to constitute preparation sufficient to make them attractive to a prospective employer. The Simmons program outlined by Ruth Leonard in 1950 does no longer exist nor have other MLS programs replicated it.

Nothing may be wrong with generic programs when specialized employers are flush with training funds and have sufficient experienced professionals to act as mentors to entry-level professionals, many of whom have never even had the opportunity to take a special libraries class. Furthermore, many special libraries have just one professional staff member with no one available to train the new librarian. If someone's goal in getting a graduate degree in LS is to be prepared to enter the job market as a specialized librarian, with even the basic knowledge and skill set relevant to an employer, he or she will need to find one with patience and a deep pocket for further training. Such opportunities are few and far between even in the best economic times. Graduate LS programs are simply not offering enough in the way of special library tracks aligned with employment placement opportunities. Again, this presumes that either the school's placement office or relevant professional associations are on top of where these employment opportunities currently exist or will most likely develop. Without a concerted effort by the graduate institutions at data gathering and analysis for purposes of guiding curriculum and student preparation, graduates will find themselves at a disadvantage in a shrinking job market. This also presumes that library school curriculum committees and faculty overall can be nimble enough to respond to the changing economic environment by offering courses aligned with what employers want.

This situation of fewer jobs and limited preparation is exacerbated when the client population being served has an increasingly sophisticated information literacy level so that an information professional must be prepared to add value beyond the basics almost immediately upon being employed. This is nearly impossible, even with a subject specialty bachelor's or master's degree, unless relevant specialized courses have been taken during the MLS program.

VALUE OF COMPETENCIES DOCUMENTS IN THE EDUCATION OF LIBRARIANS

Some of the most helpful guidance a prospective special librarian can receive to define what skills they will need to succeed in a specialized library environment comes in the form of "competencies documents" developed by various information professional groups. Associations such as SLA (2003), AALL (American Association of Law Libraries 2010), MLA (Medical Library Association 2007), SCIP (Strategic and Competitive Intelligence Professionals 2013), and specialized sections of ALA (2009) have published such documents in order to provide guidance for individuals as well as library school curriculum committees.

Focusing on library school closings in her 1999 article "Beyond Competencies: A Trendspotter's Guide to Library Education," Paris writes that these various competencies documents "illustrate efforts to codify and to promulgate commonly accepted professional standards." She goes on to observe that the last time (prior to 1999) competencies saw the limelight was in the late 1970s and early 1980s, coinciding with the first wave of library school closings when practitioners' confidence in education programs declined. Paris then asks a very forward-thinking question. "If we live to experience this phenomenon a third time, will it indicate a trend"? (Paris 1999, 33).

We would argue that we are currently experiencing this phenomenon a third time, perhaps not totally related to library school closings, but certainly in relation to the scarcity of jobs available to library school graduates and perhaps also in relation to the value practitioners put on LS education programs.

Paris also discusses the development of the ALA Accreditation Program and how it was ultimately determined that, to be accredited, all professional programs would grant master's degrees following completion of 36 credit hours. She writes, "It was assumed, at least in theory that any new graduate could qualify for an entry-level position, with the possible exceptions of school librarians and advanced technical information specialists." Underlying this assumption is the ongoing troubling notion, raised by Paris in 1999 and still relevant today, that:

> thirty six credit hours, a crazy-quilt of courses taken based on little more than when they are available, [either in the program or when the student can find the time to take them], barely prepares students for their current jobs, much less for the future. (Paris 1999, 34)

Paris is writing for a special libraries' audience. One of her concerns is whether or not there will be enough LS graduates to fill the special library positions being vacated by retirements. While today this concern is likely mitigated by a shrinkage overall in numbers of special library jobs, the core concern still remains true: whether or not there will be enough graduates who "understand the value system unique to special librarianship" (and correspondingly who know that working in a special library is quite different from public or academic service) who will be qualified to fill those jobs that do remain (Paris 1999, 36). What are we to expect, Paris asks, if, in fact, in some LS programs students' only exposure to special librarianship is through the generous invitations, year after year, of SLA members or their occasional lecture or class visit lasting an hour or less?

Paris's 1999 assessment holds true even today. With the exception of a few areas, most library school faculties have not embraced this concern about special librarianship and the requirements codified in these competency documents, nor have they used them as road maps for creating paths to survival for their graduates. Furthermore, we would argue that the associations, once these documents have been created, seem to act as if their job is done and, whether for lack of resources or interest, make little or no effort to push library schools to act on incorporating them or the spirit behind them into their curricula in very specific ways.

OTHER ISSUES OF CONCERN: STUDENTS

In 1995, Bosseau and Martin (1995, 198–99) wrote about the unusual and delayed route that most librarians took on their way to a career in the field. In their experience (and ours as well), it was reasonable to conclude that in general the profession needed to recruit and attract exceptional people right out of college. Martin and Bosseau wanted the bright, energetic, recent graduates who appeared to be headed to law school, medicine, and other seemingly interesting professions to become librarians. Well, 15 or so years later, this wish appears to have come true. At most library schools today, students are younger by and large. Whether they have selected this field because of high interest or due to the lack of jobs in other fields remains to be seen.

When the average age of a student in MLS programs was 35, many of those late bloomers had substantial experience at preprofessional positions within libraries. Others had worked as professionals in other fields. For those older and experienced new entrants to the profession, the "world of work" was familiar. And, to repeat, those without library experience could "learn the ropes" from a whole host of veterans on staff.

These new students have no work experience. While young and bright, they are entering a field they know little about. Most complete their MLS degrees with little time for internships or practicums. If they are lucky enough to find positions, the staff they join will have been reduced and the mentoring that might have been available in the past has now disappeared, as those veterans who remain are unwilling or simply unable to make up for the staff that left and were not replaced. The call for the young and brightest that Bosseau and Martin touted went out when staffing was at a high point and the long-term consequences for these students and their employability (at least in specialized libraries) was given little thought.

OTHER ISSUES OF CONCERN: FACULTY

On the other hand, library schools that have vacancies for faculty are receiving lots of applications. But this new group of applicants who will teach is very different from those from 15 years ago or even 5 years ago. These applicants are students who went from undergraduate work directly to master's programs. Library and information science (LIS) faculties, always eager to spot the best and the brightest, have talked these newly minted master's degree recipients into PhD programs.

These new and soon to be completed PhDs want to teach. As applicants for teaching vacancies, they well outnumber other applicants who have been (or want to continue to be) practitioners. This creates yet another problem in the search for the best and the brightest to join our profession.

LIS faculty and those in practice have not had a close relationship in the past. Remember Leonard's 1950 statement that "the library educator and the special librarian continue in their failure to understand each other" (Leonard 1950, 157). The demands at most universities are for research, publication, and receiving grants. Nonetheless, for those who belong to ALISE (Association for Library and Information Science Education) or ALA, faculty and practitioners at least meet on committees and at other conference events. In the past, teaching faculty had work experience which most certainly enriched the classroom, at least for public, academic, and school library classes.

Special librarians and teaching faculty rarely had this close and continuing relationship. In fact, at SLA conferences and in the past few years in *Information Outlook*, the SLA journal, LIS faculty presence is rare. This lack of interaction presents a terrible problem for those interested in a career in specialized libraries, including for-profit corporate libraries. Consider this: fewer programs offer classes in special libraries. A few schools offer a single class in special libraries, but practitioners with full-time jobs teach many of these classes. These part-time faculties appear for class and do a good job, but, while this offers at least some interaction with the real world of special libraries, after class they go back to work and the students are left with no one on faculty with even an interest in these areas. In some cases, the special library class is taught by a faculty member who has been "asked" to teach the class when no practitioner was available. With the instructor having no real knowledge of the area and no textbook to use, the class is at a real disadvantage.

In an effort to reverse the trend of second and third career students from "accidentally" finding LIS, Bosseau and Martin had put out a call to make LIS a first choice. As we have shown, even great ideas thoughtfully presented can have unintended consequences. Sure, the trend of the 35-year-old student starting a program of study has been reversed for the time being, but this has led to other issues that must be addressed. A much more dynamic integration of the various competency documents into library school curricula and with a continually reinforced understanding of the value of aligning with an employer's vision and mission incorporated into coursework, our profession can reinforce the value special librarians can contribute across all sectors, especially in for-profit organizations, and can create a more pragmatic path to employment for MLS graduates. These ideas may well be too blue sky for the realities of today's library school budgets and employer appetites for hiring special librarians. Regardless of the prognostications of some, however, the authors do not believe that special librarians, particularly in profit-based organizations, are headed for terminal irrelevance. With that baseline in mind, more discussion resulting in concrete actions around these topics could finally lead to making some progress before another 100 years pass by.

REFERENCES

AALL. "Competencies of Law Librarianship." Chicago: American Association of Law Libraries. 2010. http://www.aallnet.org/main-menu/Leadership-Governance/policies/PublicPolicies/competencies.html (accessed January 25, 3013).

ALA. "Core Competencies." Chicago: American Library Association. 2009. http://www.ala.org/educationcareers/careers/corecomp (accessed January 25, 2013)

Bosseau, Don L., and Susan K. Martin. "The Accidental Profession." *Journal of Academic Librarianship* 21, no. 3 (1995): 198–99.

Hanson, Carl A. (ed). "Libraries as Business Research Centers." In *Librarian at Large. Selected Writings of John Cotton Dana*, 67. Washington, D.C.: Special Libraries Association, 1991a.

Hanson, Carl A. (ed). "Library Pupils." In *Librarian at Large. Selected Writings of John Cotton Dana*, 97. Washington, D.C.: Special Libraries Association, 1991b.

Hanson, Carl A. (ed). "The Business Man and the Special Library." In *Librarian at Large. Selected Writings of John Cotton Dana*, 66. Washington, D.C.: Special Libraries Association, 1991c.

Hanson, Carl A. (ed). "The Evolution of the Special Library." In *Librarian at Large. Selected Writings of John Cotton Dana*, 62. Washington, D.C.: Special Libraries Association, 1991d.

Hanson, Carl A. (ed). "The President's Opening Remarks." In *Librarian at Large. Selected Writings of John Cotton Dana*, 53. Washington, D.C.: Special Libraries Association, 1991e.

Leonard, Ruth S. "Education for Special Librarianship." *Special Libraries* 41, no. 5 (May–June 1950): 157.

Matarazzo, James, and Toby Pearlstein. "Survival Lessons for Libraries: A Microcosm Points to Broader Implications – Positions Advertised in For-Profit Libraries in New England 2006–2009." *Searcher* 18, no. 10 (December 2010): 12–14.

MLA. "Competencies for Lifelong Learning and Professional Success: The Education Program of the Medical Library Association." Chicago: Medical Library Association. 2008. http://www.mlanet.org/education/policy/success.html (accessed January 25, 2013).

Paris, Marion. "Beyond Competencies: A Trendspotter's Guide to Library Education." *Information Outlook* 3, no. 12 (December 1999): 31–36.

Sass, Samuel. "A Realistic Approach to Special Librarianship." *Special Libraries* 41, no. 5 (May–June 1950): 160.

SCIP, "SCIP CIP™ Conferred by ACI Competitive Intelligence Professional Certification Program." Falls Church, VA: Strategic and Competitive Intelligence Professionals. 2013. http://www.scip.org/content.cfm?itemnumber=13117&navItemNumber=13122 (accessed January 25, 2013).

SLA, "Competencies for Information Professionals of the 21st Century." Alexandria, VA: Special Libraries Association. Revised edition June 2003. http://www.sla.org/content/learn/members/competencies/index.cfm (accessed January 25, 2013).

9

EDUCATING SPECIAL LIBRARIANS: IN SEARCH OF A MODEL

JAMES M. MATARAZZO AND TOBY PEARLSTEIN

With only a couple of exceptions, archives for example, most master of library science (MLS) programs focus on the core library science skills. When anything like a "track" is offered for students to customize their learning or training, it typically focuses on school library media center certification, the preparation for which is regulated very specifically by the (U.S.) state in which the individual wants to work. Preparation for most other kinds of information-related employment is almost always left to the students and their advisors to cobble together a program of courses that address a specific environment. Such students must hope that enough courses will be taught related to this specialty during the course of their matriculation to constitute sufficient preparation to make them attractive to prospective employers. The type of program outlined by Ruth S. Leonard (1950) more than 60 years ago and discussed in the previous chapter no longer exists. Nor have other MLS programs replicated it.

As stated in the previous chapter, nothing is wrong with generic programs when specialized employers are flush with training funds and have sufficient experienced professionals to act as mentors to entry-level professionals, many of whom have never even had the opportunity to take a special libraries class. Add to this that many special libraries have just one professional staff member with no one available to train a new librarian. If graduates have a goal in getting a graduate degree in library and information science (LIS) to be prepared to enter the job market as a specialized librarian with even a basic knowledge and skill set relevant to an employer, they will need to find employers with patience and a deep pocket for further training. Such opportunities are few and far between even in the best economic times. Our graduate LIS programs are simply not offering enough in the way of special library tracks aligned with employment placement opportunities. This presumes that either a school's placement office or relevant professional associations are on top of where these

The chapter is adapted from an article that originally appeared in *Searcher Magazine*, Volume 19, Issue 8, Pages 32–41, October 2011.

employment opportunities exist currently or are most likely to develop. Without a concerted effort at data gathering and analysis for the purposes of guiding curriculum and student preparation, graduates will find themselves at a disadvantage in a shrinking job market. This also presumes that LIS curriculum committees and faculty overall can be nimble enough to respond to the changing economic environment by offering courses aligned with what employers want. This situation of fewer jobs and limited preparation is exacerbated when the client population being served has an increasingly sophisticated information literacy level. An information professional today must be prepared to add value beyond the basics and add it visibly almost immediately upon becoming employed. This is nearly impossible, even with a subject specialty bachelor's or master's degree, unless relevant specialized courses have been taken during the MLS program.

As far back as 1999, Paris noted that the specialized literatures were mutating and multiplying at an ever-accelerating pace (Paris 1999, 31–36). And this was at the dawn of the Internet (and the attendant information access explosion) as an everyday tool in all library environments and even more so in specialized libraries. Continuing education (CE) is, of course, one critical avenue for addressing the ever more rapid changes in information sources and the analysis required to vet and deploy them. The various professional associations are all doing an excellent job on the CE front. Realistically, though, one needs to have a job to support CE both in terms of cost and time involved. It is a tall order to ask someone who has just completed a master's degree over one or more years, and likely gone into debt while doing it, to take yet more courses just to get a foot in the door of a special library. Would it not be more practical and pragmatic to provide a learning track including hands-on experience to prepare the student prior to graduation? One idea for a model of education for special librarianship in the for-profit sector would include the right training, starting early in a graduate LIS program (or even with significant outreach to high school seniors and college undergraduates). One could develop MLS and related programs that align with what employers want from information professionals even as special librarians continue to educate these employers about the value of their skill set.

A much more dynamic integration of the various competency documents described in the previous chapter into library school curricula; and with a continually reinforced understanding and commitment to aligning with the visions and missions of employers, LIS schools could provide the coursework required. The LIS profession can reinforce the value that special librarians can contribute across all sectors, especially in for-profit organizations, while creating a more pragmatic path to employment for MLS graduates. These ideas may well be too blue-sky for the realities of today's library school budgets and too rosy in judging employer appetites for hiring special librarians. Regardless of the prognostications of some, though, special librarians, particularly in profit-based organizations, are not headed for terminal irrelevance. The authors talked with a number of information professionals to try to get a well-rounded idea of what skills and experiences employers, recent MLS grads, mid-career professionals, academics, and so forth, would like to either have had when they were in school or would like their potential employees to have. (Editors' note: A list of interviewees appears at the end of this chapter.) With these conversations and other research in mind, more discussion would result in concrete actions around these topics; and this could finally lead to making some progress on a potential model for educating information professionals for the special library market.

ONE POSSIBLE MODEL: MEDICAL OR HEALTH SCIENCES LIBRARIANSHIP

One of the few exceptions to this lack of opportunity to specialize in a typical MLS program is the area of medical or health sciences librarianship. It is here that a model can be found for MLS programs to provide more specialized education and training, leading to more job placements. A substantial body of literature exists about education for medical or health science librarianship. It is obvious that those in practice as well as those who teach care about educational opportunities for the next generation of medical library professionals and act on those beliefs. Detlefsen and Galvin (1986, 148–53) found that only 10 faculty members who had medical librarianship in the American Library Association (ALA)-accredited programs were full time. These two authors reasoned that the full-time educators would "have a vested interest in, and assume responsibilities for, developing and shaping full-time curriculum." With 58 accredited MLS programs in March 2010, Detlefsen found that 43 percent of these had full-time faculty with identified specializations in medical librarianship (Detlefsen 2010, 15–16) In 12 of the remaining programs, part-time faculty taught a course, and in 15, no courses in medical librarianship appeared to be offered; five other programs listed at least one course but no instructors. What is clear, however, is that several programs have fully developed curricula for medical librarianship. Among these are programs at Pittsburgh (Detlefsen et al. 1996, 524–33) and the University of North Carolina (Marshall 2000, 17–18). Much of the literature on medical librarianship appears in the *Journal of the Medical Library Association* (formerly the *Bulletin of the Medical Library Association*). Our secondary hypothesis is that the model being used in medical librarianship bears further examination and may be an ideal one for the education of information professionals hoping to work in specialized environments. This model can be summarized in four segments, each of these is presented in more depth vis-à-vis special libraries.

- Specialized full-time faculty
- Fully developed targeted curricula
- A community of practice that seeks to improve the preparation of future medical librarians (i.e., keeping the "pipeline to professionalism" open)
- An association that supports these groups

Specialized Full-Time Faculty

If the past is any indication of LIS faculty investment for training special librarians, it demonstrates that LIS faculty members have not had a close and continuing relationship with the special library community. Tees (1989) documented a most distant relationship as measured by involvement with Special Library Association (SLA) (Tees 1989, 297–304). Very few faculty members held office in the association at any level, spoke at an annual conference, or published in *Special Libraries*, SLA's peer-reviewed journal at the time. In 2009, SLA authorized the creation of an Academic Division that welcomes "anyone working in or with an interest in college, university, or other higher education-affiliated libraries and information centers." It is geared to those working in academic libraries rather than faculty teaching in LIS and related programs (SLA *Wiki* 2011). Some faculty may have joined, but it would seem that the situation Tees described has not improved and, indeed, may have worsened. Several LIS programs offer a special library or corporate library class. But most of these are taught on a sporadic basis, making it difficult for students to plan a program of study in these areas. Furthermore, part-time faculties who typically work at full-time jobs in business or academe teach most of the courses. This limits their time for advising students interested in a career in these specialized areas. At present, the situation is even more challenging. Staffing levels at most corporate and special libraries have been reduced, thereby creating more work for those who remain and, given the amount of time and effort required to plan and teach a full semester class, it has become more difficult to attract interested special library practitioners to teach these courses. Many LIS programs are also experiencing budget cuts, resulting in cutbacks that are invariably aimed at part-time positions. This just compounds the program's inability to offer a consistent menu of special-library-related courses. Thus, a dedicated member of the LIS program faculty, with interest and involvement in specialized libraries, becomes even more of a necessity if an LIS program is to address the needs of students wanting to pursue a career in this type of library. A full-time faculty member with special library experience, involvement, and expertise is necessary, if future members of the profession are to be adequately prepared for work in these libraries. This faculty member could develop and teach one or more courses with direct application to the field. In addition, the faculty member could champion additional courses so students who wish to specialize will have a progressive array of courses and practicums for this type of library, which, at an estimate, encompasses 20 percent of the LIS profession. In light of the past evidence of little involvement with the SLA and with very few chances to meet either at the local or national level with special librarians, most faculty align themselves with associations and practitioners in their own specializations (e.g., reference, cataloging, and archives). When no one on the faculty is interested in or a part of the activities of special librarians, there is no one to champion related curricula. So if the successful medical librarianship model were duplicated more broadly for special librarianship, one critical component would be a full-time faculty member who could push for and ensure a program that supplied adequate preparation for LIS professionals in specialized libraries, one designed around the realities and possibilities of practice. It is simply not adequate to rely on intermittent offerings of specialized courses based on the catch-as-catch-can availability of practitioners to teach them.

A Fully Developed Targeted Curriculum

With a full-time faculty advocate, students could be advised about appropriate electives depending on their area of interest within special libraries. Course offerings will only be expanded through the efforts of a faculty advocate. Similarly, a member of the faculty knowledgeable about the specialization can suggest and arrange internships or field placements.

Many LIS programs have eliminated "type of library" courses. The logic appears to be that the programs are preparing information professionals to work in a variety of settings. As such, there is no need for these specialized courses. When MLS alums who were also employers were interviewed, they discussed both their own degree programs and those of recent graduates. They were very candid in commenting on significant gaps in their preparation to work in special libraries. While they do value a general set of core skills, they noted the absence of courses on such topics as budgeting for special libraries, the organizational structure of corporations, in-depth subject searching, and so forth. A senior knowledgeable faculty member can champion such courses as critical, correcting the misperception that the courses are either not required or that potential employers can be relied upon to fill in the gaps. All schools cannot be all things to all students. However, an example of how MLS programs can creatively deal with the challenge of more consistent offerings for special library courses can be seen in the Web based Information Science Education (WISE) (www.wiseeducation.org) consortium. A number of schools are members of WISE. While this type of resource sharing does have some challenges related to revenue sharing, it does allow member schools to offer specific courses not offered or infrequently offered to their students (Wise Education 2011).

One theme that ran through many of our interviews was the suggestion that cross-disciplinary courses (such as with an MBA or JD program) would be an ideal way to supplement business or subject-related courses. Some programs already offer such opportunities, and these are proven ways to enable MLS students to acquire the necessary skill set to become employment-ready for a special library situation. Such opportunities would be more vigorously explored with a full-time special libraries faculty champion.

Some of the individuals interviewed also noted that no special library survey course was offered and, indeed, that few mentions of special libraries were contained in their program of studies. This scenario will probably continue for two reasons. First, many who teach in the special libraries area have, or will soon be, retired. Second, few doctoral students and young LIS educators have special libraries experience or appear to have an interest in teaching in this area. If the future reflects the past, change is unlikely. As noted in the previous chapter, SLA published a list of core competencies with an eye toward helping LIS programs prepare students in this area. Copies of this excellent document were sent to all LIS programs and are likely posted at these schools on some bulletin board, along with the competency documents from other associations. SLA's competency document must be specifically integrated into the curriculum, however, not just posted in hopes that it will have an impact. LIS programs accredited by the ALA frequently map the program's objectives to particular courses to prove the curriculum supports these objectives. Thus, the procedure is familiar to all faculties. Both the core competencies document and the massive SLA-sponsored report published as part of the Association's Alignment Project provide a detailed map of curricular needs for special librarians, providing ample guidance for curriculum committees if they have the will and wherewithal to act (SLA Alignment Portal 2011).

One final note on curriculum. Special librarians, especially those in corporate libraries, are different from other types of librarians. These corporate librarians have to prove their value every day. Increasingly, other kinds of specialized librarians are being required to prove value if they wish to survive. Massive changes are happening in corporate libraries. Corporate librarians and their libraries are critically evaluated all the time. This close and continuing evaluation and the need to prove value every day are constants. This is the new reality, and the need for a curriculum that prepares entrants for these specializations is crucial.

A Community of Practice

The field needs a community of practice that seeks to improve the preparation of future special librarians. One of the most interesting components and elements of success of the model of education for medical librarianship is the commitment of those who are practitioners to keep the "pipeline to professionalism" open. When asked about the current preparation of MLS students for medical librarianship, Detlefsen felt that medical librarians seem to be the only specialty paying attention to the next generation (Detlefsen 2011). She noted that the industry (i.e., current practitioners and users) is driving the need for new ways to educate medical librarians, specifically the importance of students being able to participate in a "real world setting." [Note that SLA, for example., has launched its "First Five" initiative aimed at professionals in their first five years of being in the field. This is a laudable attempt but by its nature does not attempt to reach back into the MLS years.] (SLA *First Five Initiative* 2011)

When asked about whether or not new MLS graduates were "employment ready," virtually everyone interviewed expressed the need for graduates to have had some practical experience, either in the form of apprenticeships or internships. There was no question that such experiences were mutually beneficial. For the employer, this provided an opportunity to gauge the intern's potential in terms of both capability and organizational fit. For the interns, the experience was an opportunity to see if they really liked the specialized environment. (This was particularly pertinent to interns who were in an MLS program that did not offer a special libraries class and therefore had no knowledge or awareness of how such an environment differed from other types of libraries.) Internships also gave the graduates the possibility of being considered for a permanent position. Activities such as a "day on the job" where a student is hosted for a day and is briefly exposed to how a specific special library works within its organization, guest lectures from local special librarians, or visits to various types of special libraries are all well and good but do not provide anything more than a brief sampling of what it means to work in a special library. While these activities do at least provide some awareness of the special library environment, most special librarians interviewed recognized that graduates lacked even that level of awareness. Everyone (practitioners, academics, and association executives alike) agreed that the required internship for medical librarianship was essential to preparing an MLS student for work in a medical or health sciences library. The community of practice, local alumni, and others were committed to providing these opportunities.

As noted above, the same theme was heard from many practitioners, some of whom had graduated from LIS programs within the past two years and some more than 25 years ago. They felt that current graduates are simply not employment-ready. While this has much to do with faculty and curriculum, it also has to do with the absence of hands-on experience. Comments spanned a gamut from new graduates literally not knowing how to do online research to not knowing how to dress, make presentations, or generally conduct themselves as professionals. The gap between LIS faculty (many of whom have never been practitioners in any type of library, let alone a special library) and practitioners, the same gap that Ruth Leonard noted in 1950, still exists today. Most LIS programs address this gap through the use of adjunct professors. An adjunct professor is defined here as someone teaching a full semester or full credit course as distinct from a "guest lecturer," who participates in a few or only one class. This is an excellent way for the local community of practice to become involved in the LIS curriculum but does face many challenges, as discussed earlier. The reliance on adjunct instructors to provide not only a special libraries survey course, but also more specialized courses, such as legal bibliography, government documents, and business research to mention a few, is better than not offering these courses at all. However, while the community of practice can often provide the desired specialties, the frequency of offers to teach and the varying teaching capabilities of adjuncts make this an imperfect solution. Furthermore, several practitioners who have taught as adjuncts report that most schools have reduced payments for such courses to the point where the amount of work and effort to prepare and teach, amounts to a diminishing return, even among those whose commitment is high and who are willing to give a lot more than they get. Essentially, the community of practice may have practitioners willing to become involved in teaching, but often with LIS programs that are cutting resources for special libraries courses and related activities in favor of courses geared to public, school libraries, and technology. Only the last of which is supported by any evidence of the needs of potential special librarian employers. This disconnect between what LIS programs teach and what the community of practice needs will not keep the pipeline to professionalism open for various types of special libraries, with the possible exception of medical libraries.

An Association That Supports All of the Above

The Medical Library Association (MLA) is a vigorous member of the community of practice and not only subsumes what practitioners offer, but also goes beyond it to include additional support in the form of outreach to the LIS community. As with some other information professional associations, MLA is very active in supporting student groups on campus. While their overall membership is much smaller than SLA, MLA provides informational mailings (posters and such) to all LIS programs, supports career outreach activities via local chapters, and even works with some programs to sponsor career days at the high school level. Perhaps an even more important role played by MLA centers on credentialing. The Academy of Health Information Professionals is a documented program that involves a 360-degree career-development plan. According to Joanne Marshall, alumni distinguished professor at the School of Information and Library Science at the University of North Carolina-Chapel Hill, MLA members are typically "tuned into education." The membership is very "education-oriented" at the graduate level, and this focus in a fairly homogenous field makes what MLA can offer different from that of what other information professional associations seem able to do (Marshall 2010). The health sciences field tends to be very research-based, and this focus on evidence-based healthcare carries over to evidence-based research. This makes MLA very attractive to faculty and helps it mesh well with an academic environment. The availability of a peer-reviewed journal with very high standards (something no longer available in SLA) seals the deal. SLA must demand more attention for preparation of future practitioners, more than the posting of its documents on a bulletin board. Local chapters can also bring needs to the attention of programs in their geographic areas. SLA already provides a fine array of CE classes for its members at no cost via the Web. However, more emphasis is required on the programs for initial preparation in the more than 50 ALA-accredited programs, which provide the first professional degree.

CONCLUSION

As early as 1910, John Cotton Dana wrote about the unique quality of specialized libraries and the role librarians would play in supporting the business health of "scientific, engineering, manufacturing, managerial, commercial, financial, insurance, advertising, social and other organizations. . . ." (Hanson 1991, 53). The specialized librarian role he envisioned recognized the economic value provided by professionals aligned with their employer's mission. In 1950, almost 50 years after the founding of SLA, Ruth Leonard wrote about on-the-job experience as a critical component in the education of a specialized librarian and the importance of a relationship between LIS faculty and LIS practitioners in the real world. In the same issue of *Special Libraries*, Samuel Sass wrote about the importance of subject specialization and knowledge of the sources of information within a specific industry. The two major issues of how to educate someone for working in a special library and the appropriate role of the special librarian within an organization were, in 1950, still the object of much discussion and no resolution. More than 40 years later, in 1993, Tchobanoff and Price (1993, 249) writing in *Library Trends*, addressed the question of what industrial information service managers could expect of the information services (IS) educational process and further, how these managers could support that process. Much like Dana, Leonard, and Sass before them, Tchobanoff and Price recognized that there was a necessary connection between how information professionals were being educated and the roles that potential employers expected them to fill. In recognizing the gap between employer expectations and LIS curricula, they noted: "Library schools, as producers, need to be aware of consumer [i.e., industry] requirements and adjust curricula accordingly so as to produce graduates with competencies appropriate for the current job marketplace." In supporting the idea of the industry providing internships in support of practical experience, these authors were reinforcing the idea that the community of practice has a fundamental role to play in the process of creating competent special librarians. Writing in 2010 for an American Society of Information Science & Technology InfoPro Task Force, Deanna Morrow Hall echoed these same sentiments from the perspective of "The Corporation as a Stakeholder in Information Education" (Hall 2010, 43–50). She posed a series of questions around the umbrella issue of why some corporations have corporate libraries while others do not. In part, she asked:

- Can IS schools recruit, or produce, more students whose subject competencies match the core competencies of their potential corporate employers?
- Is there evidence of the need for an information professional who has more than bibliographic expertise?
- Can corporate top management be persuaded that it is in their corporation's own economic best interests to provide information professionals to manage information resources for their knowledge workers, and how can LIS graduates be better prepared to make this case?

Dana's value proposition for special librarians, the Leonard and Sass commentary, the concerns of Tchobanoff and Price, Hall's questions—all echo the same fundamental situation that we find still exists in 2011; the disconnect between the curriculum (or lack thereof) of LIS programs related to special librarianship and the needs of the employer community. SLA, American Association of Law Libraries, and other relevant associations should be encouraged to replicate the methodology outlined by Detlefsen and perform an information audit of all ALA-accredited schools to determine the extent to which courses are offered (and how often, at what times, and whether by full or part-time faculty) that enable a student to specialize in such areas as law and legal bibliography, museum and fine arts, business and finance, health and pharmaceuticals, and so forth. This audit might take the four-point model noted above and transform it into questions for presentation to each dean. The results of this audit would identify gaps in course content, faculty expertise, and course availability which, when filled, might well result in new employment opportunities for library science students. Unfortunately, all the literature surveyed here and in the last chapter has succeeded in producing little discussion and even less action. Hopefully those reading this book will generate greater discussion and, more importantly, action.

THE TIME IS NOW: CHANGE OR BECOME HISTORY!

The previous chapter posed the question, "What is the goal of graduate education in Library Science?" An initial hypothesis was that if you want to be an information professional in a specialized environment (e.g., medical, legal, government, museum, records or knowledge management, competitive intelligence) rather than in a public, school, or undergraduate academic library, or a scholar of LIS, most MLS programs provide little or inadequate preparation at best. Graduates, therefore, especially in times of a tightening job market, are left with a significant gap in relevant marketable skills that prospective employers in specialized organizations will find compelling.

CONTINUING EDUCATION

In the absence of more fully formed special libraries education within LIS programs, CE offers LIS students an opportunity to pick up additional exposure or at least to "put their toe in the water" of subjects not available to them in the formal curriculum. The WISE program discussed earlier is just one of the many options available. However, CE should not be seen as a surrogate for a fully formed MLS special libraries curriculum. As noted above, CE is one critical avenue for addressing the ever more rapid changes in information sources. CE is also a lifeline when information professionals are confronted with the need to take on new tasks and responsibilities for which they are not totally prepared. It can also be critical for information professionals seeking opportunities to survive in an alternative organization to their present employer or from that of a previous employer after a layoff or absence from the field for a period of time. Access to CE has been transformed during the past few years through the availability of online courses from myriad sources including formal MLS programs, professional associations, publishers, and vendors.

EDITORS' NOTE

Interviews were conducted with the following individuals: Joanne Gard Marshall (University of North Carolina-Chapel Hill), November 11, 2010; Kathleen Coombs and Carla Funk (Medical Library Association), November 9, 2010; Ellen Detlefsen (University of Pittsburgh), November 2010; Bill Fisher (San Jose State), March 31, 2011; Jill Strand (Maslon, Edelman, Borman, Brand LLP), April 19, 2011, July 27, 2011; Monica Ertel (Bain & Company, Inc.), April 2011; MaryAnn Cyr (3M), April 20, 2011; Ann Wolpert (MIT), April 25, 2011; Karen Bleakley (PWC Canada), July 27, 2011; Mary Lane (Lorillard Tobacco), July 27, 2011; Andrea Davis (Naval Post Graduate School), July 27, 2011; Miriam Drake (dean and director, libraries, Emerita, Georgia Tech, and former president, SLA), July 27, 2011; and Jim Tchobanoff (Information & Library Management Consultant). Conclusions and recommendations expressed here are those of the authors alone.

REFERENCES

Detlefsen, E. G. "A Snapshot of the Health of Medical Library Education and Recognition of Our Educator Colleagues." *Medical Library Association News* 50 (May 2010): 15–16.

Detlefsen, E.G., and T. J Galvin. "Education for Health Sciences/Biomedical Librarianship: Past, Present, Future." *Bulletin of the Medical Library Association* 74 (1986): 148–53.

Detlefsen, E.G., et al. "Transforming the Present–Discovering the Future: The University of Pittsburgh's NLM Grant on Educating the Training Health Science Librarians." *Bulletin of the Medical Library Association* 84, no. 9 (October 1996): 524–33.

Detlefsen, Ellen. Interview. 2011.

Hall, Deanna Morrow. "The Corporation as a Stakeholder in Information Education." *Bulletin of the American Society for Information Science and Technology* 36, no. 5 (2010): 43–50.

Hanson, Carl A. (ed). "The Evolution of the Special Library." In *Librarian at Large. Selected Writings of John Cotton Dana*, 53. Washington, D.C.: Special Libraries Association, 1991.

Leonard, Ruth S. "Education for Special Librarianship." *Special Libraries* 41, no. 5 (May–June 1950): 157.

Marshall, Joanne G. "Building Health Sciences Library Education in the 21st Century." *Health Libraries Review* 17 (2000): 17–18.

Marshall, Joanne G. Interview. November 11, 2010.

Paris, Marion. "Beyond Competencies: A Trendspotter's Guide to Library Education." *Information Outlook* (December 1999): 31–36.

SLA Alignment Portal. www.sla.org/content/learn/members/competencies/index.cfm and http://www.sla.org/content/SLA/alignment/portal/index.html. We would also recommend that readers and especially LIS faculty review the SLA Future Ready 365 Wiki at http://futureready365.sla.org (accessed January 25, 2013).

SLA. *First Five Initiative*, www.sla.org/content/membership/firstfive.cfm (accessed January 25, 2013).

SLA. *Wiki*, http://wiki.sla.org/display/SLAAD/Home (accessed August 8, 2011).

Tchobanoff, James B., and Price, Jack A. "Industrial Information Service Managers: Expectations of, and Support of, the Educational Process." *Library Trends* 42, no. 2 (Fall 1993): 249.

Tees, Miriam H. "Faculty Involvement in the Special Libraries Association." *Journal of Education for Library and Information Science* 29 (1989): 297–304.

Wise Education. http://wiseeducation.org (accessed January 25, 2013).

10

SCENARIO PLANNING AS PREVENTIVE MEDICINE

JAMES M. MATARAZZO AND TOBY PEARLSTEIN

THE CASE OF THE UNEXPECTED TAKEOVER

In a May 2009 *Financial Times* column, James E. Post noted, "The voice of change is ringing across the global economy (Post and Smith 2009). (The cartoon by Roger Beale appeared with that column.) Information professionals reading this chapter may not need Post's warning to explain the increasing number of corporate (and other) library cutbacks, disruptions, and closures. Sad experience teaches that, in times of economic disruption, libraries and the roles of information professionals in organizations come under incredible scrutiny; often totally disproportionate to their cost vis-à-vis their organization's operating budget and, conversely, almost always disproportionate to the value libraries and information professionals could contribute if retained and bolstered by their employers during these downturns. Post intended his article as a call to business schools to heed the advice of Rahm Emanuel, chief of staff to U.S. President Barack Obama, "to never waste a crisis." Nonetheless, the three suggestions Post goes on to make directly relate to the challenges facing information professionals in today's economy:

- Build scenarios for a post-crisis world
- Build for sustainability
- Promote new entrepreneurship

Scenario planning as a survival tool (which could easily incorporate the goal of sustainability and require some semblance of entrepreneurship) is suggested as a pragmatic way for managers of information services, looking into an uncertain future, to take advantage of the current crisis and create visions or, more specifically, a series of "plausible alternative futures,"

The chapter was adapted from an article that originally appeared in *Searcher Magazine*, Volume 17, Issue 10, Pages 26–30, November/December 2009.

© Roger Beale

to help forecast "what core competencies their organization needs to develop for survival and competitive advantage" (Hannabuss 2001, 168). One of the most telling points Post makes, and one that all information professionals are encouraged to internalize, is that "the management of risk has changed. Indeed, the mindset of risk versus reward is undergoing cataclysmic challenge." Envisioning new possible futures reminds us that "the future's not set. There's no fate but what we make for ourselves" (Connor 2009).

A myriad of circumstances currently affect libraries and information professionals in corporate environments. Takeovers (along with other types of mergers, acquisitions, and selloffs) usually have a profound effect on the parties' existing information services. Often this results in redundancy layoffs, closures, consolidations, and so forth. In the case discussed here, following staff reductions, albeit voluntary, and with a new parent organization and new clients, what resulted was an opportunity for the information services (IS) manager to envision a new future. No one questions the difficulty for any IS manager to take the time to participate in even a short exercise in scenario planning. However, such "preventive medicine" can immunize IS from misalignment within an organization and ensure health and sustainability. In many instances the literature on scenario planning in libraries overlaps with that on strategic planning. Since not all strategic planning involves the use of scenarios, you are encouraged to think of scenario planning as a different type of strategic tool, one that discourages trying to "map the future" in favor of an approach that recognizes the volatility of the future and seeks to answer the "What if . . . ?" question(s). By making this your mantra during scenario planning, you can begin to change your mental model and engage in a rigorous analysis of your underlying assumptions about the role you and your IS play within your organization. Giesecke describes this as "recognizing your built-in filters" and as a critical step in enabling yourself and your team to think and plan for flexibility (Giesecke 1998, x).

Simply stated, scenarios are stories about possible futures. They extrapolate from the present and challenge the conventional wisdom of the organization. Scenarios also arise from a thorough understanding of the key driving forces in an organization and thus require participation and ownership by all stakeholders. In the takeover case here, it appears that almost none of the elements of the predictive model that usually lead to severe reduction or closure applied. Users of the service were consulted, there was no reduction in customers, outside resources were available and being used, and ongoing evaluations did occur. While there was evidence of a financial crisis in the parent organization, no one imagined where it would lead. Surviving one near-death experience would send anyone in search of the right medicine to prevent a recurrence.

THE UNEXPECTED TAKEOVER

On her way home Friday evening, Jane closed her eyes and thought: "What a week! What a month! What a year!" She had put in 10 years with this firm, which was on everyone's list as "one of the best places to work." She was now the head of the information center (IC) and well respected both at the firm and within the profession. Over the years, she had grown her staff to a high of 20 and kept the center open more than 12 hours a day, 5 days a week to meet the needs of the business. Now, the staff was down to 13 and the hours drastically reduced. During this past year, as with many other companies across various industries, her firm faced unprecedented financial challenges. Jane had lost seven people in a relatively short period of time, including five of the very best researchers. The uncertainty of the times and the difficult financial picture at the firm during the past year had proved too much for them, and these good researchers had left for positions in what they felt were more stable situations. Jane thought, "I have 10 years with this company. If I leave, I have to start at or near the bottom again." She did not want that. Everyone at the company and in the field knew that while it was a great company to work for, given the firm's no-frills approach and reputation for operating very economically, all of the professional staff was underpaid relative to their competitors. Jane felt, though, that this could work to their advantage in this new financial climate. Of course, there had been signs that trouble was coming. Profits were down, and senior people had been leaving for a year before the unthinkable happened, something that no one dreamed possible. The doors were simply shut!

LOOKING BACK

Jane had spent a great deal of time each week justifying the cost of services she and her staff provided. It was hard but necessary to have to continuously prove their value. She had even outsourced some services, an activity motivated more by the demands of upper management looking to keep up with competitors and experimenting with this channel for augmenting services. The third-party provider setup involved a lot of extra work and careful management of expectations. Nonetheless, now her customers had access to some level of reference help 24 hours a day, 7 days a week. This had not been Jane's choice, and she anticipated that the outsourced service would not compare to the value her experienced research staff provided. On that Friday evening, she was just glad to be going home and looking forward to the weekend.

SURPRISE, SURPRISE

Monday morning Jane woke up to the news that her firm was effectively out of business and that her division had been sold! Did she have a job? Should she even report to work? She decided it was best to go in and at least see what was happening. Once at work, she met with her boss who informed her that the members of her division had convinced the new management team that she, her staff, and the library were essential for their work.

LOOKING FORWARD

With what seemed to be a new lease on life, Jane reflected, "If those seven team members had not left, they would still be in the information center." Despite a freeze on hiring, no one in her division had actually been laid off. "They were that good," she reasoned. So there was a high probability that the support of her customers would have helped retain the full staff. She still felt optimistic. She now had more evidence that her unit was highly valued, otherwise, why keep it as part of the takeover? Jane's thoughts turned to building on this value base to ensure that her new management had no reason to reconsider their decision.

WHAT IF . . . ?

Jane decided it was time to plan ahead, knowing that, in these uncertain times and now as part of a totally new organization, she would have to be both bold and creative. She also realized that to think productively about the future, she had to find an alternative to what had become the norm of decision making while in crisis management mode. Hannabuss (2001, 168) notes, "Faced with complexity and turbulence in their sector, many organizations are forced to look at the unthinkable (like being taken over, not surviving, restructuring, divesting a key product/service range, diversifying into unexpected product/service lines)." More pointedly, Giesecke and Hornick (1998, 19) warn, "Force fitting the future into a tunnel vision may set you up to be blindsided." Jane was not going to be blindsided again. She knew her plans for the years ahead had to include not only what "might be possible," but the unthinkable too. In committing to scenario planning as a way of envisioning the future of her role and the role of IS in her new parent organization, Jane began by thinking broadly and even fancifully about some of the abundant possibilities that might lie ahead. She thought, What if . . .

- the firm purchased another division or another company and dramatically increased the workload of her IC?
- the firm decided to sell part of her division and removed a large number of her current customers?
- the firm kept the IC staff, services, and collections, but moved it to a less-costly location—perhaps even out of state?
- after a period of time, the firm insisted that her customers do all their own research using desktop resources?
- the firm decided to expand the role of the current adjunct outsourced service and outsource all the research requests, eliminating the in-house library, staff, and services completely?

- the firm outsourced the entire operation by working with one of the database aggregators to supply desktop tools, alerts, required reference assistance, and management of a virtual IC?

- a still larger firm with its own IC bought the new organization?

- the professional researchers decided to "up their game" and take on a more analytical role, perhaps even crossing over to the role of analyst within the firm?

By allowing her thinking to range far and wide across a variety of possible alternate futures, Jane has taken the first steps toward thinking out of the box and creating the environment for a scenario planning process in which she will need to involve all of the stakeholders within her organization. The good news is that the process is well documented and, depending on the scope of the planning effort, can occur within anywhere from a few weeks to several months. Typically, there are six to eight steps for developing varying degrees of scenarios, allowing you to tailor your planning effort to the time available for planning (Giesecke 1999, 81–92). These can be summarized as follows:

1. Identify and agree with stakeholders upon the key questions or issues to be answered or considered. Example: Should we move from print to e-journals? Should we "buy" certain services we currently do ourselves?

2. Undertake an analysis to identify key strengths, weaknesses, opportunities, and threats (SWOT) in your environment. Consider: What forces are putting pressure on the key questions or issues?

3. Identify and rank the forces likely to drive changes in the future.

4. Choose the most important and most uncertain factors to form scenario plot lines.

5. Develop stories to describe two or three of the most likely futures.

6. Outline the implications of the stories.

7. Determine how you will tell if the environment is moving in the direction of one scenario or another. For example: Which leading indicators should be flagged to help guide your choice of options?

By definition, the future is unknown and therefore holds countless options. The scenarios Jane and her stakeholders choose to flesh out will help them understand what current key trends and constraints might really drive probable futures, scan beyond and behind these trends to imagine and speculate on possible futures, and develop images or visions of a preferable ideal future.

KEY TAKEAWAYS

In order to develop various scenarios or story lines and help prepare yourself to see future possibilities, the literature suggests a number of questions that you need to ask:

- What could happen?
- When might it happen?
- Why might it happen?
- What can I do to make it happen?

- What do I have to do to stop it happening?
- Where will I be if it happens?

In fact, scenario planning is a continuous cycle with these questions helping to build story lines that lead to actions which then result in another set of questions that help stakeholders evaluate outcomes and plow their findings back into new scenarios:

- What did we expect?
- In retrospect, was it the right thing?
- To what extent are others deciding our outcomes and how must we change our methods to address this?

This dynamic process of scenario planning is not about predicting the future, but rather about stimulating innovative thinking as an extremely useful and pragmatic survival tool for an IS manager. Scenario planning could help you reinvent yourself and your services to become part of a post-crisis solution within your organization.

BLUE-SKY THINKING

Whether you are involved in a takeover situation as Jane was or are otherwise looking into an uncertain future, develop a mindset for continuously questioning your service assumptions. Stay alert to warnings within your organization. Identify crisis points. Extrapolate opportunities. Scenario planning could be just the "preventive medicine" your IC needs to avoid unexpected drastic surgery or a premature demise.

SCENARIO: LIBRARIAN BECOMES MARKETING ANALYST

Today was Max's first day in his new position as a marketing analyst in the investment firm he had worked in for more than 5 years. He was terrified, but pretty excited as well. He well remembered the day several months before when he had seen the human resources posting for a market analyst and realized that his MLS and the skills and expertise he had acquired as a member of the library team could serve as his ticket to crossing over to another department and taking a new direction in his career as an information professional. He was thrilled to be able to apply his skills and broad knowledge about several industries outside the library (Simmons College 2006).

Max began by reviewing the scope of three tasks that were now his responsibility: a weekly *News Digest* providing the firm's relationship managers with top-level abstracts on the most important current events in three industries; a *Monthly Report on Market Players and Share* in which he would write commentary and assemble data digests for in-depth analyses; and, finally, participating in a weekly meeting with the relationship stakeholders in these three industries along with the department's managers, providing him with a direct conduit to learning about and contributing to new business ideas. Sitting in his new cubicle on the floor with many other analysts, Max realized he would also now have a different style of working. As part of the library team, he often had the feeling that his clients thought of him as "just a reference book," someone who would answer their question, and do it very well, but would then be "put back on the shelf" to wait for the next question. Now, embedded in the organization, he felt himself as part of the ebb and flow of daily work and viewed as a member of the "whole" corporate team, with an ongoing chance to "sell his value." Max's new manager was glad to have him on her team. She recognized that, as a researcher in the firm, Max was uniquely positioned to apply the knowledge he had gained over time and combine it with his deep industry and topical expertise. He could also provide digested results to their clients. She saw a real value to the firm in investing in the time he would need for further training to build on his already considerable knowledgebase and skill set. The fact that he brought with him significant "street cred," built up during his years in the IC, was icing on the cake. She also knew that the department's intranet would soon need an upgrade and to manage it would require someone with just the kind of information management skills Max brought to the team. It wouldn't be long before she assigned him this responsibility as well. Before getting started, Max took a moment to reflect on the irony of his situation. Some of his new tasks had been tried from time to time in the library during his tenure there, but the team never seemed to have enough time or interest to sustain the efforts. Looking back, he realized that this had been a real missed opportunity for the firm's library team. While they continued to be concerned that their place within the organization was becoming more tenuous by the day, Max was confident that his willingness to take the risk and "up his game" had positioned him to make a very visible and sustainable contribution to his firm's continuing success.

REFERENCES

Connor, John. Dialogue, Terminator 2: Judgment Day (film) http://en.wiki quote.org/wiki/Terminator_2:_Judgment_Day (accessed July 16, 2009).

Giesecke, Joan. "Scenario Planning and Collection Development." *Journal of Library Administration* 28, no. 1 (1999): 81–92, 3–5.

Giesecke, Joan, ed. *Scenario Planning for Libraries.* Chicago and London: American Library Association, 1998.

Hannabuss, Stuart. "Scenario Planning for Libraries." *Library Management* 22, no. 4/5 (2001): 168, 171–72.

Hornick, Scott, and Joan Giesecke. "Radar vs. Road Map. Developing Strategies Through Scenario Planning in an Uncertain World." In *Scenario Planning for Libraries*, edited by Joan Giesecke. 18–25. Chicago and London: American Library Association, 1998.

Post, James E., and J. E. Smith. "A New Order Fit for the Post-Crisis World." *Financial Times* (2009) http://www.ft.com/cms/s/2/486008e8–366911de-af40–00144feabdc0.html (accessed June 22, 2009). Illustration reprinted here with permission of illustrator Roger Beale (dated May 12, 2009).

Simmons College Graduate School of Library Science. "Scenario Insights Based on an Independent Study," Final Report (December 2006).

11

PROFESSIONAL ASSOCIATION MEMBERSHIP AS A SURVIVAL TOOL

SYLVIA JAMES

Being a member of professional associations has been important in my career. I'm sure I wouldn't have had the opportunities, met such a wide range of fellow professionals, or have had such a broad perspective on my career if I hadn't belonged to several library, archive, and information associations and made good use of the membership benefits and advantages they offered me over the years. The questions are:

- Is this type of membership really a feasible position for a new, mid-career, or senior information professional today?
- Do they offer anything for their members when everything goes wrong and their job disappears; when their service closes?
- What does the inherently old fashioned model of the professional association have to offer those wishing to advance their careers?
- Can belonging to an association really be a survival tool?
- If so, which particular member experience is the most worthwhile?

These are very difficult questions to answer. Belonging to any alliance of other professionals has few simple or clear benefits or advantages. The associations themselves often seem unclear about what they are really offering members as a whole and individuals need to really look at what they can take from this broad brush approach that is to help develop their careers.

Association membership is being compared to and challenged by professionally based social networks, especially by younger professionals, who have little knowledge of the history and significance of professional associations in their heyday. Compare the traditional association model to the *LinkedIn* service (*LinkedIn* 2012), which provides access to a network of business contacts. The idea of LinkedIn is that a "member" gets access to other contacts by adding their own connections and so is able to find new opportunities and broaden their network. *LinkedIn* can also be used to suggest and receive work recommendations, with user interest groups that can also point to leads and potential opportunities.

Professional associations have rarely been able to attract membership from everyone qualified to belong to them. The exceptions are when professional accreditation is essential and a legal requirement to enter and practice in the profession. Medicine and law spring to mind as the prime examples of required association membership. For information professionals there has always been a clear choice of whether to join an association or not, even when accreditation was one of the benefits offered. In addition to the option to join a professional association, there is probably a choice of specialty to be made, with libraries and archives membership associations being the usual options within a setting of a country where the professional lives. There are often also several types of library or archive associations, most usually academic, public libraries or some sort of special workplace library or special collections. Fragmentation of the professional associations seems to deter rather than attract many of those practicing and this type of association seem to struggle on with very small membership numbers, even if they have been successful in the past. The larger and more broadly based associations also seem to dissatisfy specialist library and information professionals, even if they offer distinct sections or subgroups within their structures, such as those specifically for corporate libraries. Senior information professionals also often complain that the professional associations have little to offer them and the overall membership does not benefit if these experienced people do not continue to participate fully in these associations.

NETWORKING

Conducting any survey of professional associations that asks what the main reasons for seeking and maintaining membership are, will always bring up networking with like-minded or similarly qualified and experienced individuals as one of the prime motivations for joining. Networking used to mainly mean meeting face to face at meetings like seminars or conferences, where networking was an implicit activity of the whole event. Other forms of networking were possible by joining different interest groups or sections within the membership association, with access to other specific members via some kind of directory and database and are still a crucial benefit of membership.

While there is still a very important place for this type of networking, it has been overshadowed by the replacement and near dominance of social media electronic networking that all the professional associations have had to come to terms with or perhaps risk losing relevance with their members.

Witness the enormous effort over the past 10 years made by the traditional associations in their social networking policies, offerings, and often whole sections of their internal structures devoted to the phenomenon. How much of this effort can really be seen as essential to their membership and in turn a survival tool for the struggling information professional remains to be assessed? Nevertheless, as the current treasurer of an information association recently responsible for developing the forthcoming year's budget, I moved the planned spending on all these social networking activities from the discretionary side (nonessential spending) of the budget to the nondiscretionary (essential expenditure to keep the association in business). It is impossible to imagine running a membership association without a website or some sort of social networking presence in 2013.

It is a widely expressed opinion that the successful social networks today will not necessarily be the key networks that will be around in 10 or 20 years. This was often voiced during the May 2012 Initial Public Offering (IPO) of *Facebook*, Inc., when forecasts of future performance and a perceived overvaluation of the stock price for the newly listed company could not really be justified. Can professional associations really keep up with changing fashions in this social networking world and do they actually have the funds or membership agreement to do so? The networking model is so different for the two types of organizations. It could also be argued that professional associations using social networks as part of their communications channels may confuse their members. Receiving two or more sets of messages from groups within the association, who use conventional e-mail as well as *LinkedIn* and *Twitter* and *Facebook* may be just too much for many members, who were used to just one communication channel for so many years.

For the individual professional, social networking requires some regular time and effort to achieve results from participation. Take the list from "33 Ways to Use *LinkedIn* for Business" from the Giacom blog website (Evans 2012). It could take an avid *LinkedIn* member several days to get through implementing all of these suggestions for optimal use of the service. This might be achievable and worthwhile if a member was actively engaged in looking for networking opportunities for a job search, but somehow unlikely for the average *LinkedIn* user. But the main advantage must be that all this can be done from the comfort of home or place of work, remotely. However, the obvious benefits of face-to-face networking are missing. Much has been written and discussed about the absence of the subtleties of face-to-face contact when doing purely online networking and the misconceptions and even danger of relying on the false perceptions it can bring. The traditional professional associations appear to have missed this point as one of their strengths and failed to trumpet the comparison with social networks in their important role in bringing their members together physically in more formal and informal meetings, of which they have long experience.

Most information professionals do work alone and need both social networking as well as the occasional conventional meeting of their peers. As a survival tool, there is nothing more energizing than attending a well-organized face-to-face meeting of a professional association, which can provide essential networking opportunities.

PROFESSIONAL ASSOCIATIONS AND EMPLOYMENT OPPORTUNITIES

In a pre-Internet world, many associations published all-important newsletters with job advertisements, where a large percentage of the relevant appointments in the sector were published. There was little other way of direct access to the specific employment market of the special libraries professional. This was not just the case in the information professional's world, but held true for virtually all types of professional and vocational work. The arrival in the mail of the jobs supplement or association journal with a section of employment advertisements was eagerly anticipated and new opportunities pored over. Only a few specialized employment agencies and the occasional job advertisement were found in the mainstream press, but belonging to a professional association was all important for this reason alone. Employers often only placed vacancies using this media. For several of the later decades of the 20th century, the job ad was also an important revenue stream for the associations, who charged very competitive rates to employers for their advertisement placement in their various publications and virtually guaranteed the vacancy would be filled rapidly by a dedicated and responsive readership. They are still an important feature of many associations' membership offering and many associations also actively monitor the terms and conditions and compensation levels offered to ensure they are within professional or industry guidelines.

This activity and income has now been curtailed with the development and growth of broader based Internet job seeking as the primary route for employers and candidates. Many jobs are still placed with the professional associations, who have by and large replaced their print publications with electronic journals and newsletters with the relevant advertisements. Some associations do have vacancies for their members, regularly sent by e-mail to all, or on a section of their website, behind a member log-on, as well as dedicated lists that have specific jobs advertised on an ad-hoc basis.

All kinds of other initiatives used in the past for formal notification of vacancies, such as special confidential networking employment sessions held at association conferences, matching employer and employee services and in-house employment bureaus are still in evidence, but are much less significant as the main source of employment in the sector than they used to be. It is probable that a valuable opportunity has been missed by the associations in adopting new methods of Internet employment techniques in order to become much more attractive to both employers and job seekers as the primary route for vacancies in the library and information world.

As a survival tool, relying on the formal flow of vacancies available through a professional association is not very likely to be as productive today as it was in pre-Internet days for an information professional who has suddenly had their service closed. The survivor in the know is probably far more likely to find a new opportunity by networking in any way they can and scanning any vacancy list they can find.

THE ROLE OF THE ASSOCIATION IN ACCREDITATION AND REGISTRATION OF PROFESSIONAL AND PROFESSIONAL SERVICES

Two models of accreditation and registration for information professionals are offered by the various professional associations. The individual member can be accredited to several levels of expertise by the association, or the actual library, archive, information service, or educational institution can be assessed for suitability. For both types of accreditation, the process requires considerable input from both assessors and members who are seeking assessment. Assessors are usually selected from the very experienced members of the association, who have themselves participated in a training schedule on accreditation methods and who devote their time freely to making accreditation work by then making the actual assessments. The methods used are also generally approved by a recognized educational body.

In the United Kingdom, for example, my main professional association, The Institute of Information Scientists (IIS, which was merged into CILIP, the Chartered Institute of Librarians and Information Professional in 2000) also gives professional status through accreditation, known as Chartership, which I have found very useful from time to time in establishing my credentials with employers or clients (of my consultancy). In fact, I went through accreditation to demonstrate to the other professionals in the organization where I worked at the time, that my professional association had just as rigorous a process to establish my qualifications, ability, and experience in doing my job as any of the more usual professional bodies in business.

Today, aspiring librarians in the United Kingdom study for a postgraduate diploma or master's degree at a library school, whose courses are accredited by CILIP. After two years in a professional post the newly qualified librarian is expected to apply for Chartership status which gives professional recognition and is described by CILIP as a "seal of approval" and a recognition of achievement in applying academic studies to employment. If anything, in the present economic climate, it could be argued that there is an even more important place for this "official" recognition of information professionals in the workplace and so accreditation can be seen as an essential survival tool for the individual. However, few employers in the private sector appear to have recognized the importance of accreditation as a required qualification for information professionals when seeking to recruit for relevant positions. The professional associations themselves appear to have made few inroads into bringing their accreditation standards to the attention of senior management. In the U.S., with a few exceptions (Medical Librarianship, Archives, and Records Management), such certifications and/or accreditations do not exist at all and when they do, are met with similar luke warm interest by private sector employers.

The emphasis on accreditation for libraries, information services, and archives for both individuals and services has very much been on those who work and provide services in the public sector. This seems to have had mixed results, with some employers actively requesting accreditation for every suitable vacancy, while other public sector bodies seem oblivious of the standards, even for the top positions, such as chief librarian. I can remember the disapproval and sense of shock that ran through the library community in the United Kingdom, when a spate of appointments of chief librarians of substantial local authorities were made of other professionally qualified candidates, rather than those who had formal qualifications in librarianship and accreditation and revalidation from the then Library Association (now CILIP).

As far as can be seen, this type of accreditation cannot be achieved by the business social networking alternatives at the moment and it is hard to see how this could be done effectively in a network that is for a mass market, with so many different professions and interest groups in so many different businesses and institutions.

WHAT DOES IT COST? MEMBERSHIP SUBSCRIPTIONS

Membership in a traditional association is conveyed by paying a membership subscription (i.e., dues). This has often been cited as the main barrier to joining by those who feel that these subscriptions are often set at too high a cost compared with what is actually conferred for the privilege of joining. Whether actual or perceived, what member benefits there are for the money paid has often not been clearly stated by associations and membership is seen as "expensive." In fact, many associations give very good value for money, with the monetary value of the benefits when they are calculated, often grossly exceeding subscriptions.

Association membership fees have moved from being a standard rate for all, to being based on levels of salary. Belonging to an association can be considered expensive if you are relatively well paid and are required to subscribe at the higher bands set. This has presumably brought in much needed extra funds for the association and has increased the levy on the better-paid members of the profession. The member self-certifies their salary and pays the appropriate subscription. Commonly, discounted rates are set for students, those out of work and those who have retired. Levels of associate membership can be at a lower rate for those who do not aspire to full membership or who might be on the periphery and just want to keep up to date with activities in the profession. This is particularly relevant in associations that require formal academic qualifications for full membership and accreditation.

How does a business social network compare on pricing? The core *LinkedIn* service is free, which most using the service make the best use of. Paid for levels of membership, called "premium service" are available, and it is worth looking at these in a little detail to compare with association membership subscriptions. *LinkedIn* offers three types of subscription. The most expensive level, costs $499.95 per month, which is substantially more than any membership subscription to a library or information association. It allows 50 messages to new contacts and searches for 700 profiles at a time. The other feature with this option is "Organize Profiles" allowing 25 folders to be created with notes. There are two other much cheaper, but smaller packages, Business ($24.95 per month) and Business Plus ($49.95 per month) with fewer messages and profiles. The cheapest option is probably just about the same cost as an average annual subscription to a membership association.

SERVICE AS AN OFFICER IN A PROFESSIONAL ASSOCIATION

One benefit that might be overlooked in the discussion and comparison of traditional membership associations over Internet social networks is the experience and satisfaction gained from the voluntary service in some kind of official role in the association. This might be a position in the main management of the association, or at a regional or local level, or within one of the interest groups or sections. Positions can usually be obtained simply by volunteering to serve for a year or more, or might require an election in which candidates for office at the highest association wide level are chosen by the membership in a formal vote.

Finding the time to serve in this way might be difficult for many information professionals, fighting to keep their job and information service and so dismissed as not worth any effort. Indeed, the corporate library's management might not approve of such a distraction for their employees from their main job and refuse to allow any time for association roles in working hours. Even suggesting such extra work, in office hours or spare time might be seen as putting a head above the parapet and drawing senior management's attention to the information service in a very unfavorable way.

However, this is a very short-sighted view; and any experience gleaned in this way can only add to the performance of any professional in their main employment and should be actively encouraged, rather than disdained. It can add an extra dimension to a resume and corroborate and enhance managerial experience. Having a record of working successfully with fellow professionals, with whom you have no other contact, in a team that has no cohesion from a formal salaried position in a common institution, will enhance any career. The simple fact of being able to collaborate for a common aim, in a not-for-profit environment, says much about a potential employee. Having this type of experience can really be seen as a good survival tool, a resume enhancer and is to be recommended, even if it can realistically only be done in spare time. As yet, no such experience appears to be available on a social network.

MEMBERSHIP OF OTHER PROFESSIONAL ASSOCIATIONS

This chapter has focused on professional associations dedicated to the information professional and how membership might be a crucial survival tool. Another aspect of such membership is to join an association that is aligned to the sector or profession in which you work. It may not be possible to do this without formal qualifications in a professional body, such as law or engineering. But, it is worth investigating if there is an associate or para-professional level that may accept membership from those that work in the sector, but do not hold suitable qualifications for full membership.

When I worked for a very new oil company, who was just beginning to draw revenue in the mid-1970s from the North Sea oil deposits in which it had a small share, the professional staff including myself as their Information Officer and Researcher were encouraged to join the Geological Society and the Institute of Petroleum in the United Kingdom. Membership in these distinguished bodies was thought an ideal way to develop contacts and enhance our continuing professional development. We were a very small company, with a handful of geological and engineering specialists, competing at a low level with the oil giants and needed every bit of help we could get from the wider oil sector. I also joined several chambers of commerce including the then Sino British Trade Council (for China–United Kingdom relations) to aid understanding of the potential new oil provinces in the China Sea that were opening up, so I could report to senior management, who had to make important decisions about when and how we might participate. This was my first real experience of the power of this type of networking and I was astonished at the information, or perhaps it might be termed "intelligence," I was able to pick up.

I remembered that lesson when I began my consultancy practice a decade later and have had no hesitation in joining both professional and trade associations (like the Chambers of Commerce) if I had a project in a sector I was unfamiliar with. The experience has always been worthwhile and far outweighed any subscriptions or membership fees. Attending the annual conference at much more favorable fees usually pays back the initial subscription alone. This could be a survival tool for corporate librarians, who might be looking for ways to align themselves with their business.

One word of warning; management may be very unhappy about non-front-line staff joining a professional body in this way, as they see it as the province of senior management to represent the corporation in their trade or professional association. An interesting example was described to me when I was working on a consultancy project for a private equity firm in Germany. Because there was no corporate library, research was done by a group of young analysts who were taken on after graduating with a first degree or MBA. The senior management were incensed that a lowly analyst had had the temerity to join the European Venture Capital Association, using his own funds, but without consulting his line manager. So, it is important to check the management attitude toward any membership possibilities the corporate librarian may be considering.

CONCLUSION

As I finalized this chapter, I came across a rather strange article in the *Financial Times* magazine on the *LinkedIn* service (Waters 2012, 28–31), which presented a rather mixed argument for the efficacy of networking on *LinkedIn*. The article is a profile of Reid Hoffman, founder of *LinkedIn* who asserts the networking model he has created is definitely the one that will be the future of seeking work through the much looser ties that *LinkedIn* provides. Deflecting all criticisms, especially that the network has become the haunt of job seekers and recruiters, he explains some lofty ambitions about consideration of others involved and that eventually *LinkedIn* will be able to sustain a new kind of working life. Professional associations have probably echoed similar aspirations in the past to their members, although not with the confidence of a new communication model and a vast member base.

The choice will probably be made by the next generation of professionals, whether in the information world or other professions. There are many experiences that a professional association can give that are inconceivable offerings from a social network today. Whether they are overcome successfully by the new models of interaction remains to be seen, but it seems that professional associations will be around for some time yet and very much part of the survival kit of the corporate librarian. I recommend that the reader joins one and gets fully involved.

REFERENCES

Evans, Meryl K. "33 Ways to Use LinkedIn for Business." Gigaom, http://gigaom.com/collaboration/33-ways-to-use-linkedin-for-business/ (accessed July 2, 2012).

LinkedIn. 2012. About, http://press.linkedin.com/about.

Waters, Richard. "Man in the Know." *FT.com Magazine*, March 17/18, 2012: 28–31.

12

CORPORATE LIBRARY SURVIVAL OUTSIDE THE UNITED STATES: LESSONS FROM NEW ZEALAND AND AUSTRALIA

GILLIAN RALPH AND JULIE SIBTHORPE

OVERVIEW

Events in special libraries in Australia and New Zealand mirror what is happening in North America, Europe, and the United Kingdom. Underlying economic conditions are critical to the success of special librarians everywhere in both corporate and government settings, but now there is something else at play. It is the rapid development of convergence—not only in both new technologies and the changing perception of information, but also in the convergence in the workplace of all those professions involved with information management. Professional boundaries are blurring and special librarians or information professionals need new skills and a clear voice of support. This can remind employers that special librarians or information professionals have the required skills and competencies for a role in the way information is managed in the future as it converges with technological developments.

INTRODUCTION TO SPECIAL LIBRARIES IN AUSTRALIA AND NEW ZEALAND

In a recent survey of service managers and individual library staff in Australian special libraries, it was found that 74 percent of respondents were based in cities (Australian Library and Information Association 2010). The vast majority had a staff of one to three people. Eighty percent of respondents "said there had been no change in the number of library service positions in their organisation over the last 5 years" (Australian Library and Information Association 2010, 3). Of the 358 responses 187 were from government-funded special libraries, but since 2010 and especially in 2012, this stable setting is experiencing change as Commonwealth and state government agencies begin amalgamating services. One hundred and one respondents (of the total 358 responses received) were from health or medical libraries and the rest from corporate and not-for-profit libraries.

Even in the current climate, it was found that "very few used a structured method to monitor the performance of their library service and even fewer were able to measure the cost benefit of their library service to the host organisation" (Australian Library and Information Association, 2010, 24).

The last New Zealand study of special libraries was a report by Ralph and Sibthorpe (2009). Their report found that there were a total of 292 special libraries in New Zealand. This figure is now dropping as government funding restrictions take hold, and they estimate up to 30 special libraries have closed across all sectors since 2009 so far.

BUSINESS CONDITIONS

Changes in business conditions around the world due to globalization have been dramatic. In our part of the world, businesses were more affected by the Global Financial Crisis (GFC) during the period 2008–2009, but not as adversely as those in the Northern Hemisphere countries at that time. The GFC was felt through major trading partners as most large businesses now have overseas offices or are headquartered outside of Australia or New Zealand. Now there is relative stability of corporate sector libraries including law, health, and medical libraries which were severely cut back with many job losses after the initial rounds caused by the GFC in 2009.

One positive outcome of the GFC is the advantage to libraries of a weaker U.S. dollar compared with local currencies allowing libraries much greater purchasing power in Australia and New Zealand for U.S. and European materials.

In both Australia and New Zealand the resulting restriction of government funding has placed pressure on finding cost savings in the government sector and this is leading to rationalization and centralization of government services. It is the government libraries which are reporting library job losses and space reduction as ministries and departments merge and the requirement to "do more with less" is noted here as in both Canada (where there is a campaign to protect Library and Archives Canada) and in the United Kingdom (Foster 2010).

The Australian economy remained buoyant with a slight dip during 2010, but is now back on track with a boom in the mining sector resulting in a surplus for 2012 (Lim et al. 2011). In 2012 concerns are being raised over a slight decline in the percent of gross domestic product (GDP) from 3.5 percent to 3 percent. Westpac bank predicted that the average Australian GDP growth will be about 3 percent finally for 2012 compared with expectations in February of 3.5 percent. (Westpac Institutional Bank, 2012).

During the past two years various Australian states suffered a series of natural disasters, notably the bush fires in Victoria in 2010 and the Queensland floods of January 2011, as well as extensive flooding in New South Wales in early 2012.

> Federal coffers took a $40 billion hit last financial year as the global crisis and summer of natural disasters took a heavier economic toll than expected. (Scott, 2011)

These disasters hit public purses both federally and in the affected states and have led to a reduction in public spending as costs savings are sought. A change of government in Queensland in early 2012 (from Labour to Liberal National Party) has prompted wholesale job losses in government services especially for contract staff in an effort to balance the books after the floods. In Victoria the latest budget has slashed 4,200 jobs from the public service (Sexton 2012). The result of current conditions is a rethink based on improving the economy and using technology wherever possible to create improved efficiency. This is discussed in more detail in the section of this chapter detailing Australian initiatives.

In New Zealand the government re-elected in 2011 has made a commitment to public sector reform, which is well under way. Rationalizations of government ministries and departments mean that many job losses have occurred in the information profession. For example, three government departments will merge their back-office functions as part of ongoing public service cuts. The Treasury, Department of the Prime Minister and Cabinet (DPMC), and the State Services Commission (SSC) will share human resources, information technology (IT), and management and finance functions. The amalgamation will see 16 jobs lost—three immediately and a further 13 after a year of transition (Vance 2011). Another example is that positions were lost and more will go with the establishment of the Ministry of Business, Innovation and Employment (MBIE) on July 1, 2012. The new ministry will absorb the functions of the Ministry of Economic Development, the Department of Labour, the Ministry of Science and Innovation, and the Department of Building and Housing.

New Zealand has also experienced an unusual drain on public expenditure after the earthquakes of September 2010 and February 2011. New Zealand's third largest city Christchurch needs rebuilding along with the infrastructure around it. This has to be funded and underwritten by public expenditure and resources put aside under past Earthquake Commission levies. The earthquakes meant loss of jobs, homes, and workplaces both at the time of the earthquake and subsequently. New Zealand's earthquakes have meant huge disruption to the nation and the economy, having a measured impact on productivity of over 10 percent. (Compare this to the effect of Japan's 2011 earthquake and tsunami which registered only a 1 percent impact on that country's GDP (Doherty 2011). The disruption meant having to postpone conducting the New Zealand Census in 2011 to March 2013, something which has not happened since World War II.

THE CONVERGENCE OF INFORMATION AND COMMUNICATION TECHNOLOGY

Another challenge to special librarians is the convergence of technologies and rapid changes in IT developments which provide user self-help and remote access services, as well as the sharing of information in many different ways. Information and Communication Technology (ICT) has changed how special librarians communicate with their clients but has not changed their essential duties of information management, research, collection management, and networking. They now have an amazing array of sharing technologies available such as blogs and wikis, RSS feeds, Sharepoint, inquiry tracking, digitization, web conferencing, and knowledge management systems. This same sharing technology is offering e-books and online publishing, open access sources, and complex environments to third-party access. At this point compliance with copyright requirements is presenting challenges to librarians everywhere.

New Zealand has a smart, small-scale business environment based on agriculture and is increasingly using technology to service Northern Hemisphere companies. New Zealand relies on ICT to remove the distances between it and the rest of the world. New Zealand companies are well known for expertise in software developments, IT and animation services, making New Zealand an offshore laboratory for many overseas companies. As an example, New Zealand librarians invented and developed the open source information management program *Koha,* which is now used all over the world (Koha Library Software Community 2012).

The Australian government is committed to seeing ICT used to reach all citizens within its vast borders. People in remote areas cannot always obtain the access they need to keep up with information. In the scramble to align and rationalize using ICT technologies, many other professional groups are in transition.

New Zealand and Australia are sophisticated early adopters of new technologies. Social media offer more communication possibilities which are being explored currently (mainly *Facebook*, RSS feeds, *LinkedIn*, and *Twitter*) to reach clients in locations far from centralized head offices. Many Australian and New Zealand information professionals are also Web authors for intranet and web pages. They use Camtasia and video capturing software to make instructional tools and catalogue video and audio in the normal run of information management. Creating in-house databases and digitizing of materials as solutions to information storage and retrieval management problems or for use with records and archives management, as companies are now subject to the *Public Records Act 2005* in New Zealand and the *Archives Act 1983* in Australia, is important.

All these activities bring information professionals into contact with professionals in IT divisions where good relationships are as critical as ever. One area posing a challenge for information professionals is e-books. These are desirable for small collections serving remote users, but as is being experienced in much larger libraries, licensing and the access to them for e-reader devices use is fraught and needs to improve. Many librarians are grappling with the variety of access and IT problems associated with the provision of e-books currently.

THE CONVERGENCE OF PROFESSIONAL GROUPS

Librarians in corporate, nonprofit, and government libraries, are faced with the issue of convergence with other professional groups in information management, such as Web and intranet designers, knowledge managers, researchers, records managers, and archivists. This is clearly observed in the job advertisement studies published in the past few years in New Zealand (Ralph and Sibthorpe 2009) and in Australia (Wise 2012). Job advertisement studies (Mach, 2003) find a myriad of names for tasks which fall into the realm of the information professional and even into traditional library areas, and for which special librarians could apply. With such a bewildering array of job titles, how is it going to be possible to position LIS graduates for employment and who will keep track of the transition by our LIS profession into a wider information profession?

It seems that library associations are slow to take up the collection of vital statistical information, with the exception of the Australian Library and Information Association Advisory Committee. (See Australian initiatives elsewhere in this chapter.)

PREPARING TO STAKE OUT A PLACE IN THE INFORMATION MANAGEMENT PROFESSION

Finally, there is a challenge raised by various authors including Matarazzo and Pearlstein (2012, 24–29), Hallam (2010a, 37), and Perret (2010 44–46). These authors discuss how special librarians can prepare to stake out their territory in a battle for a share of the information management market and how well they need to be prepared by library and information services (LIS) educators.

There is a need for change in the education of information professionals and to consider how we can prepare the employment market so that employers will recognize their skill set. Who will be responsible for this promotion?

A major Australian initiative to align LIS students, LIS educators, and LIS employers has been published (Australian Learning and Teaching Council 2011), which will assist LIS educators all over the world to appreciate the changing workplace and the skills needed to remain relevant. There is also a new initiative in New Zealand called The Pacific Information Management Network, which now links and supports Pacific Island and Maori librarians who work mostly in special libraries (Library and Information Association of New Zealand Aotearoa 2012).

Library associations will need to advocate for this alignment. In Australia there is already an Australian Library and Information Association (ALIA) Special Libraries Advisory Committee of ALIA which has achieved some success already and is discussed in further detail subsequently under Australian initiatives.

The Library Association of New Zealand Aotearoa (LIANZA) has moved to provide more opportunities for the training of information professionals especially via online.

The Australian and New Zealand information services industry can move quickly to identify and respond to the challenge by closing the gap between employer expectations and current LIS education. They need to work hard to dispel the old-fashioned view of librarians, and showcase the new skills and competencies of information professionals. Perhaps something similar to the Special Libraries Association (SLA) Alignment Project needs to be undertaken in Australia and New Zealand.

SURVIVAL QUALITIES FOR SUCCESS

A summary of survival qualities needed for success might include versatility, adaptation, flexibility, agility, and pro-activity. Libraries in Australian and New Zealand corporate settings are surviving well so far, however, in both countries government library services are being amalgamated and there are job losses. Special librarians are equipped with traditional library skills but they are requesting more technology and business skills training. Employers are still unaware of LIS graduate skills sets, and now more than ever, we need to lose the term *librarian*. While there have been some efforts through SLA to reimagine the profession through name changes and realignment recommendations, consensus has not been achieved (Rink 2009). In our opinion, it remains important to move forward and see a rename to reposition and promote the varied and expert skills which are needed by an information professional today.

There is a widening gap between LIS education and the skills required for a career as a special librarian or information professional. This gap has been identified in other countries, the United States, United Kingdom, Canada, and in the Australian *Re-conceptualising* . . . project report which we explore in more detail later (Australian Learning and Teaching Council 2011, 36). To information professionals around the world we can offer exciting new Australian initiatives to help shape the industry and some "home spun" advice from New Zealand information specialists.

SPECIAL LIBRARIES IN THE GOVERNMENT

In the *Queensland Government Agency Libraries Review: Literature Review*, the author Gill Hallam comments:

Governments are essentially information intensive organisations. One key focus of the government reform agenda in many different jurisdictions is the use of information and communication technologies (ICT) to ensure that government meets its objectives effectively and efficiently. (Hallam 2010a, 7)

In both Australia and New Zealand there is government sector reform underway. In New Zealand, this is as a result of a change of government in New Zealand's 2008 election (reinforced by the National party being returned to Parliament in 2011).

Across the Tasman Sea a change of economic conditions and a desire to offer better government service delivery has motivated New Zealand's wealthier neighbor, Australia, to start the reform process. The Advisory Group on Reform of Australian Government Administration "is required to develop a blueprint outlining steps to rejuvenate the Australian Public Service (APS)" to build a richer base of skill and to "foster a better environment for cross-organisational collaboration through a one-APS culture" (Hallam 2010a, 6).

In both countries the GFC had some impact but effects were not as severely felt as in North American and European countries. In both Australia and New Zealand the resulting restriction of government funding placed pressure on making savings and therefore led to rationalizing and centralizing services, including LIS provision.

In 2009 the Australian Federal Government process of government sector reform identified six significant challenges facing Australian government administration. These were: the complexity of policy challenges, increasing public expectations, demographic changes as well as the challenge of technological change, globalization, and increasing financial restrictions (Hallam 2010a, 6).

In their response to the Federal Government Reform agenda the Australian Government Libraries Information Network (AGLIN) has identified, "a move towards shared services" and "a greater requirement for coordinated procurement across government" (AGLIN 2009, 4). Likewise, national and state libraries are also conducting exercises to strategically re-align their organizations with new public expectations and using new technologies as a vehicle (Rink 2009).

The directions are clearly outlined in a review of the first of the Federal government libraries, the (now privatized) Australian Government Solicitor (AGS), where clients of the information service perceived a physical library as outdated and a cost to the organization, not as a pro-active area. A new structure now has a national library manager, a centralized research management system and "provides real value and cost savings to the organisation" (Hallam 2010a, 11).

In her initial study for the Queensland Department of Premier and Cabinet report *Queensland Government Agency Libraries Review* (Hallam 2010a), Hallam provides a literature review and discusses recent reports from the state of Victoria and provides an example of how these changes might be carried out at the state level. She observes current directions in government administration, trends, issues, and the skills and competencies of special librarians. The 2012 change of Government in Queensland since the report means restricted financial conditions and the threat of contract work ending soon. Nonetheless, Hallam has identified important issues such as being able to measure and demonstrate value, aligning information service to the organization, embedding these services, marketing and promoting them, and possessing the required skills and competencies.

It is gratifying to note the review's *Options* paper sees the role of government agency librarians in a holistic and futuristic way.

> The responsibilities of library staff cover meeting the agency's research needs, preserving unique government print resources, managing, major digitization projects and driving the innovative use of Web 2.0 tools. Their high level information skills means that library and research staff play an important role on developing the digital literacies of government officers, thereby contributing directly to the government's workforce capacity. (Hallam 2010b, 4)

Here is recognition of the librarian's future role in government LIS. Eighteen separate government libraries were surveyed with a view to rationalizing their management, pooling their resources, and centralizing services to government officers, in order to provide a better resourced and coordinated service.

However, it is unlikely that physical centralization will occur as it is acknowledged that "the embedded nature of the libraries ensures that library staff develop a broad and deep understanding of the agency's information needs, that the collections are tailored to meet those needs and that the library clients build strong relationships with the library staff" (Hallam 2010b, 11).

The review has revealed that library and research staff make a substantial, but largely unrecognized, contribution to building the capacity of the public service by teaching information skills they are actively up-skilling and reskilling government employees, thereby increasing the capability of public sector officers to seek and manage information (Hallam 2010b, 16).

More remote services using smart phones and mobile technology are expected. Consortial agreements for journal databases and books are the obvious benefits of bringing together the various agencies, along with a centralized Library Management System and unified intranet. Queensland government sees the university library model of a network of libraries and networked resources as a desirable model to follow (Hallam 2010b, 20).

Reducing piecemeal duplication of resources and services and increasing staff management and development could result in greater access for users and better economy and collaboration of government library operations overall and indeed this is the preferred option which has been put forward, however, the 2012 change of Victoria's government may delay its implementation.

In New Zealand the government has just announced a series of rationalizations and amalgamations of government ministries and departments, with an expectation that core support services will be minimized. Earlier Hilary Rendell and Flora Wallace (2009) described the efficient amalgamation of six Ministry of Education libraries into one service over a period of 18 months. Currently, ministries that are being realigned include a merger of Ministry of Agriculture and Forestry and the New Zealand Food Safety Authority with the Ministry of Fisheries to form the Ministry of Primary Industries and the combining of all services from the Ministry of Science and Innovation, the Ministry of Economic Development, Department of Labour and Department of Building and Housing into a super ministry called the MBIE. In addition, the Corrections Department has removed 140 jobs some of which will be in the support area.

The New Zealand Treasury had had a very busy information service of seven. In 2008, together with other back-office functions, this group has now been amalgamated into one information service with State Services Commission and the DPMC. We are aware job losses so far for special librarians will be significant as the smaller departments merge and are rationalized into the larger ministries.

Our 2012 brief survey of government librarians in New Zealand has found that research collections are being centralized as are budgets, current awareness services, and information services. Some librarians report workloads tripling with expectations to provide services to three not one ministry. The personal environment is stressful as for some time there has been a "sinking lid" policy of non-replacement when a position became vacant. An increased use of contract workers has been observed. Many special librarians are finding themselves ill-prepared for the job market after many years of secure employment.

Although space and physical volumes are being let go, the information professionals' skill set is still considered important to the organization. This of course needs supporting by professional training and the repackaging and representing of the profession as information professionals. The job ads studies conducted in New Zealand (Ralph and Sibthorpe 2009) and in Australia (Wise et al. 2012) indicate a much wider variety of roles and titles is appearing in job ads for information professionals. The word which is usually missing is *librarian*; however, the skills required are the same. The title of the enjoyable article from a U.S. library and information student, *61 non-librarian jobs for LIS grads,* says it all (Breitkopf 2012). With jobs and job titles changing so fast it is harder to track how many special libraries or special librarians there are now and therefore how many jobs have been lost.

Knowledge of digitization technologies, social media, and increased user desktop information provision, along with the management of e-books are being investigated according to respondents to our recent New Zealand survey. They report distant user groups, less face-to-face contact, and the reference interview opportunity as a bygone thing, now having become a "reference email." Marketing is more important than ever using bulletins, blogs, RSS feeds, and a *Facebook* page to remain in the minds of constituent users.

Overall, the Queensland Government Agencies' *Options* paper (Hallam 2010b) may mark a new perception of the role of information managers in government libraries, as long as information professionals keep up with managing digital records and archives as well as print and electronic resources, and network them to government officers' desktops all over the country.

THREE OUTSTANDING INITIATIVES FROM AUSTRALIA

The past two years have seen three projects which could lead the world in strategic planning and support for the special library sector: the ALIA Special Libraries Advisory Committee, the Australian Teaching and Learning Ltd. report on *Re-conceptualising and Re-positioning Australian Library and Information Science Education* (Australian Learning and Teaching Council 2011) and a grassroots organization called IMBASE (Nutting and Harris 2012).

ALIA Special Libraries Advisory Committee

ALIA provides the first initiative discussed here; a strategically focused committee called the ALIA Special Libraries Advisory Committee (SLAC) (Australian Library and Information Association 2012). SLAC is a group which advises the Board of ALIA. In the short time since its establishment in 2009, the Committee has identified various objectives, most of which are well on the way to being achieved. The objectives include the creation of a general set of *Guidelines for Australian Special Libraries* (Australian Library and Information Association, 2010) which has been completed. A resource sharing wiki and a mailing list have been set up. Information has been gathered to provide aspects of the value of special libraries to create a profile of special libraries and provide current data sets. The *ALIA Special Libraries Survey Report* (Australian Library and Information Association 2010a) was published in December 2010. In addition, there is an advocacy project to make sure a special libraries stream is provided at every ALIA Conference.

Although it is similar in objectives to the SLA Alignment Project (Rink 2009), the SLAC activities which have taken place are in a smaller environment and their success should be easily measured. The ALIA group is ahead in achieving some of the critical requirements for an advisory body to support and mentor special librarians, who are currently being challenged in every way.

Re-conceptualizing and Re-positioning Australian Library and Information Science Education

A 2011 report entitled *Re-conceptualising and Re-positioning Australian Library and Information Science Education for the 21st Century* (Australian Learning and Teaching Council Ltd. 2011) explains that the project was funded and supported by the Australian Learning and Teaching Council Ltd., of the Australian Government Department of Education, Employment, and Workplace Relations. It could lead the way in determining future needs in LIS education in similar countries. Twelve universities and eleven vocational library and information science (LIS) organizations have contributed to this review of LIS education in Australia. The object of the project was to develop a framework for the education of information professionals in Australia. The three key stakeholder groups of LIS students, the LIS workforce, and LIS educators were surveyed. Several key recommendations were provided. The first one is of great interest:

> It is recommended that a broader and more inclusive vocabulary be adopted that both recognises and celebrates the expanding landscape of the field, for example "information profession," "information sector" "information discipline" and "information education." (Australian Learning and Teaching Council Ltd. 2011)

Professor Helen Partridge, Library and Information Science Coordinator at the Queensland University of Technology and leader of the project advises that another of the recommendations in the report has led to a future event to be run by LIS educators at all levels, called the Australian Information Education Symposium, which is to become an annual event.

This project is unique in that it covers the whole industry, including the employers of information professionals. It is certain to create a closer alignment between LIS educators and the market they are preparing their students to enter.

IMBASE

IMBASE is a new organization for information professionals. "We saw a great need for a resource to help other industry professionals deal with the massive and ongoing transition from traditional library and information management, technologies and practices," says the joint founder Michelle Nutting, Social Media Manager, IMBASE (Nutting and Harris 2012). IMBASE plans to develop industry events, workshops, and to create resources and tip sheets for information professionals.

Australia has put forward some key initiatives to unite and promote the LIS sector. The projects will address the theme of convergence in both the technology field and the convergence of interest in information management by other groups, which has been identified as both an opportunity and a threat by many of us as far back as 1994 (Tomlinson 1994).

New Zealand special librarians have a chance to emulate the ALIA Advisory Committee activities, with the LIANZA structure, as also recommended in Ralph and Sibthorpe (2009). However, LIS educators worldwide will find the research results from the Australian *Re-conceptualising* project to be of immediate benefit in helping realign their curricula and future relationships with employer groups.

TOUGH TIMES! INTERVIEWS FROM THE FIELD

"Times have been tough!" was the conclusion of our series of conversations with special librarians in the corporate sector in New Zealand. Two years ago corporate libraries had their staff and space allocations cut. Now special librarians are providing information from "just-in-time" sources, using open access and interlibrary loan, Amazon, or the company's credit card to obtain research material for specific purposes, when needed. No more "just-in-case" philosophy. Budgets are pared down to core products, vital databases, taxation materials, standards, and there is a focus on using prior company knowledge to save costs.

They told us that user training is still perceived as a marketing opportunity to demonstrate the skills and resources of the corporate information professionals, although it is more likely to be once a month or on a one-to one basis than previously. User self-help is the key driver for this activity, enabled by branded intranet websites of library resources and links built by the information professionals. Web conferencing is a popular means for reaching colleagues in other decentralized sites. Vendor visits are an occasion to showcase and demonstrate the potential of a database.

Information professionals prepare targeted research reports that can save time for the client who knows they can request an industry or company report at short notice. Outsourcing is not a concept considered in New Zealand companies as yet. However, due to the time zone differences it is possible that companies in the Northern hemisphere could benefit from such a service located in New Zealand or Australia.

Everyone we spoke with remarked on "doing more with less," fewer staff but the same amount of work noting "thankfully the workload is steady and has not increased dramatically." Good candidates for advertised positions are around, many of them expatriates who have returned to New Zealand from the United Kingdom's adverse job market.

The experienced and long-serving librarians we interviewed are collecting client feedback with each piece of their research work. Keeping records of assistance and the high satisfaction rating from clients provides valuable demonstration of value to the firm.

Those who work in large multinationals say "keep open minded, open to ideas" and "just get on with it!" Job names and titles are not important but good service and support for the firm's objectives are what is paramount.

Relationships are critical and those who find themselves affiliated with business development, intellectual property, research and development, and marketing units within the firm are well placed. Because of the Public Records and Archives Act 2005, many of those we spoke to have had to find some training and incorporate records and archive management as part of the total information management role for their company.

WHAT TO DO WHEN YOUR SPECIAL LIBRARY IS FACING A REVIEW: MORE COMMENTS FROM NEW ZEALAND SPECIAL LIBRARIANS

New Zealand special librarians also provided useful and pragmatic suggestions and ideas for activities that could be undertaken when a special library or information service comes under review, either for the cutting of resources and services or for threats of total closure. The suggestions fell into several groupings: the external situation, warning signs, staying informed, preventative measures, your own team, obtain support inside the organization, obtain support from outside the organization, managing change, marketing your service, measuring the value of the library, professional development, and senior management.

WARNING SIGNS

How likely is the information service to encounter a review process? Are there any advance signals that a review is imminent? Echoing the predictive model developed by Matarazzo, Megan Alexander (2009) offers some general help for detecting change in an organization with warning signs indicating change:

- The first sign is cost-cutting measures being implemented throughout the organization.
- The success of special libraries (or positive perceptions of those providing information services) is closely related to the culture of an organization.
- Is your position viewed as a "revenue generator" or does your position bring money into the organization or help reduce expenses?
- Is the library situated near the major users (researchers and management teams)? Does the library have a good relationship with top management and maintain high visibility?
- Is there a key user to champion your cause within the organization?

STAYING INFORMED

When it becomes clear the library or information service is to be reviewed for cost cutting or possible closure, here are some actions to take, which might enable you to stay informed about the review process and participate to the greatest extent allowed. They are in no particular order.

- Know your team. We are warned to "be aware that personalities do change when survival is an issue." Enlist your team's support.
- Find out what is the real agenda, why is the review being conducted? You need to understand the drivers.
- Attend all meetings during this time for vital information.

- Ask to be included on the review panel, or to be able to conduct the review yourself, or failing that ask to be kept up to date with regular briefings and draft documents.
- Produce testimonials collected over time or case studies *in written form* to support the library.
- Consider Return on Investment surveys—document ways the information service contributes to the organization's bottom line. Use statistics, usage, and key triumphs or success stories. Have the facts and figures at your fingertips. Survey everything!—information needs of users, benchmark with other libraries, customer satisfaction surveys, requests and how long they take, who for and how much. Conduct a SWOT analysis and information audit. Collect specific examples and customer testimonials describing how the library has been helpful.
- Itemize the dollars you manage on behalf of your firm, and how you do it.
- Prepare and regularly update a case for keeping the library. Be aware that by the time a review is undertaken, it is likely too late to take this action. Often these things happen so quickly with little notice to the librarian, and the "new owners have a new agenda."
- Be realistic. Do not sacrifice your own values and principles—you will not be happy remaining in a place of work that holds unhappy memories. Consider if the culture has changed so much that you are no longer a comfortable fit? Are you able to contribute to the change management of the new organization? If so, you may be in a position to shape the required services.

PREVENTATIVE MEASURES IN PLACE

Before any review takes place or at an early stage of the review New Zealand special librarians thought it important to be visible and known to the senior management involved in the review process.

- It is important to continually educate them on the value of the library.
- Make a case against closure, measure the costs to the company of closure or outsourcing this function or of having no library at all.
- When presenting material to senior management some survey respondents suggested using an information professional consultant or other help to prepare these representations.
- Budget has never been large but keeping a tight eye on it, particularly in relation to usage statistics which will show where the budget has been allocated.
- Align with revenue generating areas of the firm.

OBTAIN SUPPORT INSIDE THE ORGANIZATION

In our study on trends in special library closures (Ralph and Sibthorpe 2008), we found that the users of the library or information service are not usually consulted or considered about closures of the services. We also found that an information service or library is usually highly regarded, so for lobbying purposes, and to inform the review process, involving users of the library may help.

- Consult all staff and make sure they are aware of what is happening. Drum up support especially from keen library users and key users.

- Keep the library team and other company staff members informed of the review progress and communicate results regularly.
- Publicize reactions to the review.
- Is there an inclusive process for planning and prioritizing workload with library staff, to involve them in integration projects so they can influence the direction of the services, tools, and collections?

Obtain support outside of the organization:

- Advise the union if you have one.
- Advise colleagues in other firms, and use mailing lists.
- Advise library associations, such as LIANZA, ALIA, and SLA.
- Find a source of moral and personal support especially if you are in a sole-charge situation. You need someone to talk to and mentor you.
- Look at the history of reinstatement in your organization and point out the likely incidence of reinstatement, or the need to provide information services after your service has gone.

MANAGING CHANGE

During this time of review, changes will be taking place and it is important to manage the process of change within the organization, the team, and yourself. It is also time to consider the alternative sources to gain savings in time, costs, and space for the organization. Some suggestions from those we interviewed were:

- Set up a reference group to advise on library matters.
- Refocus the library to be client sensitive.
- Increase the focus on needs of top executives and board with more self-service for other clients.
- There could be a greater emphasis on shared services and meeting with other libraries within your sector. For example, a number of government libraries are either moving to an open source shared library management system or investigating doing so.
- Use such services as videoconferencing with counterparts in other cities to keep visible.
- There is a greater expectation that everything should be available electronically and endeavor to work towards that aim.
- Introduce a service desk 24/7, an increase in self-service for clients, develop a seamless service model to overcome issues of different time zones and hemispheres.
- Look to adjust work processes where you see potential for improvement or use technology to benefit your work. Put emphasis on proactive services (e.g., monitoring) to ensure you remain visible and clients continue to rely on your services.
- Redeveloped company intranet soon to be launched will provide new opportunities.
- Greater use of social media; move to a library management system that enables end-user interaction and greater automation of library processes. Monitoring industry news via RSS feeds and Google.
- Shrink physical size and weed as you move to electronic resources.

MARKETING YOUR SERVICES

Awareness of the services available and making them an invaluable part of the organizational process is vital. The New Zealand information professionals shared the following tactics they use:

- We have a presence on the intranet but our biggest marketing of ourselves is mostly informal—making sure we are close to our client groups and know what is going on in their areas of interest and seeing if there is something we can help them with.
- Our current awareness service is a form of marketing.
- On the company website the library has several pages of information with direct links to contact the library for more information or research.
- The special librarian developed the twice-yearly company publication. She organized and gathered content written by company staff, which meant that she also benefitted in knowing what projects staff were working on and was able to provide relevant information where necessary.
- We use blogs and *Yammer* to highlight new resources for different groups of library users.
- Raise the profile of the library through simple gestures such as providing news bulletin emails to staff, consulting with them on journal renewals, promotion of new material, and so forth, and promoting that it is more than just a collection of books.

MEASURING THE VALUE OF YOUR LIBRARY

The bottom line is the key measurement method in most organizations. It is important to collect evidence of the effectiveness of your information service stated in terms relevant to your organization, regardless if a review is or is not likely. Alexander (2009, F2) suggests making sure your manager knows about your contributions and that these are in line with the goals of the larger organization. Soliciting suggestions from your manager about how you can contribute more is also recommended.

The information professionals we interviewed also suggested:

- Look for new opportunities for your department and for your organization. Show the point at which the library service enters the organization's projects.
- Prepare and maintain a database of examples of the library's contribution and cost-benefit financial savings to the company.
- Demonstrate the expertise of the staff and their (priceless) organizational knowledge.
- Consider charging back your time (if not already doing that).
- Suggest cost cutting, find savings, reduce subscriptions possibly by moving to electronic.
- Archive research results to build databases for reuse.
- Consider dispersing and embedding the library team throughout the firm to sit nearer their clientele.

PROFESSIONAL DEVELOPMENT

Continuing professional development is necessary to keep up to date with the changes in librarianship, particularly in the special library area. Many claim time commitments prohibit additional training or acquiring new skills, but it is important to keep up to date especially with the new technology.

Special librarians are aware of the need to have multiple specialist skills to accept the challenges in a special library environment and suggest:

- Using a new role as a good development opportunity for managing change and establishing services.

- Obtain new skills required by widened areas of responsibility.

- Become more flexible in undertaking "non-core library" tasks.

- Be well qualified, articulate, analytical, highly IT literate, and possess excellent communication skills.

- While as sole charge it is difficult to take time to attend courses and conferences I attend some local meetings which are held after work.

- Develop a succession plan for existing staff.

- Gain expertise in knowledge management and information management.

- Increase skills and knowledge of digitization technology and techniques.

- Become a member of professional associations, LIANZA (Library and Information Association of New Zealand Aotearoa), ALIA (Australian Library and Information Association), and SLA (Special Libraries Association, Australia and New Zealand Chapter). Attend seminars and workshops, conferences whenever possible.

SENIOR MANAGEMENT

Having support within the senior management team is invaluable to the success of the library, but it is up to the information professional to keep the service up to expectations and beyond, by providing an excellent, timely, and effective information service to the organization.

- A very forward-looking, pro-library senior management team makes a huge difference to how the library or information centre is viewed by the rest of the organization.

- A manager who recognizes the expertise, experience, and enthusiasm I bring to the role is invaluable.

Finally, Alexander has this advice:

Remain professional, positive and proactive. If job cuts are in the offing, a reputation for professionalism and a good work ethic may be enough to keep you off the redundancy list. And even if you do lose your job, it will enhance your chances of getting a new job or even being re-hired by your company when business picks up again. (Alexander 2009)

These suggestions are responses to the question, "What activities is it necessary to undertake when the library is threatened with a review?" (Ralph and Sibthorpe 2008). The full report of this survey is in *Emerging Trends in New Zealand Special Libraries* available online at http://www.lianza.org.nz/sites/lianza.org.nz/files/SzentirmayReport2009Ralph Sibthorpe.pdf).

We would like to thank the hardworking special librarians of New Zealand for their positive advice.

DISASTER AND DISRUPTION? "BUSINESS AS USUAL . . .": A CASE STUDY

Retirement of the founder and chairman, rebranding and new leadership, devastating earthquakes, and an unusually severe winter were not able to slow down a redoubtable sole-charge, special librarian in Christchurch in New Zealand's South Island.

INTRODUCTION

In 2010–2011 earthquakes shook the country particularly around the South Island city of Christchurch. Many companies had seismic safety measures in place, but the severity of the earthquakes was not expected and the central city experienced significant damage to properties and homes, and the injury and deaths of many people.

Within the organization, the company leadership has changed, and the founding director retired. The ethos of the company has not changed, that "people are the most important part of the company."

The librarian serves the head office from Christchurch and, with rapid expansion overseas, is now serving branches in many countries as well.

BACKGROUND

How did this sole charge special librarian survive in turbulent times? The company is a large, private, international manufacturing company with over 600 employees in Christchurch, and branches now in Europe, the United States, the United Kingdom, Asia, and Australia.

Nearly two years after the first earthquake in September 2010 (magnitude 7.1), many companies are still trying to cope with the aftermath of the earthquake shocks that still happen regularly. The deadly earthquake on February 22, 2011 (magnitude 6.3) was situated directly beneath the central city area of Christchurch. Many buildings and homes were destroyed and lives were lost. Earthquakes continued with further large shakes in June and December 2011.

The company repaired and strengthened the buildings on site and put in place independent sewage tanks, a diesel bunker, emergency rescue equipment, an accelerometer to measure earthquakes, and a generator. During this time the company had to keep functioning to meet international commitments and to avoid production time penalties. In place now are much sturdier "future-proofed" disaster plans and risk management processes.

While the company is situated west of the city, the library suffered only minor cracks, broken ceiling tiles, books fallen off the shelves, and more damage in the archival storage room. The librarian only lost one day of work and was able to resume quickly. Adverse weather a few months after the February earthquake, during winter 2011, brought deep snow and ice which made going to work dangerous and difficult, and caused more problems than had the earthquakes.

During this time the company leadership changed and the company was expanding, rebranding, and marketing itself internationally.

KEY FINDINGS

The librarian was moving to the provision of more electronic resources, as offices were established overseas. She picked up responsibility for the records and archives function and obtained the necessary training. She surveyed her head office and overseas-based staff to find out what information and staff training was required. Feedback indicated a high level of satisfaction from recipients of the library's information service. She also knew she needed to keep her users informed of new developments and research.

A key component of this librarian's success during challenging times was through the company intranet, a social networking hub that connects the whole company. All company announcements and news are posted on the intranet. From the library's intranet page there is an invitation to join the library (i.e., opt in to receive emails, etc.), and newsletters, new books list, and blog updates are sent by an automatic email to staff who have joined the library. The library's intranet page also pops up automatically when staff anywhere in the company start to seek information. The library intranet page offers access to the catalogue and databases, and e-books such as the *Books 24/7* collection to staff worldwide. The library's own branding identifies from where the information has come.

Reference and research training sessions are provided regularly. The librarian is well situated in a small but highly strategic team comprising R&D, IT, standards compliance, intellectual property, marketing, and project management. The librarian records and reports to management on the library's contribution to the work carried out with all teams and programs.

The library is a showcase for the company included in every tour of the plant.

LOOKING FORWARD

The librarian has coped, along with her company, with a severe natural disaster. She has been growing her services to keep pace with the growth of a rapidly expanding manufacturing company which now has branches in many countries. She is using technology to communicate and extend her services throughout the intranet network, and is arranging electronic access for all staff at their desktop. Having aligned her library with the organization, she is also very well placed strategically to market the library as an integral part of high-level strategy research and planning activity.

"Be visible!" is the advice from this survivor.

REFERENCES

Alexander, M. "Read Signs to Tell if the Axe Will Fall." *New Zealand Herald* (2009): F2.

Archives Act 1983. Canberra, ACT: National Archives of Australia (1983), http://www.austlii.edu.au/au/legis/cth/consol_act/aa198398/.

Australian Government. Libraries Information Network (AGLIN). *Statement of Strategic Intent 2009–2013* (2009), https://wiki.nla.gov.au/download/attachments/51362/Statement+of+Strategic+Intent.pdf?version=1HYPERLINK.

Australian Government. *Reform of Building the world's best public service Australian Government Administration* (2009), http://www.dpmc.gov.au/consultation/aga_reform/docs/reform_aust-govt_admin.pdf, http://infospace.ischool.syr.edu/2011/12/23/61-non-librarian-jobs-for-librarians/.

Australian Library and Information Association. *Guidelines for Australian Special Libraries* (2010), http://www.alia.org.au/policies/Guidelines.ASL.pdf.

Australian Library and Information Association. *ALIA Special Libraries Survey Report.* Canberra, ACT. (2010a), http://www.alia.org.au/governance/committees/special.libraries/ALIA_SPECIAL_LIBRARIES_REPORT_FA.pdf.

Australian Library and Information Association. ALIA Special Libraries Advisory Committee (SLAC). (2012), http://www.alia.org.au/governance/committees/special.libraries/.

Australian Learning and Teaching Council. Queensland University of Technology, "Re-conceptualising and Re-positioning Australian Library and Information Science Education for the 21st century" (2011), http://www.liseducation.org.au/resources/PP9–1326%20QUT%20Partridge%20Final_Report.pdf.

Breitkopf, Mia. "61 non-librarian jobs for LIS grads" (2012), http://infospace.ischool.syr.edu/2011/12/23/61-non-librarian-jobs-for-librarians/ (accessed January 26, 2013).

Doherty, E. "Economic Effects of the Canterbury Earthquakes" (2011), http://www.parliament.nz/mi-NZ/ParlSupport/ResearchPapers/c/4/4/00PlibCIP051-Economic-effects-of-the-Canterbury-earthquakes.htm.

Economist Intelligence Unit. "Economic forecast." *Country Report. Australia* 15, no. 2 (2011): 7–9, http://ezproxy.auckland.ac.nz/login?url=http://search.ebscohost.com/login.aspx?direct=true&db=buh&AN=58086265&site=ehost-live&scope=site.

Foster, A. "The Boss Just Said 'Do More With Less!': The Business Information Survey 2010." *Business Information Review* 27, no. 8 (2010): 1–26.

Hallam, G. *Queensland Government Agency Libraries Review: DPC Job Reference Number: DPC 45–09: Literature Review* (2010a), http://eprints.qut.edu.au/31528/1/QGALR_Literature Review_20100325_Revised.pdf (accessed January 26, 2013).

Hallam, G. *Queensland Government Agency Libraries Review: Options Paper* (2010b), http://eprints.qut.edu.au/50582/ (accessed January 26, 2013).

Koha Library Software Community. (2012), http://www.koha.org/ (accessed January 26, 2013).

Library and Information Association of New Zealand Aotearoa. (2012), PIMN SIG, Pasifika Information Management Network Special Interest Group, http://www.lianza.org.nz/community/group/pimn-sig (accessed January 26, 2013).

Lim, G. C., C. L. Chua, E. Claus, and J. Kim. "Review of the Australian Economy 2010–11: Growth, Jobs and Debt." *Australian Economic Review* 44, no. 1 (2011): 1–12.

Mach, M. "Real Job Title for Library and Information Science Professionals." (2003), http://www.michellemach.com/jobtitles/realjobs.html (accessed January 26, 2013).

Matarazzo, J., and T. Pearlstein. "Survival Lessons for Libraries." *Searcher* 20, no. 2 (2012): 24–29.

Nutting, M., and K. Harris. IMBASE: *Information clarity* (2012), http://imbase.org/sb_clients/imbase/bin/home.cfm (accessed January 26, 2013).

Perret, R. "A New Look at the Background and Work Experience of Business Librarians." *Journal of Business and Finance Librarianship* 16, no. 1 (2010): 44–46.

Public Records Act 2005. Wellington: Archives New Zealand, http://archives.govt.nz/advice/public-records-act-2005 (accessed January 26, 2013).

Ralph, G., and J. Sibthorpe. "Emerging Trends in New Zealand Special Libraries." (2009), http://www.lianza.org.nz/sites/lianza.org.nz/files/SzentirmayReport2009RalphSibthorpe.pdf (accessed January 26, 2013).

Ralph, G., and J. Sibthorpe. *Special Librarians without Special Libraries*. Paper presented at the LIANZA Conference, Wellington. (2008), http://www.lianza.org.nz/resources/conference-proceedings/2008/special-librarians-without-special-libraries (accessed January 26, 2013).

Rendell, Hilary, and Flora Wallace. "A Model for Difficult Times: The Merger of Special Libraries." Paper presented at the LIANZA Conference, Wellington. (2009), http://www.lianza.org.nz/resources/conference-proceedings/2009/model-difficult-times-merger-six-special-libraries (accessed January 26, 2013)

Rink, T. SLA's Alignment Project (2009). http://www.sla.org/PDFs/alignment/AlignmentProject_Rink.pdf (accessed January 26, 2013).

Scott, Steven. "Disasters, Dollars Hit Budget." *Courier Mail*, September 30, 2011, 1, http://www.couriermail.com.au/ipad/disasters-dollar-hit-budget/story-fn6ck4a4-1226152312119 (accessed January 26, 2013).

Sexton, Reid. "Job Cuts Headline Toughest Budget in a Decade." (May 1, 2012), http://www.theage.com.au/victoria/job-cuts-headline-toughest-budget-in-a-decade-20120501-1xwki.html (accessed January 26, 2013).

Tomlinson, Janet. "Will You Survive the Electronic Library?" *The Journal for the Serials Community*, 7, no. 1 (1994): 37–41, http://uksg.metapress.com/content/e0m4q6bcnw01fycv/ (accessed January 26, 2013).

Vance, Andrea. "More Job Cuts in Govt Mergers." (2011), http://www.stuff.co.nz/dominion-post/news/politics/6094342/More-job-cuts-in-Govt-mergers (accessed January 26, 2013).

Westpac Institutional Bank. "Westpac market insights." Sydney, Australia, May 2012, 32, http://www.westpac.com.au/docs/pdf/aw/economics-research/MarketInsights.pdf (accessed May 2012).

Wise, S., M. Henninger, and M. A. Kennan, "Changing Trends in LIS Job Advertisements." *Australian Academic and Research Libraries* 42, no. 4 (2011): 268–95, http://www.alia.org.au/publishing/aarl/.

PART III

SO WHAT DOES YOUR MANAGER THINK?

INTRODUCTION

JAMES M. MATARAZZO AND TOBY PEARLSTEIN

Parts I and II of this book have focused on the perception of survival from the point of view of information professionals. In this final part, three nonlibrarian managers of information services (IS) tell how they perceive the value of IS and why they think these services survive in their organizations. Since the alignment with your employer's mission is critical to sustainability, it is important to reinforce understanding of how decision makers outside IS think about your contribution.

The three contributors represent sectors of the economy, financial services, and professional services, which have experienced incredible turbulence over the past decade and especially since the recession of 2008 began and consequently are uniquely positioned to provide us some insight into sustainability. In a companion essay, "Investment Management, Buy-Side Research, and the Information Professional," Sylvia James addresses the type of "buy-side" research that occurs in two of these organizations and suggests some opportunities that might yet be found there for the enterprising information professional seeking to succeed in this challenging environment.

COMPANION ESSAY

Investment Management, Buy-Side Research, and the Information Professional

Sylvia James

It will come as no surprise when you read this group of essays on "What does your Manager Think?" that they came from three professional services firms and that two of the authors were senior managers in the large and well-known independent investment management companies, Fidelity and Putnam. It was obvious as long ago as January of 2003 (James 2003, 1–5), that new areas for corporate information professionals had to be identified and that investment management is and would continue to be a really important area of employment for them in the broader financial services sector.

As the headcount of information professionals in the major corporate libraries of the mainstream investment banks that served the needs of vast corporate finance teams waned during the past decade, and many of the services they had performed so successfully in the 1980s and 1990s were outsourced to companies in India, switching to serve the research needs of investment management information teams seemed to be picking up. This author's prediction that the "buy side" (a term for all the investment management functions in investment banking), existing as it did across a Chinese wall from the investment bankers and particularly their corporate finance business, would readily take up and use all the information expertise and build new corporate "libraries," looked as if it might be proved right. The "buy side" was certainly expanding globally with the development of all kinds of retail long-term savings products to the proliferation of hedge funds for private investment for the very wealthy.

The part of the investment banking business known as the "sell side" (or trading activities; that sold to the "buy side") had never had much of a requirement for information services (IS) from the large corporate libraries that had supported the information-hungry corporate finance activities. The "sell-side" analysts who researched and wrote the analysts' or brokers' reports, with their blanket recommendations on a company or sector, for distribution widely to clients (and increasingly to the wider public through the media), was in itself a research and information function, but surprisingly, these analysts had never sought much backup or expertise from information professionals in the main corporate library. In the many surveys this author carried out over 25 years of IS consultancy in investment banking, rarely could one find more than five percent of the information work being done being provided to the "sell-side" analysts. Often these analysts seemed disdainful of any research that could be done by the corporate library. A detailed explanation and paper on the work of the "sell-side" analysts (James 2009b, 1, 4, 6) discusses how the reports they write should be viewed by a legal information professional, which more fully explains the scope and purpose of these reports.

"Buy-side" information needs were evident in the rise of a new type of "buy-side" research that had been developing during the 1990s. Senior management in these firms began to see a need for confidential proprietary research to be done in-house, with a dedicated team of analysts, who would be supported by well-qualified and trained information specialists. This would augment and supplement the vast range of sell-side analysts' reports that flooded in to their institutions from every brokerage firm and investment banks. The Research Department at Putnam Investments, described by Patrick O'Donnell in Chapter 15, which took over the line management and absorbed their corporate library into its structure, is exactly that type of department.

The idea for this type of research had originally been an extension of the work of the "quants," who had come to work alongside portfolio managers in the investment management companies. These were the quantitative analysts with advanced numerical prowess, who developed their facility in math into even greater technological skills in analyzing company equities and especially bonds, as automation and computing power increased. Combined with the increasing lack of confidence in the "sell-side" analysts' reports that came to a head with the exposure of the false and appallingly optimistic forecasts for many of the profit and asset-poor newly listed dot.com companies in the late 1990s, "buy-side" research gained traction in the firms that developed the specialty.

"Buy-side" researchers are especially regarded in the independent investment management companies. Spotting this trend, the author advised and worked closely with a recruitment agency in the late 1990s, which specialized in "sell-side" positions who wanted to diversify their business. New services was developed identifying and selecting "buy-side" analysts to fill these new positions. Recruiting information professionals to some of these analytical positions had some success and many were able to develop their skills into full analyst positions, much in the way Patrick O'Donnell describes.

The 2007 global financial crisis changed everything. The vast investment banks that had grown top heavy on the back of balance sheets stuffed with toxic asset-backed securities collapsed and were merged, bought out, or went bankrupt. The "sell-side" trading and corporate finance activities shrank dramatically and with them decimated many of the supporting back-office departments, including the corporate libraries, which are now shadows of their former substantial units, if they still exist at all.

The independent investment management firms like Fidelity and Putnam came out of the crisis in much better shape than their competitors that were subsidiaries of the investment banks, because they had no other lines of financial businesses in retail and investment banking in which to fail. In fact, there were much smaller numbers of independent investment management firms operating by 2007, because so many had been acquired by banks because they wanted to operate in all areas of financial services and benefit from cross selling to clients. These types of banks are known as universal banks and have been widely criticized as being near-impossible to regulate and so seen as the root cause of the ongoing global financial crisis. Many financial regulators are now proposing to break up these very large banks and will probably require the splitting of investment banking functions from retail banking and investment management. This will probably result in new standalone "independent" investment management firms, which ironically will probably lead to more opportunities again for information professionals in their newly created buy-side research functions.

Investment management did not escape from scandal during the financial crisis. The largest Ponzi scheme ever uncovered, exploded in the media in December 2008. Bernard Madoff had been running a series of much favored investment funds for over 30 years that actually never existed. The breadth and depth of the financial crisis was the reason that the fraud was finally exposed as investors swamped the Madoff funds for the return of their capital to pay off other losses. The capital of course didn't exist. All the returns that had been paid to existing investors in the Madoff funds came from the money deposited by new investors as they clamored to join Madoff's funds; the classic Ponzi scheme. With this fraud came all the investigations into the failure of the regulators to spot this problem and much more interesting from the perspective of corporate researchers was the completely inadequate due diligence that was carried out by the institutional investors in the Madoff funds, known as the feeder funds. After reading all the books possible about the failure (James 2010, 1–5), it would seem that none of these feeder funds had effective research routes for checking the funds they were introducing to unsuspecting clients, let alone the corporate librarians who could do the basic research on these counterparty investments. Admittedly, these would have been complex searches and would have needed some experience and knowledge to track down information. But, the information and the warning signs were there in the public domain and when uncovered, would probably have changed decisions to invest. These signs and implications for business research are discussed in an article about the books written on the fraud and another article (James 2009a, 1–5), where a clear case is proposed for recruiting business information researchers, who would understand how to do the ongoing due diligence for any "buy-side" fund.

The best endorsement of all for special libraries and librarians on the "buy side" came in a book, *No One Would Listen,* published later by the renowned "whistleblower" in the Madoff case, Harry Markopolos (2010). The book is a detailed account of how he went to the Securities and Exchange Commission (SEC) (the investment management regulator), no less than four times between 2000 and 2009 to try and expose the fraud, but as he put it in the title to his book *No One Would Listen.* In the "Epilogue" to the book Markopolos (2010, 275) suggests a series of steps that would transform the SEC into a respected agency, which it clearly was not at the time it was supposed to be regulating the Madoff funds. The startling challenge to the SEC and it's research capabilities is described in the sixth step as "book 'em" and Markopolos describes the "well-stocked library" of the investment industry firm (Markopolos probably means those firms in both the buy and sell side), with a range of professional journals such as the *Journal of Portfolio Management* and *The Wall Street Journal* available to staff. Compare this to the offices of the SEC, where there is probably no investment library or subscriptions to significant investment journals:

> So where do SEC staffers actually go to research an investment strategy, or find which formulas to use to calculate investment performance, or even figure out what a CDO squared is? Apparently the SEC staff uses Google or Wikipedia—because both of them are free. Good luck to a man or a woman attempting to figure out a complex financial instrument using free Web resources. The SEC makes sure its staff will remain uneducated—by not providing the educational tools they need.

The breakup of the financial services sector into its component subsectors by most regulators in North America and Europe following the global financial crisis now seems inevitable. This can only be good news for the corporate librarian with initiative, who can spot new opportunities to make a case for an excellent in-house research function in the smaller financial institutions that emerge. One good example on the "buy side" may be that when one of the great casualties of the financial crisis, AIG, the vast insurance conglomerate had to break up, as a result of taxpayer funding to keep it alive, an information professional developed a research service and offered it specifically to some of the former subsidiary companies that emerged as independent insurance and investment management companies. Many of the professionals in these companies were accustomed to the good IS provided by the AIG Research & Development Service and were very happy to have a new provider as a short-term measure while they worked out whether to set up their own in-house service.

So, to come full circle and reiterate the advice from 2003 that the "buy side" may well be a shining light for the survival of the corporate information professional who has worked or would like to work in financial services. The author is absolutely sure that there are and will be many opportunities for both full-time in-house positions and independent research services in this corner of the financial world.

REFERENCES

James, Sylvia R. M. "The Future of Financial Services and the Information Professional." *Business Information Alert* 15, no. 1 (2003): 1–5.

James, Sylvia R.M. "After Madoff and Stanford, How Do You Research These Firms?" *Business Information Alert* 22, no. 2 (2009a): 1–5.

James, Sylvia R.M. "Using Broker/Analyst Reports." *Legal Information Alert* 28, no. 3 (2009b): 1, 4, 6.

James, Sylvia R.M. "Seven Books about a Scandal." *Business Information Alert* 23, no. 8 (2010): 1–5.

Markopolos, Harry, with David Fisher. *No One Would Listen: A True Financial Thriller.* Hoboken, NJ: John Wiley & Sons, 2010.

13

WHAT THE LIBRARY HAS TO DO TO BE SUCCESSFUL

CHUCK PICKELHAUPT

Today's libraries face an increasing challenge: the ongoing commoditization of information and information technology. What has not been commoditized, however, is insight. For a decade at our corporate library at Fidelity, we have provided valued content in various formats to many thousands of employees. However, we always get the strongest net promoter scores and the deepest engagement when our librarians get involved to curate content and help inform people's thinking. Success may be defined in many ways, and I offer six action items to guide yours.

HIRE BRIGHT, INQUISITIVE MINDS

Nothing inspires learning like interacting with others who have a passion for knowledge. We have consistently hired our librarians from high-quality institutions like Simmons College. As well, each year we offer multiple internship positions, where graduate students continually bring us new ideas and perspectives in exchange for valuable, real-world experience.

AUGMENT INFORMATION WITH INSIGHT

I like to organize content into the categories of Know, Think/Discuss, and Do. Some content purely educates and informs, telling the reader what things they should know. Some content provokes the reader with alternative points of view and questions to consider, suggesting what insights beyond the text should be thought about and discussed. Some content provides calls to action, specific recommendations on how to apply the information, and insights to enrich the reader's situation. Setting aside social interaction for a moment, each customer of the library is seeking to know more, think about impact and alternative views, and/or clarify what to do next. Although recommending action can require a deep understanding of the customer, libraries should always try to enhance purely informational sources with insight in the formats the user prefers most. By inspiring thoughtful consideration and critical thinking, libraries can provide added value that enhances customer engagement and their own brand.

MINIMIZE COSTS FOR IT INFRASTRUCTURE AND SOFTWARE

Open source software and cloud-hosted services can bring high-quality information technology to libraries with little external expense. A dizzying array of valuable open source software is available for libraries, including the popular Drupal, Koha, and Apache Solr. Both corporate and public libraries have embraced these low-cost options, although some corporate libraries seem to prefer proprietary applications.

INVEST IN PREMIUM CONTENT

Few libraries are blessed with huge budgets. With the money you are not spending on IT, invest in pay-wall sources that bring insight as well as information and then track usage diligently. Valuable information will always be locked away from widely used search engines, and by understanding library customers' interests, librarians can use those sources to maintain and even grow their impact.

BE WHERE YOUR CUSTOMERS ARE

For us, this includes delivering fresh information to their browser home page, in their email inboxes and office mailboxes, on their mobile phones and tablets, alongside their electronic productivity tools, at their strategic planning sessions, and so forth. It also includes staying in the front of their minds with marketing messages in their new employee orientation training, in their staff meetings, at company trade shows, in the cafeterias, and on their screensavers. We have also embraced social interactivity, from provocative book clubs, to internal micro-blogging, to embedding on teams. Our goal is simple: Ensure every customer and prospect knows exactly how we can help them be more successful—and be there whenever they think of us.

EMBRACE CHANGE

This is perhaps the toughest part, because it asks libraries to think not about what they were in the past, but rather how they will add value in the future. For us, servicing customers with disparate physical locations forced us to provide all of our services online years ago: from multiple online pay-wall collections, to online book collections, to asking a research question. Those services now need to work with whatever device the customer has with them, whenever they need us: PCs, Macs, Androids, iPhones, iPads, and so forth, used during the day or late at night and on weekends, when their busy days are paused and they have the time to access content and request assistance. Like any well-run company, libraries need to regularly analyze their customer transactions, charting quantity of engagements, surveying quality of engagements, graphing return on investment for paid services, tracking modes of interaction, and so forth. If the data say something isn't working, strategize how to fix it. If the data say that something isn't wanted or needed anymore, take a deep breath and boldly let it go.

In short, to be successful, a library has to deeply understand its customers' and sponsors' stated and actual needs—and its librarians must be passionate customer service representatives that deliver insights along with information. Not coincidentally, that's exactly the kind of library where I want to be a patron and an employer.

14

INFORMATION SERVICES AT BAIN & CO., INC.: ADDING VALUE TO THE FUTURE OF THE FIRM

MICHAEL ZIMMERMAN INTERVIEWS STEVEN TALLMAN

Recently I had the privilege of speaking with Steven Tallman, Partner and Vice President of Global Operations. The topic for discussion was how the Information Services (IS) Department at Bain added value to the overall operations of the firm.

Steven, a 25-year veteran of Bain, has filled several roles within the organization since joining the firm as an Associate Consultant in 1986. Having overseen Global Training and working to help create Global Services, Steven understands the vast importance of knowledge-related services at Bain.

Today as Vice President of Global Operations he is over the Technical Services Group (IT), Information Services, the Customer Insights Group (Market Research), and the Bain Capability Center, a centralized analytical resource located in India. We discussed how IS at Bain adds value to the overall organization.

Tallman started our discussion with a very basic question: "Why is Information Services important"? The answer, in his mind, is tied to how Bain serves its clients. "We tackle their toughest problems and answer their most complicated questions." Therefore he pointed out, "we need not only to have the right insights, but the right data at our fingertips. To be able to accomplish this consistently we need the right level of access to data, both internal as well as external."

When asked how the role of IS has changed over the past five or six years he pointed to three significant fundamental actions: regionalization/globalization, industry specialization, and embedded case team researchers.

Tallman views Bain's approach to globalization and specialization as very complementary to the structure of the organization and different from their competitors. Six years ago Bain was very local in operation. He characterized the period since as moving from offices, "doing their own thing," to a more regional model where people share best practices.

Based on an interview with Steven Tallman by Mike Zimmerman, Information Center Manager, Bain & Co., Dallas, TX. in March 2012.

This new approach to research, he noted, "has allowed us to have researchers in each region, resident in local offices, who have a greater depth of expertise and become more knowledgeable in Healthcare, Industrial Goods, Financial Services, etc. They also become more efficient in knowing how and where to get at the best data sources to help the various case teams they serve." Adding to this model of globalization and the depth provided by industry specialization is a significant investment in desktop resources providing "ready access to really great sources at our consulting staff's fingertips."

The value of having local information staff in place then plays out three ways: "First, training our consultant staff in using these desktop resources; second, being in place as a ready adviser as to which resource is the best to answer their question; finally by enabling the consulting staff to do some of their own research, the IS team becomes available to help case teams research their more complicated multilayered assignments."

This helps in making the model consistent. "We make a much heavier investment in sources than our competitors do, yet maintain a much leaner staff in terms of researchers." But this staff is involved in a higher value-added work, and hopefully most of the time is involved in working within a specialization. Also, we have improved the "embedded" librarian approach by moving away from a "help desk mentality." The embedded approach allows each researcher to become much more attuned to the needs of the team and much more relational to their teams. Tallman went on to say, the IS model is "consistent and has grown and evolved well over the past six years."

Under this model there is now a deepened career path for the IS researcher, he noted. "Before, we had the researcher and the manager and that was about it. Now we have industry specialist researchers, we have team leaders working with researchers around their region, and now on a global level, we have regional directors; so the career path has grown."

When asked for his thoughts on the value of IS metrics, Steven briefly listed the metrics that have been tracked over time. "First and foremost we have always tracked customer satisfaction with IS. It allows us to get a view into which offices are doing well and where there may be some concern."

The second metric relates to productivity and shows the overall IS costs versus firm revenues. This metric also shows if IS is scaling with the growth of the consulting staff.

The final metric they track is the satisfaction the IS team has with Bain. Measuring how IS team members feel about their jobs and the firm is extremely important in making sure the teams feel that their work has value and as individuals they are continuing to grow.

Tallman also pointed out that many of the IS team have very long tenure with Bain, which is incredibly valuable. This tenure gives IS a strong sense of history and strong relationships within the firm. And new team members are valuable as well, bringing fresh ideas and new perspectives.

I asked if it was still true that Bain's ability to collect data and know more about the client's business than they themselves did still "bought a seat at the client's table," given that today many clients can access more data on their own. Has this bar been raised and how does IS contribute to supporting this? He felt that certainly to an extent the client's reach was further, but Bain is also able to take insights from one industry and bring it to bear in another industry. This cross industry, cross-functional thinking is something that clients cannot do on their own because they are so deeply seated in their industry. To be able to do this we have to have the best people and the best data coming to the table. IS has been a key part of this. IS has been proactive in driving their strategy in sync with the company's direction. He believes

IS has stayed ahead of the curve by keeping a close eye on the firm's strategy and building their services to support it.

Our interview also touched on the topic of outsourcing. IS has been proactive in approaching this issue. A regional and global structure has allowed IS to take advantage of a virtual model. By getting in front of the issue, IS had built on the value of growing industry expertise, leveraging capacity across offices and regions and providing access to a rich array of data sources across all offices. The model of investing heavily in electronic desktop resources, utilizing local IS researchers to advise and guide the consulting staff about how to use these resources successfully and efficiently, and embedding researchers into case teams demonstrates the true value of IS and how it fits well within Bain's global structure.

Looking ahead to the future, Tallman sees the IS model expanding even further. As an example, the appointment of Global Industry Team Leaders was a logical next step to stay aligned with the firm's structure and allows for even more sharing of valuable information. Another logical next step he noted was the expansion of global distribution rights for their data contracts. Perhaps another logical step will be to find a way to offer 24 by 7 services though this will take very careful and thoughtful planning.

As a bottom line, IS needs to continually be aware of the company's needs and structure and build an IS team that supports these. IS needs to stay ahead of this by anticipating directions and offering the firm's leadership value-added advice. It will ensure that IS continues to be a key contributor to Bain's success.

15

PUTNAM INVESTMENTS CORPORATE LIBRARY

PATRICK O'DONNELL

In the mid-1990s, the Corporate Library at Putnam Investments in Boston was an efficient, well-managed repository of information, principally corporate filings and documents. It also had a powerful database-search capability staffed by extremely well-trained librarians. The purpose of the library was to respond as quickly and efficiently as possible to inquiries from any sector of this large firm, which managed in excess of $300 billion in mutual funds and institutional investment products. It was wholly successful in its mission.

During some discussions among the firm's top managers a question arose about the library's natural home among all the different departments. The question was whether the library should be supervised by somebody in administrative operations, since it served the entire firm. This was at the time the traditional arrangement in most big companies. However, we decided to take another approach.

At the time I was the Managing Director of Worldwide Equity Research. My department's job was to know the world's major publicly traded companies thoroughly enough to provide investment opinions to our colleagues who managed portfolios. Essentially, we were constantly trying to refine our understanding of the world's major industries and to determine whether the companies in various sectors were undervalued relative to other companies.

My proposal, which was accepted, was that the library's most natural home was in the Research Department.* Although the librarians were principally involved in information retrieval and the research analysts were principally involved in sifting through and evaluating information, there were, I thought, basic affinities between librarians and analysts. The best librarians and the best analysts are keenly curious, aggressive in pursuit of the truth, and intellectually fussy in an entirely laudable way.

---

*Here I might add that ever since I was a small boy roaming through the Coventry Branch of the Cleveland library system, I have loved libraries, which I understood to be potentially huge continents of the mind, able perhaps to provide wisdom and always with the suggestion that something even more interesting was on the next shelf. A nice librarian let me check out a book on the Dead Sea scrolls in 1957, when I was 11, even though I was not eligible to do so. I will always be grateful to her and the other kind, thoughtful ladies who fed my curiosity.

Our first move was to integrate the librarians into daily life in the Research Department. Each day began with a Research meeting, in which analysts would make recommendations to portfolio managers and in which both would discuss the investment decisions that were in process. The librarians were not only invited to the daily meeting, but they were also expected and encouraged to understand the issues being debated. Moreover, there were frequent meetings of various groups of analysts, those covering the banks, for example, or the major manufacturing or consumer sectors. Each of these analytical teams was joined by a librarian, who came to know what work the analysts were doing. This integration would not have been possible without first-rate leadership, so we were lucky that Ellen Callahan was already the head of the library.

In other words, we integrated the library into the research department by making the librarians close, daily working associates of the analysts. We also, however, brought the library and the librarians into the middle of the research department, in a literal way. We moved the library from its rather elegant quarters into a smaller space next to the analysts' offices. The librarians were happy to give up some prime real estate (on a different floor and on a different elevator bank) in order to be in the middle of the daily flow. The results were immediate: research requests doubled in the first month and grew steadily from this new base. This is proof of the adage "In sight, In mind."

The charge to the librarians was to use their searching and gathering skills to help the analysts as directly as possible by knowing as much as possible about the work being done. The librarians quickly understood the major problem faced by investment analysts: The world is so awash in statistics, opinions, news, secondary and tertiary sources, proprietary work, propaganda and just plain informational junk that the discernment of useful facts was a challenge that required a specific set of professional skills. It is like reducing a tsunami to a useable flow of water. It is difficult and when it is done well it creates a meaningful competitive advantage.

This was, however, an exciting challenge to the librarians, whom we all knew were capable of high-level creative work; they sharpened their evaluative capabilities. The analysts did not ask, for example, "what were auto sales in China ten years ago and what are they now?" but rather said, "you know I am trying to figure out the potential for auto sales in China, how can you help?" The librarian would then not simply find basic statistics, but would advise about potential problems with the quality of the numbers and the sources, and, because she was familiar with the analytical process, would be enterprising about what else to supply. She might find insight into the ways in which other developing countries adopted and adapted to the automobile; might look into the problems of distributing major consumer durables over large swaths of territory; might try to get some insight into whether the paint for these cars could come from a company we covered (by, let us note, somebody who was not the auto analyst). To a fertile imagination, these are engaging questions which, when answered properly, provide a huge collegial contribution.

There were other advantages, some of which we had not anticipated. The librarians became, for example, such experts on their industries and sectors that they became excellent teachers for new analysts, who quickly learned both the major sources for their specialized researches and the best ways with which to work with expert librarians, a new experience for all of them.

Incorporating librarians directly into the research process as value-adding investigators worked very well. The firm's investment results benefitted, the analysts enjoyed highly literate searchers and evaluators to work with and the librarians enthusiastically accepted the challenges of their new roles. We (i.e., what we used to call "the library") still answered all the inquiries from the rest of the firm, but we knew that the best intellectual and professional pleasures were in the Research Department.

INDEX

About the Authors

JAMES M. MATARAZZO is Dean and Professor Emeritus at the Graduate School of Library and Information Science at Simmons College. His previous books include: *Closing the Corporate Library*, *Corporate Library Excellence*, and *Knowledge and Special Libraries*. His doctorate is from the University of Pittsburgh School of Information.

TOBY PEARLSTEIN is retired Director, Global Information Services for Bain & Company, Inc. the strategic management consulting firm. Most recently she co-authored the series of articles in *Searcher Magazine* on survival skills for information professionals on which this book is based. She holds a doctorate from the Simmons Graduate School of Library and Information Science in Boston, MA.